A
SCORPION'S
LAIR

A BITTER LEGACY

(VOLUME 3)

A SCORPION'S LAIR

A BITTER LEGACY

(VOLUME 3)

EARNESTINE M. WALDEN

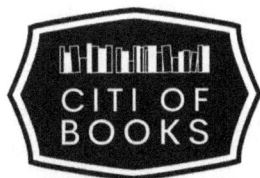

CITI OF BOOKS

CITIOFBOOKS, INC.
3736 Eubank NE Suite A1
Albuquerque, NM 871113579
www.citiofbooks.com
Hotline: 1 (877) 3892759
Fax: 1 (505) 9307244

Ordering Information:

Quantity sales. Special discounts are available on quantity purchases by corporations, associations, and others. For details, contact the publisher at the address above.

Printed in the United States of America.

ISBN13:   Softcover   979-8-89391-146-6

Library of Congress Control Number: 2023913587

It all began when, Blake Colwell the firm's Attorney and personal friend of the family received a call from a former colleague, who telephoned informing him of the Business scandal. In a shocked tone, he asked the caller,' What in heaven's name is this, and why after the deaths and not before?" Neither one had an answer to those very two important questions. Blake informed the caller that he was going to look into the matter further and see what he could learn. But if what he had conveyed to him turned out to be valid, it could mean big trouble for the firm not to mention the effect it was bound to have on Claudia, after what she had already been through. Finally, he said, "I have the unpleasant task of apprising Claudia of the nasty situation which I don't believe she's aware of, or she would have called me. I'll telephone her to meet with me here this morning then I can explain everything to her uninterrupted he said with a light Chuckle," thereby concluding the conversation. Blake sat silently gazing at the notes he'd taken during the conversation then suddenly asked himself,' I wonder what's really going on and just how deeply is the firm's involvement to be implicated in such a scandal and Charles, is it possible that he's aware of this atrocity? I'm still the firm's attorney contrary to what he might feel, so I'm going to pay him and the firm an unexpected visit, but first, I'll make some informal telephone inquiries before contacting Claudia.' His inquiries proved to be quite fruitful with the cooperation of a number of sources. As he began to compile the information, it became obvious that the situation could have a far more reaching effect than he would ever have imagined. "Hello! The voice on the other end responded by saying, Claudia, this is Blake, I'm pleased to see that you're back did I awake you?" "Good morning Blake no, you didn't awaken me, I've been up for quite some time now. I returned home late last night." "Will it be convenient for you to meet with me at the office this morning, say around eleven-thirty?" She noted a tone of urgency in his voice indicating that the call was very important. "What's wrong, she asked?" "A matter of great importance has come up requiring our immediate attention and we need to discuss in *private, he said." Without further questioning, she said, "Yes, I'll see you at eleven-thirty." Slowly and deliberately, she placed the receiver in its cradle. Leaning back letting her head rest on the chair, her small hazel eyes shifted upward to the wall-mounted antique clock, the hands on the clock read eight-thirty a.m. A somber expression fell upon her face as she briefly recalled the conversation between her and Blake, and remembering the tone in his voice, she realized there was something definitely disturbing him and wondered if he was concealing something from her. He'd always been protective of her, but whatever the problem, they would just have to deal with it.*

Claudia was grateful that, the morning traffic to Blake's office was moderate. She never did enjoy driving in heavy and congested traffic anyway as long as she could possibly avoid it. She entered the Law office at precisely eleven-thirty and was greeted by Blake who was waiting for her in the opened door. Taking her by the arm he led her to a mahogany velvet plush cushioned chair with side arms resembling a lion's head that had been placed directly in front of his large matching well-polished desk. After seating her, he walked around the desk and seated himself. There was a brief silence then he called his secretary, informing her to hold all his calls. Looking at her through clear, steel grey eyes and slightly arched, handsomely shaped eyebrows he asked, "Just how are you Claudia, I mean really?" Without even a flutter of her long thick eyelashes, she immediately replied." "I'm gradually getting there by taking one day at a time," while giving him an assuring smile. He didn't care about pursuing it any further because he knew she was still struggling with pain and sorrow and the best way he could possibly help her get through it all was to just be there for her. However, Blake was well aware of her pain, for he too was experiencing it, but for a different reason and in a much different way. Shifting his eyes to a neat stack of papers on his desk and not so much as a glance in her direction. He began the conversation by saying, "Prior to my calling you, I received a rather disturbing telephone call from an old colleague bringing this matter to my attention. It appears that the firm is being implicated in some sort of Business scandal. As she moved to the edge of her chair and looked directly at him, her eyes widened with apparent disbelief as she calmly asked," Blake, exactly what kind of business scandal are we talking about here?" Look, I know you're trying to protect me, but I'm no longer a little girl who's in need of protection from the "Buggy Man," and I have to know the truth whatever it is, she said in a very determined tone. Looking at her, he knew very well that her mind was made up and there was no way in which anyone could influence her decision, but how could he possibly tell her, the whole story without going into detail, this was exactly what he'd hoped to avoid. "Yes, you're right, you're no longer a little girl, but a beautiful and vibrant young woman, and please forgive me, he said smiling." "You're forgiven, she said returning the smile." On a more serious note, he said, Claudia, as it stands now, it appears that someone is trying to ruin the firm by creating this whole nasty mess. I made some informal inquiries to see what I could find out, and the effort paid off. The sources whom I spoke with validated the rumor, but we need more concrete information to establish what is really going on and by whom because at this point, I believe a full investigation into the situation should be implemented but first, I'll need your approval." Her eyes still focused and looking directly at him she said, "you have it, and asked, do you have someone in mind that can be relied upon to do the job well?" Blake's response was, "as a matter-of-fact, I know just such a man and he's the best in his field. He went on to say, his name is Bradford T. Maxwell and he's a private investigator. We've known each other for many years." She saw a glint of sparkles in his eyes as he spoke and sensed there was something very special about this man of whom he spoke. "This is fine by me, you know I've always had confidence in your judgment she said with a smile. But I'm puzzled by all of this, you know I was away for only three days which means this developed in my absence yet; Charles didn't say anything to me about it when I returned last night, and I'm curious to know why he didn't?" Blake looked at her for an instant and said, "I don't know, but don't you be concerned about Charles, I'll handle him when the time comes." After a brief period of silence, she finally said, "But I'm very concerned because he's becoming distant, and when I asked him what was wrong, he nonchalantly said, there were things on his mind and walked out the door." "When did you first become aware of this change in him Blake asked as if to be thinking?" She finally said, "A few weeks after my parents' deaths. I asked why was he spending so much time at the office and he told me there were things that he should be personally taking care of and that I shouldn't worry. But the fact of it is, I believe there's something more than just the usual office business." "Just what do you think it could possibly be Claudia, he asked her?" She said," I don't really know, it's just a feeling I have and I don't like!" Blake made no comment, just pushed the chair backward away from his desk stood up, and walked across the room stopping in front of a large brown, metallic file cabinet and pulled out a drawer. As he was going through what appeared to be neatly kept folders and after fingering through them, he finally pulled one out looked at it and pushed the drawer back into place, and returned to his desk. After giving her a quick glance he said, "I've been tied up here with a number of cases and haven't had much time to get by the firm because up until now, I assumed everything was going alright, but I see I couldn't have been more mistaken. Perhaps I'll go by there this afternoon. There are some things I need to check on anyway. As for you, young lady when was the last time, you were out on a shopping spree?" Not waiting for a response, he stood up walked around the desk smiling, and said I've got some more telephone calls to make." Returning his warm, gentle smile, she walked towards the now-opened door, turned around to look at him briefly then gently closed the door behind her.

After Claudia departed, Blake returned to his desk and opened the folder that he'd retrieved from the file cabinet earlier and began reading the papers it contained only stopping occasionally to absorb; perhaps evaluate specific contents that he felt were significant. He neatly gathered the papers and replaced them in the folder. Opening the attache case that was already on his desk and, before placing the folder inside he briefly looked at the label that read: "Lansing Contractors' Firm." An expression of deep sadness and apparent regret appeared upon his face as he slowly closed the case, at that time, there was a gentle knock at the door and, looking up he said," come in Jenny ."With a notepad in her hand, she said, "I'm sorry to interrupt you Mr. Colwell, but you asked me to remind you of the luncheon appointment with Mr. Wilham at one-thirty this afternoon and it's one-ten now." Looking at her smiling he said," "thank you, Jenny. I didn't realize the time. I'll be out of the office for the remaining afternoon, so I'll see you in the morning smiling." She said, "yes, and have a pleasant afternoon sir." "Thank you, he said as he was leaving out of the door."

The following morning Blake arrived at the office at eight-thirty a.m. As he unlocked the door to his office and began to enter, he saw his secretary, Jenny sitting behind her desk. "Good morning Mr. Colwell, she politely said." "Good morning Jenny, he said smiling, then asked," were there any calls?" "No sir, she replied." After consuming a delectable breakfast consisting of a mug of hot steaming coffee, creamer, sugar, a spoon, napkins, and two Danish pastries with the aroma of having been freshly baked. He called Jenny at her desk informing her that he would be making some important calls and asked her to hold all incoming messages, but if Mrs. Carrington should happen to call, she could ring her through. After completing the calls and finally realizing the complexity of the whole situation, he decided that now was the time to make his call to Maxwell because there was no point in postponing it any further. He only wished that he'd been successful in obtaining more information. Reminiscence of the past, Maxwell was a no non-sense man with a reputation for being mild-mannered, resourceful, and could be very dangerous if ever pushed too far. There was one thing for certain, he'd never desire to have him as an enemy because it would be like finding a keg of *dynamite that was about to explode! They had met each other while in the Military and formed a bond that had been a long-standing one and he was a man who valued his friendship with others.*

Finally, he thought to himself, with a sigh of relief as the doors to the elevator opened on his floor. He walked down the long-carpeted hallway to his office. Stopping in front of the door, there was an embossed plaque that read Bradford T. Maxwell Private Investigator. Beneath the name was Suite 315. He unlocked the door and stepped inside, and as he closed the door behind him the telephone on his desk began to ring. Taking a long stride across the room he hurriedly sat his briefcase down on the floor with one hand while reaching for the receiver with the other and in his baritone voice he said, "Hello, you've reached the office of Bradford T. Maxwell, how can I help you?" A familiar voice responded by saying, "you're still the best I know in the field and this is why I need your expertise Brad." "Blake Colwell, what a pleasant surprise, as I recall it was around six months ago; when we last talked and the conversation was brief because we were both pressed for time, he said." Blake said, " you're right as usual and a number of unpleasant events have transpired since then. Hearing a note of apprehension in his friend's voice he asked, "This isn't a social call is it?" "No, my friend, I'm afraid it isn't. Are you available to meet with me in my office tomorrow afternoon around two-thirty?" "Yes, I'm free tomorrow, as a matter of fact, I'm in the process of tying up some loose ends from a previous assignment, he said." For a fleeting moment, Bradford's thoughts of his friend were, 'something had deeply stirred him 'A few seconds had lapsed when he said o, I'll see you tomorrow in your office at two-thirty sharp?" "Yes, and thank you Brad, was his reply." There was a click and then nothing but silence. Inhaling deeply and then exhaling, he leaned back in the large tan leather swivel chair with fingers interlaced behind his head, he extended long legs crossed at the ankles on top of the desk. As he slightly shifted his broad shoulders to a more comfortable position, his thoughts again reverted to his friend, and with a broad smile asked himself;' I wonder who or what has caused so much anxiety in him?' well, it's been quite an eventful day and a rather enjoyable one after all.'

The following day, Bradford arrived at the Attorney's Santa Monica office at precisely two-thirty sharp, as he was closing the door behind him, Jenny the secretary was standing behind her desk and greeted him with her genuine adorable smile saying "Good afternoon Mr. Maxwell, Mr. Colwell is expecting you." "A good afternoon to you Jenny and thank you." As he was turning around, Blake was already standing in the doorway with a wide grin on his face and an extended hand, briefly glancing up at the wall clock he said," Punctual as always I see." " I try to be, was Bradford's instant response." As they started through the door of his office a soft voice behind them said, Excuse me, Mr. Colwell, would you like for me to hold your calls, sir?" "Oh yes, by all means and would you also reschedule this afternoon's four o'clock appointment please?" "Thank you, Jenny." Closing the door behind them he motioned to the large chair opposite his desk then seated himself. "Would you care for a cup of coffee or perhaps a soft drink Brad, he asked?" "No, thanks, I'm fine thank you, he said." On top of his desk were three folders, but only one appeared to be open, and right beside was a notepad with special notations written on most of it. Bradford knew Blake had been at work on something so, he patiently waited in silence until he was ready to begin. As if reading the other man's thoughts, Blake leaned back in the large leather chair while focusing his eyes directly on the tall, handsome six-foot-four man, sitting in front of him. He began the conversation by saying," I appreciate your coming and if I understood from our conversation yesterday, you're not presently on a case. "No, I'm not, he replied." "I'm pleased to hear that because I'd like for you to handle a very important case for me, he told him while leaning forward and placing folded arms on the desk." Casting a brief glance at the opened folder Bradford asked," so, what do you have?" Blake said, "What I'm about to tell you I believe with great certainty is going to require someone with your expertise. I need a man whom I can trust and that man my friend, happens to be you. Look Brad, as I stated before you're the best I know in the field, besides as I recall, you've always enjoyed a challenge and this case is a rather complex one I can assure you, he said with a broad grin." "Let's just say, I like what I do, was his immediate response bringing a hearty laugh from the both of them. "Then on a more serious note, Blake said approximately six weeks ago the owners of a Contractors' Firm I represent were killed in an automobile accident. They left behind a daughter Claudia, who is twenty-nine years old and sole, Heir to their wealth. Uncrossing his legs while leaning slightly forward and gazing into Blake's eyes he said, "wait a minute." About six weeks ago; I was up North on a case there was headlined news of a well-known Businessman and his wife were both killed in an automobile accident while vacationing somewhere in Arizona. Their Attorney was the one who notified the daughter who was out of the country at the time of the accident." Blake, not saying anything just lowered his eyes to the desk. Bradford broke the silence by saying, "and you're the Attorney." Finally, looking up again he said, "one and the same," with deep sadness in his tone of voice and his eyes revealed the same. Bradford said, "man, this is rough to hear, Blake I'm truly sorry. I never made the connection until now, why didn't you contact me?" "Everything was so chaotic I had a very difficult time, trying to think clearly so; don't be disturbed, Buddy. There was no way that you could've known. Anyway, there's more which is why I need you to take this case for me." "Go on he said, in his mild-mannered tone as he leaned back in the chair again crossing his legs also; still very much aware of the strain that appeared on the man's face. " Blake said, here's what I've been able to learn so far, it appears that after the deaths occurred, the Firm's name has been implicated in a large business scandal asserting a series of unethical business transactions and applying strong-arm tactics to undermine other companies especially, the smaller ones. I need not tell you, this means big trouble and the consequences could be serious enough to *possibly ruin the firm, and as of right now, we don't have a clue as to "who is responsible and what the motive behind it all mean?" Claudia is married, but only she and I've discussed this terrible situation and there's a mutual agreement that a full investigation is in order. I also informed her that I would be more comfortable with you handling the case, she consented without question, he said.' Bradford asked, "what about the husband, I assume he wasn't included in the decision making he asked, looking directly into Blake's eyes?" "Your assumption is correct and until we can determine where he stands in all of this, perhaps it would be wise if we allow things to remain as they are at least; for the moment anyway." Bradford gazed at him and casually asked, "I sense there's something exceptional about this case, what's your stake in all of this Blake?" His response was, "let's just say, at this point we're not certain about him. You see, during our meeting Claudia expressed reservations regarding her husband's loyalty. "Point well taken, Bradford spoke." "Unfortunately Brad, the integrity of the firm is going to be severely compromised by the scandal and I'm afraid the organizational structure within will be fragmented. I've made a few inquiries already and that is where we stand as of now. Adding insult to injury I've been informed that there are recurring events and this my friend is greatly enhancing an already situation by casting further suspicion upon the firm. I've already spoken with some drivers and delivery men who were incidentally, reluctant to talk to me until I offered them a little friendly advice then they were more than willing to cooperate, he said smiling. They were quite nervous and I got the distinct impression that they're more afraid of whoever is giving them orders than of me." After Blake had finished speaking, they did an assessment of the situation and concluded that what was known so far, the incidents were not isolated, but well and deliberately planned by someone. Looking at him smiling broadly Bradford asked, "when do you want me to start?" At that question, Blake expressed a deep sigh of relief and, reached into his desk drawer, giving him a ring with a number of keys on it explaining that they were to the firm's* building and David Lansing's private office. "Brad, I don't believe Claudia has made up her mind to go in there yet, she spent a great deal of time there. Helping out when her parents were alive, he told him." "I imagine it's been pretty rough on her loosing both her parents at the same time that way, as he spoke in a very soft tone." "Yes, it has been rather difficult for her, but she's beginning to lighter up a bit now. She's a very strong young woman, Blake said with apparent admiration. Then with a wide grin and eyes squinted he said, to answer your question, You're officially on the case as of when you answered my plea for help and, thank you Brad." Both men were now standing and looking fondly at each other after shaking hands, he escorted Bradford to the door, but before leaving he turned around and said," Man its great seeing you again. I very much regret that it has to be under these circumstances though." "You know the feeling's mutual, was Blake's reply. "I'll be in touch Bradford spoke, as he was gently closing the door behind him." With fond memories of the man whom he'd relied upon for assistance in a situation that was becoming crucial by the minute. Blake stared at the closed door for a time. Returning to his desk, he picked up the folder and started towards the file cabinet when the telephone rang. "Excuse me sir, Mrs. Carrington is here to see you." "Thank you Jenny, and please ask her to come in."

He greeted Claudia with a soft kiss on the cheek and taking her by the arm led her to the big chair opposite his desk, then seated himself. "How are you my dear, he asked her?" "Oh I'm just fine thank you for asking, she replied with a smile." "And Charles, how is he Blake asked her?" "Well, that's a difficult question to answer, since our conversation this morning was rather brief." "I don't understand, Blake said in obvious bewilderment." "At breakfast, I informed him that I plan to leave the city for a few days." "Oh, and what did he say, if I might ask?" "Nothing really, he just looked at me in silence for a few seconds then managed to ask when am I expecting to return?" "Blake asked her, he didn't bother to ask you where you're *going or why?" Her response was no, and that's the odd part about it, he only seemed to be interested in knowing when I'll return she said with some skepticism." That is odd to say the least; 'Blake thought to himself, then with uncertainty, he asked her, "When did you make the decision to take this sudden trip Claudia, he questioned?" "She said, it really isn't that sudden. After our meeting the other day, I didn't go on a' shopping spree' as you suggested, but went for a long drive instead. I've been thinking for quite sometime, about getting away just to clear my thoughts. It has been difficult for me to really focus on anything and now this scandal involving the Business. I need to adjust to things being different now and I haven't reached that point at least; not yet anyway." At that moment, he was completely lost for words, and was thankful when she suddenly interrupted his thoughts by saying, "they've been gone nearly two months now. And I've been in the house on several occasions, but haven't had the courage to go into their bedroom, or Dad's private office. There are personal effects that I should attend to and soon. My friend Sharon is back in Santa Barbara. She telephoned me a couple of weeks ago to ask if I would come up and spend a little leisure time with her, while she's on Spring Vacation." He smiled at her and asked, "What did you tell her?" "Well, I didn't give her an answer because I wasn't certain at the time, so I told her that I'd get back with her in a few day's. This is the first opportunity we've had to see each other again at least; our being together will be more pleasant this time, she said." Suddenly, Blake felt a sickening feeling in the pit of his stomach as he watched the strain on her young face, then managed to say, Claudia my dear, you've had a very traumatic personal experience and I'm afraid it's going to take some time to bring closure. As for the situation with the firm, there's no further need for you to be concerned because as of today I've already seen to the matter and I'm confident that it will be resolved in a timely manner." As soon as he had finished speaking she said, Blake, I hadn't realized it until yesterday, but you my darling man, influenced my decision to accept Sharon's invitation." "What's this he, asked her?"*

Surprised at her direct statement. Looking at her with a steady gaze and not daring to take his eyes off her, he was even more bewildered by her actions, as he watched her slowly stand up and walk over to the large window and began to stare outside. Neither one said anything. There was a still silence in the room except for an occasional honking of horns coming from the streets below them. After standing there for a few seemingly long minutes, she returned to her chair and resumed her same position with her long legs crossed. Seeing the expression on her face, he couldn't help but wonder just what was behind it all. At one point he had a strong desire to say something, or perhaps ask her a question, but decided to wait until she was ready. Finally, she said Blake, I haven't said anything before because I wanted to be certain it wasn't just my imagination getting the best of me, but now I know it's not, everything's too real and I'm having a terrible time trying to cope with it. I'm certain Charles is having an affair, she said in a mild subtle tone." Shocked to hear this coming from her he asked, "how can you be so certain?" Looking directly into his eyes with a slight, but confident smile on her lips said, "Oh, I'm quite certain believe me, a wife can tell." Blake really didn't know what to say at that precise moment, but he continued to look at her with anger in his heart and being careful not to give her any indication that he'd been suspicious of Charles for quite sometime. Finally, he asked her, "When do you plan to leave?" She replied, "I have a few errands to run first, then I'll drive up this afternoon." He asked her, "so your mind was already made up before you came?" "She said yes it was, I just wanted to let you know." She sensed an uneasiness of mind in him and said, "Oh, don't be an old 'worry-wart' I promise to telephone you when I've arrived there." Gazing into her eyes he said "Claudia, I'm very concerned for your happiness and well being he assured her." "I know you are and I love you for it. But Blake, I think this trip is precisely what I need so, stop worrying I'll be just fine she said with a smile, and looking into his deep penetrating eyes she said, I'm going to miss you also and gave him a big hug and kiss on the cheek." She walked slowly towards the door glancing around to look at him before finally closing the door behind her. After informing his secretary that he'd be out of the office for the remaining afternoon, Blake decided it was time to pay the firm an unexpected visit. Just as he was arriving in the firm's parking lot he spotted Charles and an attractive young woman entering his car, and immediately recognized her as someone he knew, but why was she leaving in the car with him? He had a sudden desire to halt them, but thought better of the concept and continued on his way however; still puzzled by the event also, remembering the conversation between he and Claudia earlier. He entered the firm and made his way to the Bookkeeper's office, he was met at the door by a tall, slender man in his mid-fifties with greying hair and wearing a 'Prince Albert' mustache that was neatly trimmed. Smiling at each other Blake said, "hello Robert how have you been? " But before responding to Blake's question, he took a quick glance outside and quietly closed the door. After asking him to have a seat pointing to the chair opposite his desk that was neatly cleared with the exception of one large black leather binder, he said. "Oh I'm alright Blake thanks for asking and frankly, I've been expecting you." This situation with the firm has everyone up in the air because they don't know what is going to happen including myself, he said." Blake was fully aware of the man's feelings as he spoke, and understood. He'd been employed there since the firm's change over many years ago. And seeing the grave concern on his face he said Robert, "I fully understand all of the anxiety, it's not an easy thing to accept because unfortunately, it places everyone under suspicion especially, since the assertion is that it's someone associated with the firm. Without taking his eyes off the man Blake said, "from all indications it appears that someone is deliberately trying to ruin the firm and as yet; we haven't a clue as to whom or why. The only thing we have so far; is the approximate time frame that it actually began, and more events continue to occur which is very disquieting. Suddenly, shifting his position and sitting more erect and focusing his eyes directly into Blake's he asked, "I've noticed your use of the term, 'we' tell me what, is going on Blake?" Seeing the anxiousness on the man's face he leaned back in the chair and with a broad smile said, "Robert, I've hired a private investigator to search out the truth in the nasty mess and bring it to a resolve. His name is Bradford T. Maxwell and he's very good at what he does so; I'd appreciate your full cooperation when he comes to you and I know he's going to because, he doesn't believe in leaving any stones unturned." As he was speaking, he saw the man's eyes widened and his face took on a surprise look. Slowly leaning forward and placing both hands on the desk, Blake immediately noticed that his voice had become an octave lower when he asked, "Not the Bradford T. Maxwell who has his office on Wilshire Blvd?" Blake began to chuckle and replied, one and the same.' Then he asked, "do you know him Robert?" His voice began returning to its natural range when he said, "only by reputation and that's enough for me, and from what I've heard he's not one to fool with either. But I wasn't aware that you know him." Responding with a smile Blake said, he's a very mild-mannered man until crossed and then he's like a Scorpion that's been disturbed. He's quite resourceful and energetic. There was a brief period of silence and Blake saw the tension line slowly leave the man's face as he was speaking and recalled his own relief, when Bradford agreed to take the case. Returning to a more serious note he said," you keep records of all the firm's payable and receivable accounts, transactions and so forth. We can certainly use your help on this one so, is there anything you can tell me, perhaps; it was something that didn't appear to be significant at the time?" Without hesitating he asked him, "Blake do you recall when I took two weeks off from work after the funeral?" "yes, I recall you calling the office to inform me that you felt the need to get away for a couple of weeks." "Well, when I came back to work and was going over some of the books I ran across a number of discrepancies. I still haven't gone through the rest of them yet, nor all of the paper work. Look Blake, give me a few day's to get all of the other books, I can go through all of the paper work and files and see what exactly I can produce for you." "Blake said, that will be just fine Robert, in the meantime, I've got some more checking out to do myself, I'll be in touch with you."

Bradford began the process by methodically making inquiries and performing close observations, he started out by going directly to the sources of complaints first. Some of the small contractors informed him that they'd been receiving only about half of the materials and supplies ordered and was told by some individual in the front office that they should consider themselves lucky to be getting that much. Eventually, after numerous complaints they found themselves being blackballed, facing strong-arm tactics and verbal threats by some of the larger companies and from some of the drivers at the firm. they decided to form a small alliance in their own defense because it seemed that nothing was being done to rectify the situation. He was given the names of two other construction companies who were also dissatisfied . Later that afternoon he visited two of the large construction companies, he also informed them that he was investigating the complaints alleged against the firm. They were very cooperative and explained that they'd never had any problems with the firm before, but after the deaths things began to change, and they could give him no explanation as to why. However, he was told that a number of new people had begun working there. The assertion was that they were being over charged for materials and small rental equipment and some of the badly needed supplies ordered to complete a job was never received. He spent several days gathering information, visiting and observing different sites of particular interest including activities at the firm. Taking time out to compile and analyze the information he'd gathered there still remained too many unanswered questions for his comfort. While carefully documenting the information he still had a distance to go because he'd just begun in the preliminary stage. He became more persistent in his inquiries and closer observations in the hope of getting some sort of lead. He visited construction companies and interviewed private contractors who were doing business with the

15

firm. Nearly two weeks had passed when he finally got his first lead from an unidentified source. Who a name and the location stating that he might find it to be of interest, but said nothing more. At first he was hesitant and then considered the fact that it might be worth checking out so he did just that. Bradford had no concept of who he was going to meet, or why, so he'd just have to use caution and play that one by ear. After driving some distance he finally reached the location that he was given and slowly observing his surroundings while getting out of his car suddenly, he felt a big knot in the pit of his stomach ,but he was determined to continue the distance. As he entered the double glass doors leading into the building and walked inside, he was immediately, greeted by a man in his mid-sixties, with a broad rugged face, hostile blue eyes and greying hair who introduced himself simply as Mr. Chatsworth. And asked what could he do for him? At that very instant and without any reservations he realized that he'd jut entered the 'Meltingpot.' And it was apparent that he was looked upon with obvious suspicion that was indicative of the false assumption of appearance. Which was the true state of mind of a bigot and witnessed the onset of asperity as he introduced himself and presented his credentials of course. It wasn't anything that he was unaccustomed to. Besides, the more things change the more they remain the same. After a brief, but calculated inquiry which came to an abrupt halt when two henchmen who'd been standing nearby, and who appeared all too anxious were ordered to escort him outside and away from the premises. By that time, he assumed Chatsworth to have been the Head Man. Walking in the direction of his car he observed a small gathering peering out of a large bay window opposite the parking lot as if, to make certain of his departure. Driving away smiling and thinking to himself, the trip out there wasn't a complete washout, but he had to find out more about this 'elite' group and wondered jut what was his source's intentions when he sent him there in the first place? However, Bradford had no concept that more encounters with Chatsworth, and his men were just the beginning. It was late afternoon and as he was returning to his office, he began to have a 'gut' feeling at that point perceived caution to be his alto-ego.

Bright and early the next morning he decided to play a hunch and revisit a couple of locations, one in particular had stood out above the others. At the construction site he visited was privately owned. The owner and a small group of his employees agreed to speak with him and there, he was informed that the firm had a rather shifty background before the present situation developed. The consensus among those who spoke out explicitly stated that the deceased owner was a dictating tyrant who was dominant as well as vicious, a tone that indicated there was no love lost by his absence. After concluding his inquiries he gracefully thanked them and headed for his car. Something's wrong her, he thought to himself as he was leaving the site. Intuitively looking in the rear view mirror he spotted a familiar car about two car lengths behind as he periodically changed lanes so did the other car, and as it came closer he recognized one of its occupants the driver, whom he'd seen on two previous occasions. The car finally drove up along side him and the passenger rolling down the window yelled out, 'stop snooping around in thing's ain't your business." 'Thanks for the advice, and tell your boss I'll surely keep that in mind." He immediately retorted. The car abruptly sped off into traffic. Still watching them he said,' now this is more like! Back at the office he made note of the newly acquired information. He re-visited one of the main construction sites unfortunately, someone had gotten there ahead of him because that time, no one was willing to talk to him however; someone did quietly suggest that he leave and then he said, 'man don't come back'. It was obvious from the man's action that he was being closely watched, and taking heed to the advice he promptly left the premises. While driving back to his office he thought to himself, 'this case is becoming a cascade.'

Late one afternoon Bradford sat in his car parked directly across the street that would give him an adequate view of the firm's front and back entrance and exists. Sorting through some notes he suddenly peered up and said, "well, well what have we here?" He saw Steven Chatsworth, the 'Head Huncho' and his two henchmen exiting the entrance of the firm. Their appearance wasn't unexpected he just didn't know when, but there was one thing for certain, he was going to find out what the connection was between Chatsworth and the firm, especially, since he'd any sort of business dealings with it during the inquiry. The following day he went to the firm to speak with Robert the bookkeeper. He'd just pulled out of the parking lot and turned the corner when he heard the screeching of tires behind him. Looking in the rear view mirror he saw the same car that had exited the parking lot just two days earlier except this time, the Passenger was someone else that he hadn't seen before. Smiling and casually asking himself, 'oh, oh now what do we have here this time?' They hit the rear bumper a couple of times, and as they were passing he quickly glanced in their direction and saw the two of them laughing while speeding off into traffic. The driver he knew, as for the passenger, he'd know him when they met again. After that little display he was counting on it! After that incident, his instincts began sending warning signals which he never took lightly and that was his 'cue', and nor was he inclined to believe for one fleeting minute those two goons pulled that stunt on their own. He considered the emerging obstacles as becoming more than potential 'road blocks'. It had been obvious for awhile that someone didn't want him asking questions and was going to great lengths in an effort to impede his investigation, but he wasn't about to be intimidated by anyone. It was late in the afternoon and after making a couple of stops he returned to his office to burn the 'midnight oil'. He'd learned from years of experience that things weren't always as they might appear, but expect what wasn't obvious. An analysis of the information he'd already gathered by the many inquiries and observations definitely validated the assertions against the firm, and he didn't like the picture that was in front of him.

Early the following morning he'd had a restful night's sleep and a hot, soothing shower Bradford sat at his desk eating a fresh glazed donut and slowly sipping on a cup of freshly brewed coffee. He began to re-examine all of his data and looking at the situation from a much different perspective his theory was someone had devised a very deliberate and elaborate scheme to divert attention away from their true motive, and once he learned who then he'd know the why. He'd known for quite sometime that something was very wrong about the case, now he was convinced with great certainty that the assertions were only a small piece of a much larger puzzle and there still remained a lot of work to be done. Slowly with deliberate accuracy going through the process he realized there was much more to the case than he previously suspected. Bradford was certain that something far more significant than a Business scandal was involved, because there were too many variables. With that in mind, he decided that it was time to take a closer look inside of the firm itself, and that meant everyone associated with it was still under suspicion excluding those whom he'd ruled out at the beginning stage of the process. There were two major questions that had lingered in his thoughts from the onset, 'why after the deaths and not before/' Perceiving caution while theorizing, he was willing to bet a gold-plated dollar that something had transpired previously to influence the present situation, but what could it have possibly been?' There were too many pieces that still didn't fit together and was annoying him Big time! Carefully considering the magnitude of the whole situation the odds of bringing an early resolve as the Attorney hoped was rapidly decreasing because his perception was that he'd merely touched the tip of the iceberg. The answers were out there and he was determined to find them, but he was totally unaware of the changes about to occur that would further enhance his suspicions leading toward the firm itself. It was time to have a meeting with Blake Colwell, but there were a few places that he wanted to check out first, before going to him with anything. Claudia returned home after her two weeks stay in Santa Barbara with her friend Sharon. It was early afternoon when she tried telephoning

Charles, but was unsuccessful in reaching him, so she telephoned Blake's office and Jenny, his secretary immediately put her through to hid desk. Blake upon hearing her voice delightfully welcomed her back. She explained that she'd just arrived back a short while ago, and her trip was quite an eventful and exciting one, but it felt good to be home again. He insisted that they have luncheon together the following afternoon around one-thirty p.m. He told her that he was quite anxious to hear all about her trip, and she readily agreed. After the telephone conversation with Blake ended she thought that she might as well go by her father's office after lunch. She felt that she'd finally come to terms with their being gone and nothing could change that!

He was leaning against the large brown file cabinet while half facing the door. The second drawer from the top was pulled out and in his hand she saw a folder and another one tucked beneath his arm, he was shuffling through the papers then stopped abruptly. What ever he was reading had his full attention because Claudia was standing just inside the doorway when he finally took his eyes off the paper and saw the somewhat puzzled expression on her face. They just stared at each other for a minute or so then they both began laughing at the same time, with a fixed gaze on her he said," you have to be Claudia Carrington." She said right on cue, and you're Bradford T. Maxwell." "Affirmative, he said smiling." Thinking to herself 'my, but he's quite a handsome man.' He broke the silence by asking her, "when did you get home?

"Oh, I returned yesterday afternoon. Blake said that I should expect you, he just didn't say when, she said smiling." Claudia, he said I'm going to be up front with you, I've been making a lot of inquiries as well as observations and the picture I'm getting is placing the firm in a very unsatisfactory light. I've still got a few more areas to check out first though. "Looking directly into his eyes she said, "Bradford, I haven't the vaguest concept of how all of this can be happening or why, nor am I aware of anything remotely similar to

this predicament occurring before or who is displeased enough that they're attempting to ruin the fire." Seeing the pain and near tears in her eyes and carefully choosing his words, Claudia, up until now I've shadowing in and around the firm, but when I learn whom? Then I'll also know why. The answers are somewhere and I will find them, he said with an air of determination." With eyes fixed directly on him she said, "Now I truly understand the admiration Blake has for you. So do whatever is necessary I won't interfere in any way and if there's any way I can be of assistance in the ungodly mess please don't hesitate to let me know." "Thanks! He said with admiration, thinking to himself, she's quite a strong beautiful young woman." Suddenly remembering the folders while holding them up he explained." I'm going through these to see if they might give me some sort of clue as to what's happening. I hope you won't mind, he said." "she said no, not at all take whatever you need. There are also two safe's. One is here and one in their home. Dad had the combination changed on the one here just before leaving on their trip. I'll give you the numbers to the other one. This is the first time that I've been inhere since they left, she said sadly." "Well, its going to take you some time to finally come to terms with it, but you will, he said compassionately."

/The following day, he headed directly for the bookkeeper's office just as he began to knock, the door opened, and before he could speak a man's voice behind him was asking, can I help you?" Slowly turning to face the speaker he said, "no thanks anyway, I see the man I'm looking for and turned to face Robert who was broadly smiling." He ushered him into his office and closed the door behind them. They were both still standing when he said, "I'm Bradford T. Maxwell." "I know who you are, and I'm Robert Sharp." While shaking hands and asking him to have a seat. After seating themselves directly across from each other, Robert smiling said, "I've been expecting you for quite awhile." Bradford gave him a wide grin and said, "better late than never." Then they both laughed. "I was told that someone was looking for me yesterday, and I just figured it was you. I'm sorry to

have missed you , but I was out on an errand." "yes, I did come to see you and apparently someone was keeping tabs on me." "What do you mean, he asked him?" "Oh, it was just a little minor incident, nothing I can't handle he responded." "I'm sure it isn't, Robert said with a broad grin and his 'Prince Albert' mustache flickering upward." On a more serious note he said, "Look Robert, Blake has already assured me of your loyalty and I trust his judgement. I've been on this case three and a half weeks making inquiries and doing close observations and I'll tell you, I don't like the picture because everything is pointing back to the firm. Now I know this isn't easy for you, but everyone here is under suspicion with the exception of the three I've eliminated and they're Blake, Claudia and your self to be precise. From the information I've gathered so far, and not nearly done, someone is definitely out to ruin the firm of this I'm certain, it's too pat. I'm going to come in closer to home now, and I'm still covering other areas as well while doing so. Looking at Bradford for a full minute then he said, "Blake told me you're good and and I'll be dog-gone if he wasn't right. Now what do you need from me, he anxiously asked him?" "Robert this is undoubtedly, going to be difficult for some people, but I was hired to search out the truth and bring this situation to a resolve, and this my friend is my primary objective. Looking at his wristwatch and abruptly standing he said Robert, I hadn't realized the time, there are a couple more areas that I plan to check out. I'll see you again in a few days and I'll have a list that I would like for you to go over with me. This time, I'll call to see if you're in first he said smiling." Robert was now standing as well and said, "Bradford you're up front all the way and I respect that in a man. Looking around he said, "this place used to have a pleasant atmosphere now this nasty situation has created division here, Robert spoke in a dismayed tone." "Perhaps; this is precisely what someone had in mind from the beginning, and thanks, so do I Bradford said as he was leaving." After the meeting with Robert Sharp convened, Bradford telephoned Blake's office and his secretary, Jenny informed him that Blake was out of town on a case, and would be gone for a couple of days at most. He left a message asking Blake to get in touch with him when he returned. It was now late evening, and feeling a bit hungry Bradford stopped and ordered a 'Chew Mein' dinner on the way to his office. Sitting at the desk while slowly consuming his meal and reading the files from David Lansing's office suddenly, the telephone rang, it was Claudia asking, if he could meet her at her parent's home around eleven a.m. the following day?" "He replied yes, he'd be there." Chatsworth's name apparently, the two had signed an agreement pertaining to some sort of new land development they were involved in, but he found nothing more that would indicate his involvement in the firm. Although he felt that he was somehow, but first he had to find proof that would substantiate his involvement.

Bradford and Claudia met at her parent's home at precisely eleven a.m. sharp. She was already parked in the driveway when he arrived. After getting out of his car and taking long strides toward her smiling he said, "good morning hope I haven't kept you waiting long?" Slightly craning her neck to look up into his deep penetrating eyes she smiled and said, " Good morning and no, you haven't kept me waiting as a matter-of-fact; I arrived here just ahead of you." They both turned and began walking toward the front entrance of the large two-story home. It was sitting on a hillside over looking the city of Bel-Air. And judging from the architectural design of the home he estimated that it was complimented by one large smoked glass window on each side. The house was white with no trimmings. Walking up the cobblestone lined semi- circled driveway he thought it thought it was a beautifully well kept estate. After a short walk they finally reached the house, she unlocked the doors and once they were inside she said, "Brad, this is the first attempt that I've made to go through my parent's thing's, oh, I've wanted to, but I just couldn't find the courage to do it." Looking down her for a few seconds before speaking. In a very soft tone he said, "Claudia, its never easy to accept the death of those we love especially, the way your parents left, but once you're over the initial shock and come to terms with their deaths, the pain lessen with each passing day. You're a strong woman and you will go on with your life because they'll always be in your heart. As far as I'm concerned, you're moving in the right direction because you're here today doing something that you've been postponing, and in my book that's courage." With tears in her eyes and looking up at him she reached up giving him a hug and said," Thank you Brad for the encouragement." "You're quite welcome, he said with a broad smile and twinkles in his eyes." She said, "let's get started here shall we?" "I'll take you into the study and open the safe then head upstairs." "Fine by me, he said." Upon reaching the top of the stairs, she held on to the staircase for a couple of minutes and after taking a deep breath she slowly walked down the long carpeted hallway stopping in front of her parents bedroom. She looked at the door for an instant then slowly turning the knob continued on inside, Everything had remained as they'd left it. Walking over to the large picture window she slowly opened the blinds that had been half closed. Then turning away from the window she walked to the middle of the magnificent room and standing there, she recalled the morning they were leaving on their last and final trip. Her mother holding both hands in hers whispering how much she loved and would miss her, while her father was standing in the doorway encouraging her to come on because of the long drive ahead of them. Smiling at him and then her, they hugged each other tightly. She walked over to the door giving her father a big hug and he kissed her on the forehead as he usually did. Charles was standing there beside her, but when they began to drive away suddenly, she felt a void. Apparently Charles had been observing her because he asked, if everything was alright?" And with tears in her eyes the only response she could give him was 'yes. I'm fine,' but down deep inside she wasn't, and she herself was leaving in two days on a trip abroad for a two weeks stay with her God-parents. Claudia hadn't realized she was sitting on the foot of their bed until she heard a deep, but mild-toned voice asking,' if she was alright?' Abruptly wiping the tears from her eyes and remembering, Bradford was down stairs she quickly replied, 'oh yes

Brad, I'm fine thank you.' 'You're so quiet up there I was beginning to wonder if something might be wrong, he said in a concerned tone.' She finally stood up asking herself, 'Where shall I begin?' She eventually started by going through her mother's things, there were no cartons available she'd have to get those later, after going through everything first, she'd planned to give them to her mother's favorite charity anyway. She'd gone through most of the drawers when she came upon a small book with a black leather cover, she asked, 'what's this?' She removed the book from its place of concealment and looking at it she realized she'd discovered her mother's personal Journal. Slowly she rubbed her hand across the smooth surface. Skeptically, she wondered if it was right for her to open it after all, it was personal and she felt as if she would be invading her mother's privacy. Suddenly, as if something; or someone was encouraging her to open it she untied the beautiful pink lace ribbon that bind it closed, at that very moment she has a strange feeling that something was guiding her through the motion. She opened to the first page and stared at the all to familiar handwriting and a sudden sadness began to engulf her. Her eyes began to fill with tears, after all, they were very close and her mother was her confidante and best friend. Regaining her composure she started to read the first page and observed that her mother had begun her Journal with the history of the family-owned enterprise, and thought 'how strange for her mother to have begun her Journal in such a fashion. Abruptly, Claudia stopped reading, ending with the second page as she remembered Bradford was still down stairs. Closing the journal, began placing things back as they were until she could return at a later time. Still astonished at what she'd read she quietly closed the door behind her and headed back down stairs. As she was entering the study Bradford looking at her with a broad grin said, 'hi, thought I'd have to call the rescue squad for you." "I'm truly sorry Brad, but I found something in mother's belongings that I never expected and became completely distracted, she told him." "I see he said, while observing her." He wasn't going to pry, she'd tell him whenever she was comfortable in doing so. In a *more serious tone he said, "Claudia while going through your father's files, I came across a number of things I'm not quite certain about yet, then looking at her he asked, would you by any chance happen to know a Steven Chatsworth?" Looking directly at him for a time, she was well aware that he had a very good reason for questioning her so she said, "I only met him three times. The first time, I was helping out at the office, he came in to see my father and we were introduced. The other two occasions were here at my parent's dinner parties. Its strange that you should ask about him because my mother never cared for him at all, and for some strange reason I can't explain why, neither do I! "I know my mother said they'd known each other for many years and she only tolerated his presence in fairness to my father, but why do you ask Brad?" "Claudia, remember the two folders I took from your father's office?" "Yes, I remember." "Well Steven Chatsworth's name is in one of them, and today, I find more with his name in them here. I'm not ready to say for certain until I get back to my office , but I'll tell you this much, there's something going on and Chatsworth is a part of it. First, I've got to analyze all of my information before I can make a determination either way, he said." "you know, you just might be right because for one I never trusted him, and yet; I don't know why she told him. And there's something else, I only read through the second page of mother's Journal, but I've never seen a 'personal Journal' written in the way mother wrote in hers, there's something very strange about it, she said." "Strange in what way he asked her?" "I don't know exactly; I've only read the first couple of pages. She began the Journal with the history of the contractors 'firm, she said." "That is strange to say the least, he told her." Looking at his wristwatch he said, "I believe I've everything I need for now, how about you?" "Oh, I'm done here until I get some cartons to pack thigs in. Hey, I'm getting hungry how about you, she asked him?" 'Oh, I'll grab a Chinese dinner on the way to my office. I've still got a lot of work ahead of me. Claudia, this situation is far from conclusion, and I'm still searching for clues, perhaps, in a few days I'll be able to give you something solid." " I believe you*

Brad, do what ever is necessary for you to find who ever is responsible for all of this happening. In the mean time, I'm going home and get back to reading my mother's Journal." "Asking out of genuine concern, will you be all right?" "Oh yes, I'll be fine. I'm just going to look around a bit more before leaving, and thanks for the concern.. "You're quite welcome."

Bradford checked in with his answering service there were no new messages so, he placed the folders on top of the desk beside his food, after washing his face and hands he sat down and opened the two containers and a soft drink. He knew that he was going to be there for quite sometime, for the moment, he just wanted to relax and enjoy his meal hopefully without any interruptions. The meal was finally finished and after discarding the containers he opened each folder on his desk while still sipping on his soft drink. Leaning back in the large chair he focused his eyes on the papers in front of him. Where and how Chatsworth fit into the picture especially, since he'd retired? Yet, he's signed an agreement with David Lansing just weeks prior to the accident, and today I find his name on other papers as well. He visited Lansing at his office at least once that Claudia knew about, she also stated the he and her parents had known each other for years. I saw him leaving through the entrance after he'd flatly denied having any business dealing's with the firm, then just who was he seeing and what was he doing there? He's up to his racist neck in something and I'm going to find out what it is, David Lansing is dead. Is there a connection between him and the situation that's developed? The 'goof balls' who've been playing footsy with me and a couple of guys working for the firm is also working for him. I know who they are so, I'm just going to let them play out their hands. Blake is scheduled back in two days it's time, for me to meet with him.

The following day, Claudia telephoned his office at ten a.m. asking if she could meet with him there? He asked if she knew how to get there? She replied, Yes! He hadn't scheduled anything for the morning anyway. That's the advantage in working for yourself he *thought; (smiling) recalling Claudia's voice on the telephone and she wasn't her usual pleasant self either. He didn't want to speculate on anything so, he'd just await her arrival. Bradford wasn't aware that his special treat was going to come from a very unlikely source. Hearing a light knock on his door he immediately pushed his chair back from the desk and walked across the room and opened it. Claudia was standing there with red swollen eyes. Looking at her in astonishment and in a mild tone asked her, "Claudia, what I heaven's name is wrong?" While taking her by the arm and leading her to the chair opposite his desk, he gave her a cup of water from the cooler then sat on the corner of his desk, waiting until she was ready to talk. She began by saying, Brad, remember when we at the house yesterday, and I told you that I'd found my mother's Journal and what I considered to be a strange way to begin one?" "Yes, I remember and when were getting ready to leave you told me that you were going home and get back to reading it. Am I correct?" "Yes, and I did just that and now I regret having found it." He held a steady gaze on her while asking in a soft, but serious tone, Claudia, what could possibly be in your mother's Journal that would stress you out this waw?" "Brad, when I was in college, one year I came home on Spring break, Mom and I had gone for one of our long walks because she enjoyed it so much especially, since Dad was making frequent out-of-town trips. Anyway, she stopped and while holding both hands in hers and said, 'darling whenever you make a promise to someone full fill that promise even if it take you half a life time. Brad, the significance of it really hadn't registered in my mind until I was reading this Journal. I never knew my grandfather he died long before I was born, but when I was younger, I remember my mother telling me that she'd whispered a promise in his ear as he was dying, and she kept it. When I removed her Journal from her drawer I was hesitant in opening it, but it was as if someone kept nudging me until I did. And I believe in my heart that you're going to find some of the answers to your questions, because there's something in there that you should know." Tearfully and with trembling hands, she gave him the Journal and said," after you're finished, you can burn it up because I don't ever want to see it again, she said in a very determined tone." Holding the book and looking into her eyes he said, "Claudia, I'm truly sorry for the pain you're enduring. Is there anything that I can do?" "Thank you Brad, but you're already doing what you do best , and all I'm asking is when and wherever you find the missing pieces put an end to it." "You 've my word on it! After Claudia assured him that she would be all right and left his office, Bradford returned to his desk wondering just what was in the Journal that had influenced her to become that bitter. He returned all of the papers to their folders and picking up the Journal looking at it for a couple of minutes decided that the only way to find out exactly what was written inside, was to open it and begin reading. So, after pouring himself a cup of coffee he settled back and opened to the first page. "How strange indeed, and justifiably so, thinking to himself."*

November 16, 1967-

This is the true history of the Contractors' firm. My father, Karl Henderson the original founder, owner and operator of his own company was a well-established building contractor. It took many years of hard labor to develop and establish the business that now is. He had a reputation for being a man of integrity and honest.

June 12, 1964-

David Lansing a young land surveyor and I were married. David began his new job in the company soon after our return from the honeymoon trip abroad. He was an energetic young man who was quite eager to learn more about the contractors' aspect of the business. There was a substantial a mount of work and they appeared to be working well together.

July 10, 1965-

There was a formed partnership for the purpose of expanding and establishing a family-owned enterprise. The partnership was a voluntary consensual relationship, and was not imposed by any law.

By forming the partnership they became co-owners, and principals to transact the business of the firm. They each would have a fractional interest in the enterprise.

December 12, 1965-

There was a mutual agreement to change the name to Henderson & Lansing Contractors 'firm. At that time, the firm had begun to generate more contracts and David began his apprenticeship under my father.

July 20, 1967-

Two years later, father began to exhibit signs of illness. My father became an unwilling prey. His condition worsened and he reluctantly cut back on much of the physical activities because his health was on a steady decline. To have witnessed the diminishing health of the man who had fulfilled a very important roll in my life was both painful and frustrating because he was my beloved father, and there was nothing that I could do, but observe time running its course. At that time, there was also an unwelcome change occurring in David, he was appearing to be more interested in the financial affairs of the company than anything else. He was becoming decisively ambitious. On the pretext of being concerned about my father's health he had begun resorting to duplicity to further enhance his own personal financial gain. I was later informed that one day during my absence, David accompanied by someone else had made a special visit to his home and the question was why? During day's visit, I was given the answer to my question.

September 8, 1967-

David had become the universal agent for the business, father had given him a blanket power-of attorney to do anything that must be done during his absence. When I learned of this betrayal, I was shocked because that issue had never once been discussed. It took all of my strength and will power to maintain composure in the presence of my seriously ailing father. After our return home, I accuse him of having committed an insidious act against my father because I knew he'd manipulated him into giving him that authority. I asked why had he done it? He gave me no verbal reply, but the sinister expression that appeared on his face at that moment, led me to believe without reservation was the direct response to my question, and it tore at my very being. I questioned myself as to what manner of man had I married and was rewarded with a disturbing thought. David had begun to potentate his newly acquired authority by reducing my father's authority in his own firm. However; by the time this happened the illness had progressed to it's chronic state and he was hospitalized. My father has been for a period of two weeks and already David has grasped complete control of the firm, and I've characterized his demeanor as being desensitized and ruthless. He's begun to make abrupt changes in the firm as if no one else was involved, or even matter. I must acknowledge the fact that I've allowed a parasite to enter into our lives, and the thought of it is quite disturbing. Today when I went to visit my father, by some means he'd learned of David's flagrant deceptions and treachery from his hospital bed, I was faced with his reaction to the news and there was intense sorrow, anger and disappointment. I soon realized that my efforts to console him were futile. What David has done is indescribable, so I softly whispered in my father's ear to set things straight.

October 10, 1967-

Karl Henderson my beloved father expired in his hospital bed. Later, the medical examiner ruled his death as the result of a massive coronary, but I most certainly believe that y father died of a broken heart, and my husband David Lansing is responsible. Unfortunately, he never lived long enough to terminate David's authority as an agent for the firm. Exactly one month after my father's demise, David changed the name to Lansing Contractors' firm When I objected he became enraged because his perception is that, women are subservient to men. I've also been aware of his unsavory life-style for quite sometime. There is an unquestionable about him that is appalling. From this day forward there are no more delusions regarding our marriage, my attention will most certainly be focused elsewhere.

November 16, 1967-

One afternoon I was on my way to David's office as I came near there were voices coming from inside, and I wondered why they were there? As I approached the door was slightly ajar, I immediately recognized each of the voices. Steven Chatsworth was a land developer whom I loathed. My father and e had a big disagreement a few years prior, and he'd told me that Chatsworth was big trouble he's a racist and Dad was not. Nathan Thompson is a large building contractor, and Matthew Crawford is a Corporate Attorney. I stopped in my tracks when I heard David tell the others that first, they should get rid of some of the smaller contractors because they were becoming a big nuisance , and then they could proceed with their next plan. At that moment, I became infuriated at what I had just witnessed, and wondered 'what in heaven's name were they planning to do? After over hearing their conversation, I walked back to the office. Besides, I needed time to think before confronting David on this issue. Anyway, I don't trust him to be truthful with me, and I definitely have no qualms about mistrusting Steven Chatsworth. But what brought them here and with Chatsworth? The more I thought about it the more curious I became There was definitely something going on, and I could sense it wasn't good. The following morning David informed me that he would be out of the city for a couple of days to take a look as some new construction sites. That afternoon two men who were small building contractors asked to speak with David. I explained the he would be out of the city for a couple of days and asked if I could possibly be of any assistance to them? They explained that on two separate occasions David had come to them trying to pressure them into selling their businesses. They are small true enough, but this is their livelihood and there is no need for any negotiations because they're not interested in selling no matter what amount, the offer is. Looking at them standing in front of me for a moment and having listened to them, memories of my father's struggle years ago returned and I recalled his stout heartedness and determination. Finally I asked them, did David ever tell either of them why he was interested in buying their businesses? Both ther responses were no! But one of the spoke and said about two weeks prior, he'd met another building contractor who told him that some land developer (that would be Steven Chatsworth) was trying to buy his business and he just flatly said he wasn't interested. I assured them that when David returned I would try to find out exactly what was going on. After their departure, I suddenly remembered the conversation in David's office, and recalled his statement in reference to some of the small contractors. I'm in no way considering what is, happening to be purely coincidental, and then this sudden out-of-town trip soon after the meeting. Acknowledging both David's and Chatsworth's background in deviousness, my perception is that they're up to something sinister. However; I still don't have a clue as to precisely what, or why? And those men appearing when they did tied in with the meeting . David returned two days later as scheduled. That evening I informed him that there was something that, we need to discuss. Sitting down facing me he nonchalantly said, 'I'm listening, what is it that you're so anxious to discuss? Abruptly I informed him, of what had transpired at the office during his absence, leaving nothing out. I directly asked him, 'what was the rationale for what he'd done? In a rather stern tone he told me that it didn't concern me. Of course; I disagreed. And casually reminded him that the business is also mine, and I have a right tobe concerned. Whether he agreed with me or not, was not the issue, but what I was most interested in knowing was what were he and that group of men up to? He was becoming furious, and at that point, I didn't care. Suddenly, his eye's widened when he asked me, what group of men was I talking about? I told him that since he was pretending ignorance, I would gladly tell him what group. The group that was in your office the day prior to your trip, and you're all up to something I know it! You're wrong, all of you are. He sat there staring as if uncertain of how to respond. He had never seen me that resolute before. I imagine he finally reconciled himself to the fact that I knew about the meeting, but what else did I know and just how much? He seemed to realize that the only way he'd really get the answers was to ask me directly, so he did and my response to him was 'I was there and heard your every word, but what I don't know is why? He immediately retaliated by asking me, what did I mean I was there? I explained every detail of the meeting to him including, the statement he made. He quickly accused me of eavesdropping. No, your door was ajar apparently, you'd forgotten to close it, or perhaps thought no one would hear you, but I did hear you David. He quickly said that he had no idea of what I imagined to have heard. I interrupted him without giving him an opportunity to continue because I knew he was only stalling for time. I wanted to know why he was trying to as was stated, buy up their businesses? There was no reply, so I asked him again. He said, I didn't understand that was big business and the contractors companies were expanding. I had to firmly stand my ground, and focused my eyes directly into his. I said in other words, you're trying to convince me that with all the land still remaining undeveloped you also want their businesses and for what, just to tear them down and reconstruct something else in their place? Just to refresh your memory, my father developed this business from scratch and he struggled for years to accomplish what you walked into, but of course you wouldn't know about that or eve care. Those men are trying to do the same thing for their families, and how dare you attempt to elevate yourself above everyone else especially, after what you did to my father. He stood up and looked at me with cold, penetrating eyes and said, so, that's what all of this is about, your old man? I said no David, it's about you and your greed. Apparently, angry and frustrated over the entire issue, he suddenly threw up his hands and stormed out of the room. By that time, I was infuriated to the point of tears, but I refused to let them come. A week had lapsed before either of us began to speak to each other again. He came into the office one afternoon and gave me some papers to look over and sign. Two days later, he invited me to dine out with him and after giving it some consideration I finally accepted. Thinking to myself, that wasn't an apology, he's up to something I know it! I had no intention of allowing myself to be deceived by his noble gesture especially, since I'm fully aware of his history for being devious, manipulative, and insensitive to others.

December 12, 1967- Their actions were so subtle that when I finally realized what was actually taking place David, Steven Chatsworth, Matthew Crawford, Nathan Thompson and a number of others had formed an alliance against the smaller companies. And those few of the larger ones who openly opposed their method of doing business came under scrutiny. The flagrant deceptions were such that I could never have imagined it's ever happening in my entire lifetime. Many of the properties acquired were indiscriminately and, insidiously obtained. There was large scale cheating by mis representation such as, defrauding and depriving people of what was rightfully and legally theirs. Business dealings in which David was known for his expertise in forestalling to prevent competitive trading was unscrupulous. He influenced the larger contractors to raise their bids to such a high level that the small companies especially the less stable one's didn't stand a chance. David Lansing was said to be manipulative and cunning in his business dealings. He himself fraudulently acquired certain properties and re-sole them for out standing profits including the fixed assets of businesses. The corruption included bribery and selling of certain favors in an effort to maintain controlling influence against opponents Coercion, obstruction and strong-arm tactics were used to prevent normal negotiations among other contractors. Where as opponents and smaller contractors could not participate and this was referred to as- high undermining. The circle that evolved was unlimited, chaotic and profitable in the struggle for the absolute that was being sought. It was felt and known through the region as being ruthless and brutal in nature. Having such an enormous impact that it obtained a reputation of the worst kind.

April 15, 1968-

A number of businesses that had managed to survive the chaos by eventually pooling together in defiance of the brutally formed alliance became pawns in the power struggle. Former associates as a dictating tyrant who was ruthless referred to David Lansing. With morals where and when ever, money was involved. He even had a greater air for deviousness and insensitivity when it came to, human suffering. Quite sometime later, I was informed that upon witnessing the terrible aftermath of it all; Nathan Thompson thought their actions had gone too far' and Matthew Crawford said, he'd seen too much and finally had enough. They broke rank from David and the others and each had gone his separate way. I believe the results of the struggle for power were important factors, and the immediate results were these:

Businesses, both large and small folded, homes were lost or cheated out of, including the two men who had come to the office that day. One lost his business, home and family. The other not only lost his business, but also suffered permanent paralysis of the lower extremities as the result of a severe brutal beating. Physical and psychological suffering was induced by threats of violence and brutality. The long-term results were these: The circle of destruction has left an everlasting effect, and the amount of devastation in the region is beyond comprehension. So many lives were affected by the abhorrent acts of injustice that nothing remains, but fear, pain and oppression. My self-observations, personal feelings and lasting reflections are these: David's ruthless decisive ambition was directly motivated by his greed to be both wealthy and powerful. As for myself, I feel remorse, shame and humiliation, and all of the self-anguish for allowing him to completely dominate and control my life all those years, as he has others. I've written this Journal in memory of my father, Karl Henderson as a promise that has been full-filled. Claudette Henderson Lansing. After having read the Journal in its entirety Bradford's sentiments toward it's owner were: it was very unfortunate that she had no clue tat at the time, he grasped control of the business it was a matrix. And according to what I've read, he had no concept of how she was thinking, or what she was doing. Claudette Lansing was by no means a weak woman, she accomplished her goal, and that took courage. Now I understand the rationale for Claudia's sudden emotional behavior, this has to be rough on her. Leaning back in his chair and eyes fixed on the now closed Journal Bradford thought to himself, I've really got to have a talk with Blake. I'm interested in finding out just how much does he really know about Crawford and Chatsworth's involvement with David Lansing prior and up to the time of his death. As a matter-of-fact, there are a number of things we need to discuss ASAP. In the meanwhile, I'm going to call Mathew Crawford, he was next on my list anyway. 'Now I'm certain to find out how many crevices are there in this situation?

"Mr. Crawford, a Mr. Maxwell is here to see you sir." "Thank you Cindy, and send him in." As he walked in through the opened door a man who appeared to be in his early sixties was standing up behind a large polished walnut colored desk. "He said hello Maxwell, I've been expecting you . Have a seat pointing to one of the two leather chairs that was positioned in front of his desk. Looking directly at Bradford as to be sizing him up he said, considering your reputation you're a bit younger than I had anticipated." "And just why is that, he asked with a slight grin?" "Oh for now, let's say when Blake Colwell told me that you were on the case, and with your reputation I expected to see someone much older." "Oh I see, would it have made a difference?" "Taking into account your expertise I'm going to say no.""Good! Now that we've established that, I'd like to ask you a few questions." "Sitting further back in the chair while folding his arms across his chest appearing to be more relaxed and half smiling he asked so what are your questions?" "Since you've already spoken with Colwell you also know why I'm on this case, but what I'd like to hear from you is what connection if any, was there between Chatsworth, Lansing and yourself prior to his death?" "Bradford's direct question appeared to

have caught Crawford off guard because he was suddenly becoming noticeably tensed when he said, I don't know what you mean by connection." Looking directly into his eyes Bradford said, oh come off it Crawford I didn't come here completely ignorant of your background so, let's not begin by playing the cat and mouse game. I'm only interested in getting to the bottom of this situation and resolve." "Leaning back in his chair and not taking his eyes off Bradford he said," I broke ties with Lansing and Chatsworth years ago because I didn't approve of what was happening and wanted nothing more to do with it; or them for that matter. And when I learned of this situation I immediately telephoned Colwell. Listen Maxwell I didn't care for David Lansing, but his daughter Claudia doesn't deserve what's happening here. However, I do know that none of this took place until after the deaths and that's the puzzling part about it. You're privileged to believe what ever you will, but as you can see there's no connection as you might assume between the three of us." All right, let's just say for the sake of argument that what you've said is true, and you've no involvement with the two of them. Are you aware of any business dealings between Chatsworth and Lansing prior to his death?" "No, I'm not, but I wouldn't be at all a bit surprised if they were." "Why is that?" "Because neither of them, ever seemed to have enough of anything." "I hear you there, some people are just that way." "I've been on this case over three weeks now and everything is pointing directly at the firm. David Lansing is dead of this, we're certain, but is it feasible that Chatsworth is working with someone else within the firm?" That question seemed to have struck a cord because Crawford sat up right in hi chair. "And looking directly at Bradford said, there's a remote possibility that you've hit on something here Maxwell." "Come on man what is it, Bradford ask anxiously?" "Well when you mentioned someone within the firm, the first person that came to mind was Charles Carrington the son-in-law. Have you spoken with him yet?" "No, I haven't why? What are you suggesting ?" "He's much like David Lansing was, arrogant and unscrupulous. I never knew all of the details, but about two months before the deaths it was rumored that Charles and David had a big confrontation in which David had given him an ultimatum of some sort. It was intimated that a woman was involved, everyone was aware of David's unsavory life-style, and no one else knows what the ultimatum was, but I believe it's worth taking a shot at anyway." "I believe you're right, I spoke with Robert the bookkeeper and now I'm going deeper in side." He stood up and said, thanks Crawford for your help I appreciate it." "You're welcome, and I believe Blake made an excellent choice in hiring you for this case Maxwell, now I understand why, so if I can be of any further assistance please don't hesitate to call me," "Thank you." Bradford believed in keeping a leverage, he had no intentions of informing Crawford that he'd already observed Chatsworth and Carrington at the firm together. Thinking to himself, Crawford confirmed what was written in the Journal of him, that he had broken ties with the others. It appears that at least, some of the pieces are beginning to fit together, so its Chatsworth and Carrington. I've still got to get the facts that will tie them in together. Before I pay Robert a visit again, its time for me to have a meeting with Blake. He should've returned from his trip by now.

It was still early afternoon when he telephoned Blake's office and Jenny, his secretary, immediately put him through stating, 'Mr. Maxwell is on the line sir,' "Thank you Jenny. Hello Brad, I was just thinking of calling you." "Well, how about that see, I've saved you the trouble. I called to see if you had returned. We need to have a talk ASAP. " "That's fine with me. I arrived, a couple hours ago so I'm free for the remaining afternoon. Good! I'll see you in about half hour then." When he arrived at the Law Office Blake's door was open and after their greeting" Jenny said, you may go right in he's expecting you sir." "Thank you Jenny." As he was entering the door Blake stood up and extended his hand across the desk and after the handshake, "he asked Bradford to have a seat," "Thanks! I called your office and Jenny informed me that you'd be out of the city for a couple of days *on a case, how did it go for you?" "It went quite well thank you, but you know Brad, this situation has even reached the Ventura area. The second day in court I ran into an attorney I hadn't seen in nearly two years who said it was in the news papers up there. It appears that bad news still has a way of traveling faster." "It does appear to happen that way sometime." "I did get your message, but since it wasn't urgent I decided to wait until I returned." "Now that's what I consider to be logical thinking he said, and they both smiled." " Sitting father back in his chair focusing his eyes directly on Bradford Blakes asked, so what do we have now?" "At that moment Bradford leaned back in his chair crossing his legs while never taking his eyes off him said Blake, I've obtained quiet a bit of information and none of it appears favorable for the firm." "Sitting silently lowering his eyes to the desk and up again at Bradford he finally said, give me what you've got Brad." "First of all; everything I've come up with during the process is leading back to the firm and I'll tell you this much Blake, from all indications I've found the allegations against it to be valid. I understand this isn't the news you were wishing for, but my friend, we've an in depth situation here, and I'm only about half way through it. This is a very big puzzle and some of the pieces are just beginning to fit together, but they're not the major ones I'm seeking. And as it now stands, I believe an early resolve is out of the question. As Bradford sat looking at Blake an obvious strain was making its appearance on his features. "And as he spoke there was a deep a deep sadness in his tone when he said, Brad, when I first received news of this pickle situation from Crawford, I became alarmed and furious now, I'm more angry than mere words can express. What you're telling me is that someone in the firm is responsible for all that's taking place?" "Blake this is precisely what I'm saying, but someone else is also involved, I'm working on just how deeply and with whom? Incidentally, I interviewed Crawford and if I'm any judge of character, he appears to be on the up and up with this. I have some background information that once linked Lansing, Crawford and Chatsworth together and when I brought this to his attention, he stated that he hadn't associated with either of them in years. How long have you been the firm's attorney?" "Giving Bradford a quizzed look he said, since nineteen sixty-nine. I was asked to represent them by a senior partner in the firm I was associated with at the time. Why do you ask Brad?" "I'm trying to establish something here." Like what for instance?" "A connection between Chatsworth and Lansing." "why is that important?" "You weren't around when David Lansing seized control of his father-in-law's business and Chatsworth was involved with him then." "Just what do you mean, he seized control of the business Brad?" "Blake, we'll leave that question open for now, later I'll supply you with full details. He continued, when I went to Lansing's office I came across some papers with Chatsworth's name along with his, they were involved in some sort of land development deal, and that was just prior to the deaths. Yet, when I interviewed Chatsworth he vehemently denied having any business dealings with the firm." "Wait a minute, you 're telling me that you went to Chatsworth? "Yes I did, the visit was a rather short one, but it wasn't a complete wash out.." "What do you mean, Brad?" "In addition to being a racist he's also a liar." "There was an expression of embarrassment upon his face when he said, Brad I'm truly sorry." "Don't be, you of all people know as well as I that his way of thinking comes with the territory and I'm definitely not intimidated by it. The point is, he lied." "What do you mean, he lied?" "Number one, a few days after I'd spoken with him I was observing the firm when I saw he and two of his henchmen exit through the rear entrance. Number two, three incidents have occurred involving his men since our little chat. On one occasion, I was warned to stop meddling into things that's not my business. Some of the people, whom I interviewed earlier, are not afraid to speak with me again. This is indicating to me that I'm getting too close to something. In addition, number three, I observed Chatsworth and Charles conversing in the firm's rear parking lot. Now Lansing's dead so, what was his business there?" "You actually saw he and Charles there , together?" "Yes I did, and they weren't boxing. What it is, he's up to his neck in it." At that statement, Blake slowly leaned back in his chair and became silent. Bradford never altered his focus on him. Something was revolving around in Blake's mind and he knew it. "Finally, he came forward placing both hands on the desk while interlacing his fingers and said Brad, I don't understand why Charles would be speaking with Chatsworth. And in light of what you've just conveyed to me I'm now convinced that you should've been informed of this from the beginning and at the time, I thought your investigation would prove the assertions to be false, but I've been completely in error. Steven Chatsworth was David Lansing's silent partner." "Abruptly uncrossing his legs and sitting upright in the chair he exclaimed what! "with a sudden apologetic expression on his face he said please Brad, just hear me out. As far as I'm aware of he took no active part in the transactions and was virtually unknown to the public. I had no knowledge of any land development deals between the two of them until just now. I became aware of this act years ago; that David Lansing was the kind of man who did a lot of things on his own, and informed you of what and when he wanted you to know, no more and no less with a period. If you're asking why I represent the firm," observing the pressure on Blake's face he resumed his most obvious sitting position by leaning back in the chair and again crossing his legs then he said yes, that question has entered my thoughts." "Realistically I agreed to represent the firm because of Claudette. I knew she and her father quite well. David was a few years older than she and I." "All right, I suppose that's understandable, but what do you know about the bad blood that existed between Lansing and Carrington?" "Oh, so you heard about that huh?" "Yes, from a number of sources I must say." "Brad, I never really knew what that was about, but I'll tell you this, whatever transpired between the two of them infuriated David to the point that he immediately minimized Charles's authority in the firm. This took place shortly before the deaths." As if being awakened by a sudden jolt, "Blake sat straight up and without taking his eyes off Bradford said, while we've been sitting here talking different thoughts have been revolving around in my mind that's been there all along. But I was too pre occupied to realize what it was that's been so disturbing to me. Brad, this situation began shortly after the deaths and I couldn't possibly imagine anyone with this kind of bitterness or resentment who would have a rationale for what's happening. That is no one, but Charles Carrington. I recall during one of our conversations, Claudia informed me that she'd observed a change occurring in him soon after the deaths, and he was spending a great deal of time at the office. I believe this was the time Robert the bookkeeper was still on vacation. When she questioned him, he told her there were things at the office that he needed to take care of personally. You've already observed he and Chatsworth together in the firm's parking lot. Charles is quite arrogant and a lot like David was in many ways. As for Chatsworth, I've never trusted him anyway, and I expressed this to David more times, than one. Staring at him and asking Brad, "do you believe it's possible for the two of them to be responsible for the situation?" "Yes, from all indications I'd say it's quite possible, but first, I've got to get solid proof tying them in together along with who ever else that is involved with them. Right now, it appears that someone doesn't want me asking questions, little do they realize I've many more to ask before I'm finished." "Blake viewed him for awhile before speaking then he said, look I'm fully aware of your capabilities for handling yourself, but Brad please be careful from what you've told me, this situation is really becoming sticky." "Will do, but I've got to get all of the evidence not just some to resolve this thing." "yes I know, but it's becoming far more extensive than I could ever have anticipated it to be." "Oh by the way, I met Claudia. I was going through some of Lansing's files when she came in. She's a very lovely young lady Blake, it's a shame that she has to endure something that she had no control over." "Yes, I agree with you completely." "Obviously you haven't had the opportunity to speak with her since your return have you?" "No I haven't, has something happened during my absence?" "I believe that you should speak with her at your most earliest convenience Blake." He eyed*

Bradford skeptically. "I'm only telling you this so you'll be prepared when you do." "Prepared for what Brad?" "Claudia asked me to meet with her at her parent's home because she was going to take care of some of their belongings, and in the meanwhile, she would open her father's personal safe for me, and I agreed. While I was going through Lansing's personal files she went upstairs to start sorting through her mother's personal belongings. Blake, she discovered her mother's personal Journal, which she said was a surprise to her because she never knew her mother had kept one. It contained the complete history of the Contractors' firm. Chatsworth and Crawford's names are written in it. The following day, she called me at my office to see if I was going to be in for awhile, I said yes. When she arrived I could visibly see red swollen eyes and the devastation on her face I asked her what was wrong? 'After a short while and finally gaining her composure enough to tell me that she wished she'd never discovered her mother's Journal.' "I asked her why was that?" "She looked at me for a couple of seconds then said there was something I should know. She gave me the Journal and said, she believed I was going to find the answers to some of my questions, and when I was finished I could burn it up because she never wanted to see it again. On her way out she stopped long enough to tell me that when and wherever I find the missing pieces to the puzzle put an end to it! After Bradford had finished, Blake sat staring as if he was in a trance. "Then finally speaking in a trembling voice he said Brad, this is disheartening news indeed. I had no concept of what you were about to say , but this definitely wasn't it. Do you still have the Journal and if so, may I please see it?" Now there was a deep sadness in his voice and also in his eyes as well. He stared at the man before him who appeared to be aging by the minute. Looking at Blake, Bradford was beginning to wonder if there was something more significant about the Lansing's personally, especially Claudette than he was willing to admit. And of that, he was quite certain however, to "Blake's question he said yes, I still have it I thought you might want to read it for yourself. I'll get it to you very soon." "Thank you." "No problem he said smiling." "I've *definitely got to talk with Claudia now speaking in a low voice." "I'm sorry Blake." "So am I Brad and thanks." "Any time, he said with a wide grin. Now standing he said, I'd better be going there's still a lot more work to be done, I'll be in touch with you later."*

On the way back to his office and remembering their conversation he realized Blake wasn't aware of all Lansing's deals. But Chathworth was involved in the take-over of the firm and apparently, that's when he became the silent partner and now here he is again, only this time, it's with Lansing's son-in-law. The question is, 'what is he planning this time? I'm willing to bet he has his own agenda and it doesn't include Carrington. There's something very wrong with this picture.' I'm anxious to find out just what they're up to. In the meanwhile, I'm going to go through all of the information that I've obtained including the talk with Matthew and Blake. I want to see if I'm missing anything so far. Upon returning to his office and checking his messages, Robert the bookkeeper, had called him twice, stating it was urgent. After finding his number in the locator on his desk he telephoned him, hoping to find him still in the office. "Hello Robert, this is Maxwell I just returned to my office and received your messages. I take it you have something for me." "That's affirmative Brad, and I have quite a bit that I believe you'll be interested in." " This is the best news I've had all day. When are you going to be available?" "As a matter-of-fact, I'm available now, and I'll be here until six this evening." "Well, it's only three fifteen now, it'll take me about forty-five minutes to get to the firm with the traffic the way it is right now." "That will be fine, I'll be expecting you." "Right! After replacing the receiver, he leaned back in his chair closing his eyes for a few minutes with a mental image of what has already come into play so far. After he's seen what Robert has, he'll take it from there.

Blake received a rather disturbing call from Steven Chatsworth immediately following his meeting with Bradford inquiring about the investigation. He demanded to know how his name had become involved in the situation? Blake said, "look Chatsworth it was *unavoidable, everyone who is associated with the firm is under suspicion, including yourself! Chatsworth was silent for a brief period, before saying ' I don't like what's happening here, and I sure don't care to be explaining my business to a high-minded black, Investigator or not. Blake said listen."* Bradford is thorough and quite resourceful and he's no pushover. In fact, he can be a man's best friend, or worst enemy he always give you a choice, but when crossed he has a potential for being deadly. He's only doing the job that he was hired to do, so my advice to you is to cooperate with him." "He snapped, like the devil you say." Blake thought to himself, 'I'd say this man's in for a rude awakening.'*

At precisely four p.m. Braford was walking towards the office when Robert appeared in the doorway, and smiling he quickly ushered him inside and immediately closed the door behind them. They shook hands and Robert pointed to a chair in front of his desk and invited him to have a seat. Bradford immediately observed a few folders and papers on top of the desk. "Brad, I've gone through the books and paper work, the accountant has been assisting me with all of it. This is what we have as of now and it's by no means favorable. First; when I returned from my trip I was informed that some of the long-time drivers for the firm had been terminated and Charles hired new inexperienced ones. Having through the records it appears that the amount of materials on a number of prepaid orders, approximately twenty to forty percent that has been delivered to buyers were below the amount they've actually paid for. And numerous complaints are coming in saying that only about one-half of the materials and supplies ordered and paid for are being delivered to them. What I find to be ironic about the whole thing is, someone has signed off saying all of the materials were accounted for. From all indications, someone is deliberately skimming off materials and cutting back on prepaid orders. Brad, there's also some undermining going on here." "Like how for instance he asked him?" "Delivery orders of building materials, and supplies to a number of small contractors has been terminated suddenly, and some are complaining that some of the quantities of goods was offered for sale at a certain price, but when they came in to make the purchases the price had been hiked. According to Blake, Charles's authority to represent the firm has been minimized, and he's not authorized to negotiate any business deals without Claudia's or his approval. He's negotiated business deals with some of the larger companies as the firm's legal representative by offering to furnish them all of the supplies and materials need for their jobs, while at the same time, he's been cutting back on regular up front paying customers for sizeable commissions. There's a profit being made here, according to the books it's not coming into the firm's account." "Robert, during my meeting with Blake, and what you've just shown me confirms our suspicion of Charles, but he's not the only one involved here. I've got to find out who all of the players are. Who's been signing off on these delivery orders?" "A guy by the name of Phillip Brandt, who incidentally works for one of the larger construction companies you visited. Brad, I have one question to ask." "What is that ?" "Why is Charles and who ever else doing this?" "Robert when I get all of the pieces to fit together, then we'll have our answers. It's also time for me to have a little chat with Charles. Anyway, it's getting late and I've got a busy schedule ahead of me tomorrow, and thanks for your help. I'll be in touch." "You're more than welcome Brad, I'll be seeing you."

Early the next morning the first stop on his agenda was the firm. He was about five feet away from the front entrance when the door opened, looking at the man that was coming out he said "Charles Carrington I presume." Staring up at the over six foot tall man that was standing in front of him, with a blank expression from the apparent unexpected appearance he hesitantly responded saying" Your presumption is correct, but who the devil are you?" "I'm Bradford T. Maxwell, and I'd like to ask you a few questions." Staring at him for a moment then with an air of arrogance he questioned, so you're the one who's got everybody up in the air around here. Therein lies your problem my dear Charles, you're too arrogant for your own good. With eyes fixed steadily on him Bradford said, "no, someone else has and that's why I'm here. "What do you mean?" "Oh come now Charles, don't play coy with me you know precisely what I mean. Why are you cutting back on orders to the small contractors in favor of the larger ones, and some aren't even receiving the amount they paid for, and what are you getting out of this?" "I don't know where or how you got your information, but it's a lie" "Is it now, do you know this is considered as undermining?" "I don't know what you're talking about, and I have an early appointment." "Then by all means, I suggest you keep it, but remember this-I'm going to find out who ever created this situation and why. I'll be in touch with you again, you can count on it!" He observed Charles's demeanor changing as he spoke and he was obviously becoming nervous as he abruptly turned away and headed for his car. Smiling and thinking ti himself, 'my, he's in a big hurry.' Later that afternoon as he was entering one of the larger construction sites that he'd previously visited, he observed a big disturbance in the middle of the yard and wondered to himself, 'what was happening? ' The answer to his question came just as he was locking the car door when a man came bouncing off the hood. Seeing the injured man attempting to stand he abruptly went to assist him, and began to question him regarding his injuries, which didn't appear to be, life threatening. He just asked the man about the disturbance when he was snatched from behind, and instantly his reflexes kicked in, a minute later, a stocky built man was lying flat on his back in front of them out cold. By this time, a small group had gathered around them, they were all staring down at the still out cold man on the ground and Bradford immediately recognized him as the same one who'd told him to stop meddling in something that wasn't his business. Finally, someone poured a pail of cold water over him, and he eventually began to moan and groan while holding the side of his face, and as he tried to speak they realized that he'd sustained a broken jaw. Bradford learned that his name was Jason Stevenson, and the one who was unsuccessfully attempting to help him up was William Hackford. They both engaged in strong-arm tactics, and worked for Steven Chatsworth. He was told by some of the men that they had gathered at the site to negotiate bids, and the tactics were applied to prevent them from doing so. After speaking with the group he learned that some of the larger companies as well were experiencing the same problems. During that time, Bradford also discovered that Charles was involved in unfair competition by combinations, and contracts, this was involving him along with Chatsworth. After leaving there, he decided to visit the Construction Company where Phillip Brandt worked as a dispatcher. He'd just entered the area when he spotted Charles Carrington's car, no one was inside therefore, he was somewhere on the premises, but what was he doing there trying to negotiate more deals?' He wondered to himself.' He was headed for the front office when a man came out, and he asked if he could tell him where he might find Phillip Brandt the dispatcher?" "Staring at Bradford curiously for a minute or so before answering then asked, "who wants to know?" "I'm Bradford T. Maxwell and I'd like to ask him a few question." "About what, he asked him?" "He'll know when I ask him, was Bradford's response." "Well he's not here right now." "When do you expect him back?" Hesitating for a couple of seconds before answering he said, "He said in about an hour." "Good, then I'll be back." "Suit yourself he said, as he abruptly turned away and went back inside. 'Something's wrong here, I can feel it. Ten to one he's here and so is Charles he thought to himself as he walked back to his car.' Taking a quick glance at his wristwatch he decided that in the meantime, to pay Chatsworth a visit at his home this time.

Apparently Chatsworth and his passenger had arrived at his residence just ahead of him the head huncho. Because they were still sitting the car as he pulled up behind them, and got out of his car. Thinking perhaps he'd been seen in the rear view mirror suddenly, the passenger door opened and one of the same men who'd escorted him out of the golf club came rushing towards him, at that same, instant he saw Chatsworth hurrying out of the car. He came within arm length taking a swing at Bradford he sidestepped snatching the man from behind and throwing him across the lawn. Looking down at the man sprawled on the ground, shaking his head and mummering something unintelligible, then returned his focus on Chatsworth who was stating at him with obvious hatred in his eyes said, "this is the second time that you've injured one of my men." "with the same gaze who's counting? He asked, in a very serious unfeigned tone.." "What do you want here now boy Chatsworth asked him in a voice that was quite hostile?" "First of all, I came here to discuss your involvement with the Lansing contractors' firm you adamantly denied, but I see that's out of the question now. Second, do I look like a boy to you?" "All your kind are boys to me." "And just what might be my kind?" "you're black, and that's enough for me." "I see, is that the best excuse you can give? So, when do boy's become men to you Chatsworth?" "When they're dead and buried." "Then I'd say you're living a terrible nightmare because I'm a m who's very much alive, and I definitely plan to remain that way." "Look Chatsworth you're up to your neck in this situation, and I'm going to find out why, you can count on it. Oh yes, a small piece of free advice, the next time, your little shirt-tail flunky bounces upon me I'm going to send him skidding right between your lanky racist leg's." Changing his focus directly on the other man who'd finally managed to stand on his feet he said as for yo, consider yourself forewarned." Then gazing at the both of them for a full minute neither of them spoke a word, he turned away walked back to his car and drove off.

In keeping his word, Bradford returned to the Construction Company. This time, he didn't see Charles's car in the area. Slowly getting out of his car and walking towards the building, he noticed activities around the site appeared to be busy as usual. He knocked on the door and a familiar husky voice from within said, "it's open come on in." When he entered the room a large stocky man was sitting behind a metal desk that was stacked with papers, and immediately looking up he smiled and said, "hi Maxwell it's good seeing you again take a chair." "The same here Bradford replied as he began sitting down." "By the way, I hear you've been pretty busy doing some chastising he said with a hearty laugh." "Let's just say, I have a thing about people grabbing me from behind.." "That one has been itching for something like that for a long time, and from what I've heard he approached the wrong man that time. So, what can I do for you? I was informed by one of the men that you'd been here earlier, but I was tied up on another job." "Look Kendall, the last time we spoke you gave me some advice regarding Charles Carrington, and you were right on the mark." "What'd you mean?" "I mean he's right in the middle of this thing if not at the top which I'm rather doubtful, because he's not that brilliant ." Are you certain about this? Because this is a big mess involving a lot of people, and he's still trying to do business with some of the contractors. Since you started the investigation, a few of them are backing away from doing business with the firm." "I see. And to answer your question, yes I'm certain, but he' not the only one that is involved in this situation, I know you've been experiencing some problems too, and that's why I came here earlier. I understand you have a man by the name of Phillip Brandt working for you as dispatcher." "That's right, but why do you ask?" "For starters, his name has come up a number of times during my investigation and I believe some of your problems are coming from within your own company. " "Looking directly at Bradford and seeing the seriousness on his face he asked in a rather shocked tone, are you telling me that someone is undermining me in my own company?" "I'm afraid so, but right now I'm working on gathering all of the facts that will substantiate this." "Then what does Brandt have to do with any of it?" When I first drove in I spotted Carrington's car. Abruptly interrupting him he asked, you what? Looking at the man's wide-eyed expression he continued the sentence. "As I was saying, I saw Carrington's car as I was headed this way when a man suddenly came out to meet me. I asked if he could tell me where I might find Philip Brandt, then he ask, who wanted to know? I gave him my name and explained that I just wanted to ask him a few questions. Then he asked me about what? I just said, he'd know when I asked him. He told me he wasn't here, that he'd be back in about an hour. I told him I'd be back. His abrupt rudeness gave me the impression that he was withholding something and wanted me out of here pronto. I don't know his name because he never gave it to me.'

"His name is Hank Meadows one of the Forman's he told me that you came by, but he never said anything about Carrington being here, or your wanting to talk with Brandt. Now I'm wondering why?" When he'd finished speaking Bradford asked him, "did anyone know you were going to be delayed?" "Why yes, I telephoned Meadows explaining that I'd be tied up a bit longer than I'd anticipated." "When was this?" "I guess a little before noon.." "Was Brandt here at the time?" "He should've been he comes in every morning at six -thirty." "Listen if you don't mind, I'd like to have a talk with Brandt and also go over the log manifests with you to see what we come up with." "Sure no problem, you've got me curious now, and I'd really like to know why Carrington was here anyway. I'll call him to come over here." When Haskell telephoned the dispatch, no one answered. "That's odd he told Bradford, no one's answering over there." He then called for Meadows to come to the office immediately. About ten minutes later, he appeared and it was quite obvious that he was surprised to see Bradford again. "Haskell said, Meadows you've met Maxwell, his response was yeas, "I met him. " "First of all where's Brandt he's supposed to be at his post, but no one's answering the telephone over there?" His sarcastic response was," I don't know." "I'll tell you what, you locate him and tell him that I want to see him here in my office, like yesterday Haskell told him. " He abruptly turned, but before leaving he gave Bradford a hostile stare which didn't go unnoticed by either of them. After the door closed Bradford looked at Haskell and said, "I've got a bad feeling about all of this, something's wrong here." "How do you mean, he asked?" "I didn't see Carrington, only his car, which means he had to be somewhere on the premises and Brandt's not answering your calls. I also noticed that

Meadows never mentioned that Brandt was supposedly to have left and return in an hour. One other thing you weren't here, so who Carrington visiting? Haskell, how long has Meadows been employed here?" "Let's see he said, as he stood up and walked across the room stopping in front of a large grey file cabinet. He pulled out a drawer and after fingering through folders, he removed one and opened it then he told Bradford, "He's been here two and a half months. Suddenly, looking at him he said, Maxwell, he was referred here by Charles Carrington." "His reply was, you don't say! "And just when did you start having these problems ?" Staring at the folder in his hand for sometime, before answering him he said, "shortly after he came here. Looking at him curiously he asked, "Maxwell just what are you thinking?" "That this is too much of a coincidence." "I agree, but just what do we do now?" "I suggest nothing until we get Meadows and Brandt together , and go over the log manifest.. I believe we're going to find a few discrepancies, some of your supplies and materials are going elsewhere. This is why you and some of the others are coming up short. Someone is signing off that you're receiving the correct amount. I'll lay you odds ten to one that Meadows is also on Carrington's payroll if not the both of them." "I've a hunch you're right, but I've been looking other places and it's been right here all along." "Haskell, you're one of the larger construction companies and from what I've seen, and what I've been able to piece together is that companies such as yourself, are being forced compete against each other for a profit. While cutting out the smaller ones by not allowing them the opportunity to compete, and you know that's called, unfair competition." "Man this is bad news." "You're telling me, but Carrington isn't the only one that's involved, there's a larger fish I'm going to catch." Just as Bradford had finished speaking Meadows came trough the door, and looking at the both of them he said," I couldn't seem to locate Brandt anywhere MR. Haskell." Bradford had an amused expression on his face when Haskell shouted ",what do you mean, you can't locate him, who's at the dispatch office?" "No one right now, he said. I went over there all the books and everything's gone including Brandt." By that time, Bradford noticed that Haskell was obviously steaming, and staring at Meadows in a tone that was anything but light(looking at the man who was now standing reminded Bradford that at one time, he'd worked as a timber lumber jack) when he said, " I have two questions to ask you, why did Brandt leave his post without first clearing it with me for replacement, and what was Charles Carrington during here?" "I don't know why he left, I didn't ask him." His demeanor was noticeably changing as he was being questioned by Haskell. With the last question he was appearing more nervous when he said, "Mr. Carrington wasn't here." With his anger now quite apparent. Haskell said, "you know the rules here. You didn't bother to inform me of Brandt's absence, neither did you tell me that Carrington had been here." Bradford thought it was time, for his intercession and looking directly at Meadows he said, "he was here I spotted his car as I drove onto the site. Which means he was seeing someone here.." He quickly turned to him and said, 'you're mistaken I don't know what you're talking about." "I'm talking about your being on Carrington's payroll, and you know it's true." By this time he knew he'd been wedged in. To Bradford his reaction wasn't totally unexpected when he stared at him in a challenging tone and cold eyes asked, "you think you have it all together don't you?" But you haven't! "No, but you've simplified things because you're another piece that fit the puzzle, he said in a confident tone. " Haskell had a disgusting expression on his face as he stared hard at Meadows and said, "as of now you're no longer employed here. I'll call payroll, you can pick up your check leave these premises and don't come back." Meadows never said anything, but gave he and Bradford a smirked look while slamming the door shut behind him. They both sat silent for a few minutes and Haskell was the first to speak. "Maxwell, from what I'm seeing there's much more to this situation than I originally thought, something's really going on, and I really want you to level with me. " "Looking at him for a speaking he began by saying, "Haskell, what you've just witnessed is only a small part of a much larger picture that's beginning to come into focus. You see, before the situation can be resolved I have to connect everyone that's involved and that means going after the big fish as well, and I've already begun that. Meadows isn't the only pawn there're others as well." "man, this sounds like some sort of chess game." "Believe me Haskell, this isn't a game, but the real Mccoy. They're out to ruin the contractors' firm, and using strong measures to so. " "Just who do you mean, by they?" "Your assumption about Carrington was correct, but he's not the only one involved there's also Steven Chatsworth." "Wait a minute Maxwell, are you certain about, Chatsworth's involvement in this?" "I'm quite certain. I've also observed he and Carrington together at the firm." "You stated that they're out to ruin the firm, but why?" "That's what I'm going to find out." He sat gazing at the man that was sitting in front of him and admired him for his strength and determination, because he knew he meant every word that he'd spoken. Finally he said look, "If you're as certain of Chatsworth's involvement as you've said, and I believe you are then, I suggest you watch your back. He's a big man who doesn't play fair, and it's a known fact that he has little tolerance minorities." Bradford leaned back in the chair, and with a sudden smile that was quite noticeably serious said," affirmative on all counts, but big men have been known to fall just as easily at the right given time. I've already been introduced as to how he plays. As for his racist concepts we've already had somewhat of a discussion about that." Haskell leaned forward on his desk and without taking his eyes off Bradford he asked, "you mean to tell me that you've already spoken with Chatsworth?" "As a matter-of-fact on two occasions, and I'm going to see him again. At this point it's irrelevant whether he wants to see me or not. Right now, I suggest we focus our attention on your missing dispatcher. How long has he worked here?" "Now that you've asked, he came here about two years ago, said he'd worked for a transportation company and when they downsized he was laid off. " "Has anything like this happened with him before?" "No, but I believe he had a gambling problem though, or something." "Oh, why do you believe that?" "For one two days after payday he was broke, then I heard from a couple of the men that he'd started borrowing money from them. Twice he's asked for advance on his pay. I didn't question him because I felt it was personal. And there was never any complaints regarding his work performance that is until now, but for the last couple of month's he'd done neither, so I just assumed whatever problem he had was resolved." "Has he paid the men back the money that was loaned to him?" "As far as I'm aware of yes, no one has said anything else abut it." "Doesn't it strike you sort of odd that his routine has changed this way. Shall we take a wild guess?" "Are you telling me that he was a plant too?" I really believe he was a plant because he's been here for two years and nothing like this has happened with him before. One, he might have agreed to do what they asked for a certain amount of money. Now whether he left on his own, or was coerced, or threatened we don't know. Two, the simple fact is he and the paper work's disappeared and I think you've been highjacked, so to speak by your own employees, just maybe this was the purpose of Carrington's visit. Either way I'm going to find out. I'm also going to try and locate Brandt if so, perhaps I might be able to get some answers from him. By the way, do you have an address on him?" Haskell said yes." And wrote it on a piece of paper from his note pad. Maxwell took the paper, looked at it and said, "I rather doubt he'll be foolish enough to go there, but I'll try it anyway. In the meanwhile, I suggest you contact some of the contractors, who have larger projects and find out who's received their correct amount of materials, supplies and rental equipment without any hassle. We already know the ones who've had problems including yourself. Also see if you can possibly get it narrowed down to one or two because they're the one's I'll be going after. Which means they're the one's Carrington negotiated deals with." "Maxwell, do you realize this is a tall order?" "Yes I do, but I need your help on this." After gazing at him for a couple of seconds Haskell finally agreed. "With a broad grin he said, thanks as he was heading for the door."

At the time, those events were taking place, Claudia herself was occupied with the task of clearing er father's safes and delivering everything to Blake. She decided to have a face to face talk with him only this time, the conversation would be far more different, than all the previous ones. When she arrived at Blake's office he was standing at his secretary's desk. Someone was assisting her with the cartons, and Blake directed them to his private office. After the men had gone he led her to a chair walked around his desk and seated himself. There was a few minutes of silence then Blake's fixed gaze was directly on her face and he said. "you're one up on me," "I don't understand, what do you mean she asked him?" Smiling he said, "I was just about to telephone and ask if you would come to my office." "Oh I see, she said solemnly." "Look Claudia, I'm not going to ask if you're all right, at this point that would be an unfair question because it's visibly clear you're not, and I do understand why you're so upset. Brad informed me that when the two of you were at you parent's home you discovered your mother's personal Journal and your reaction after reading it." As Blake sat looking at her there was a distorted expression on her face that was impossible to over look. In her eyes were anger, pain and terrible sadness. In his mind, it was as if she'd become a different person and seeing her that way disturbed him greatly. Sitting farther back in the chair and eyes focused directly o him she said," Blake first of all, I'm beyond being upset, I'm down right furious and I don't believe for one minute that finding my mother's Journal was by accident, contrary to the way it might appear to someone else. I can't explain it, but among all of her personal belongings I was led to a particular drawer, and there it was. I never knew she kept one. I was surprised to see it, but even more so to actually read what was written inside. Frankly, I didn't understand her rationale for writing it the way she did until after I had managed to read it through. He never interrupted her, but just continued to sit back and listen. Claudia turned her head for a moment in the direction where the cartons had been stacked she looked at him and said, Blake I've some questions to ask you up until now, there had been no need to." "What is it that you want to ask me my dear?" "Second of all, you've been the attorney for this firm since before I was born correct?" "Yes, that's correct." "Then tell me, why did you accept the position?" While maintaining his focus on her, his inner thought was 'oh , oh what is she leading up to?' "Truthfully, I agreed to represent the firm because of your mother. I knew she and your grand father quite well." "What about dad, she asked him?" "What about him?" "Just how well did you know him?" "Not that well, he was a few years older than your mother and I." "I see, she said. " "So you're aware that my grand father was the original owner and when he became ill dad deceptively and treacherously cheated him out of it that is, he and Steven Chatsworth." He came forward a bit never taking his eyes of her and said Claudia, I was away at the time, and by the time I returned those changes had occurred. There was a lot of speculation, actually happened, I can't say because your mother and I never discussed it. So, your mother wrote all of what you're telling me in her Journal?" "That and much more she said bitterly" "I always knew there was why mother could barely stand to be in the same atmosphere with Chatsworth, and I never cared for hm either. I didn't trust him then and I definitely don't trust him now." There was a deep smile on his face when he said" Claudia, just remember this, your mother loved you with all her heart and why she wrote this way, I can't say." She stared at him hard then said, well I van. She kept the promise that she'd made to my grand father when he was dying." "And what was that my dear, he asked ?" "That the truth regarding the contractors' firm be known." Blake leaned ack in his chair looked away for an instant then at her again and said, "My word, all of these years she'd been keeping record of those events, and no one ever knew, not even David. She was an amazing woman. Suddenly, smiling Blake said something that surprised even himself. "Your parents are both gone, but Chatsworth is still here, and we'll just see what happens next, he spoke confidently." She stared at him in bewilderment. He gave her a broad smile when he said," things are beginning to shape up quite nicely. Oh incidentally, has Charles said anything to you recently regarding the firm's situation" "no, he hasn't, but I've noticed that he's becoming quite edgy." "In what way?" "Oh he seems to be more nervous with each passing day, but why do you ask?" "Because Bradford has spoken with him regarding the situation and he high tailed it out of the parking lot fast." "Oh you don't say! Well, if Bradford spoke with him all I can say is that he definitely has a reason to be nervous, then she began to really laugh." Seeing her do so uplifted his spirit and knowing Bradford as he did, he too began to laugh.

The next day Bradford paid a visit to the apartment building where Phillip Brandt was supposed to have lived. He was informed by the manager that he'd left the previous day obviously in a big hurry because he didn't bother to leave a forwarding address so his deposit could be mailed out to him. Bradford asked him if he was alone?" The man looked at him for a minute or so, then he asked him, "did you say you're a private investigator?" "Gazing down at the man he said, "yes I did, but why do you ask?" "Well, you asked me if he was alone and that's ironic because it's as if you already knew he wasn't." "How's that ?" "There were two men with him, one remained in the car, a big husky fellow, and the smaller one stood on the sidewalk looking up and down the streets as if they were expecting somebody you know?" "I see. By the way did you happen to notice whether or not he was carrying any luggage?" "Yes, he had a suitcase and a couple of small boxes, but he seemed awfully nervous to me." Chatsworth's goons he thought to himself. His hunch was correct, Brandt's disappearance wasn't of his own choosing. After leaving the apartment building Bradford thought he'd stop by David Lasing's office to see if he might have over looked something significant. However, he had no way of knowing that Claudia had completely cleared away the safe and all files. Obviously someone else didn't either because he'd just turned the corner headed for the office when suddenly, he spotted a man trying to break in. Apparently he was so preoccupied with his efforts that he never saw or heard him coming. Abruptly snatching him from the back and turning him around he asked the would-be burglar, "Just what do you think you're trying to do?" Looking at him obviously startled by Bradford's sudden appearance he said, "None of your business." "Then I'm making it my business as of right now, so I'll ask you again this time, in a different way. Why are you attempting to break into this office?" He became arrogant and asked, "who wants to know?" "I do. Bradford knew only too well that the man was being evasive and he was still holding the screwdriver in his hand. "Look, you're going to give me the answers I want one way, or another." "He said, I'm not telling you squat." And at that same instant, Bradford saw him slowing raising his hand, and as he brought it up, he grabbed his wrist twisting his arm to the back until the man screeched in agony. "Now fellow I'm waiting." For a couple of seconds he said nothing, but just then Bradford tightened his grip he yelled out like a wounded animal and said, "alright I'll tell you what you want to know." "That's more like it. Let's start with your telling me why were you trying to break into this office?" "I was paid to break in and steal some sort of folders in a file cabinet." "what kind of folders?" "All the ones marked confidential." "All right, one last question and it had better be the right answer. Who hired you?" He was still whimpering and holding his arm when he said, "man he'll have men done in if I so much mention his name." Gazing at him for a minute Bradford smiled and said that's it, I've had enough of your stalling" then he started towards him and the man loudly said, "Charles Carrington paid me to do it I swear." Looking down into the frightened man's face he said," Alright get out of here and if I ever see your face around here again I'm going to break both your arms into parts, do you understand me?" "Yeah, I hear you, while looking at Bradford briefly then left." Waiting a few minutes before using his keys to unlock the door, he thought to himself, the way these locks are made I seriously doubt that he would've been successful in getting in anyway smiling. Unlocking the door he walked inside slowly looking around everything appeared normal except when he began opening the drawers one at a time in the file cabinet. It was completely empty of its contents. Asking himself out loud, 'what in tarnation has happened here?' Everything had disappeared, but the file cabinet, desk and chairs even, the telephones. His immediate instinct was to telephone Claudia, but thought better of the concept, and decided to call Blake instead. Either way, he'd have to use his car phone. After taking a last look around he went out securing the door behind him. He called Blake from his car phone and apprised him of all that had transpired at David Lansing's office. When he'd finished speaking Blake informed him of Claudia's visit to his up to and including all folders and files, at which Bradford gave a sigh of relief. But then both their concerns were why had Charles hired someone to break into the office, and just what could possibly be of interest in Lansing's files"? He explained to Bradford that he hadn't the opportunity to go through any of them, but planned to do so very soon. And he would definitely keep him apprised if he found anything of interest pertaining to the case. After the conversation with Blake was completed he decided to go on to his office, compile and make an analysis of his data including the latest event. After which, he would decide what his next plan of action was going to be.

After leaving Blake's office Claudia didn't go directly home, but went for a lengthy drive by the ocean side instead, so it was late evening when she finally arrived home. And to her surprise, Charles was there for what she considered t have been an unexpected change. One which made her quite suspicious and as she went inside closing the door behind her she viewed him standing in front of the large bay window with a martini in his hand. Her inner thoughts were what is he up to now? Here is the man she's married to and yet, she's becoming uncomfortable in his presence. With a smirk on his face he said, "so the dove finally returned home. With a steady gaze on him she asked, "Have you been here very long?" He returned her gaze and said, long enough to have downed two of these." Shifting his eyes to the glass in his hand he asked her, care for one?" "No thanks, I'll have a cup of coffee instead." "Fine by me, just thought

I'd ask, he said sarcastically." After brewing herself a cup of coffee she returned to the living room. This time he was sitting down on the sofa still clinging to his martini, while she sat in the large opposite him with apprehension. As she sat cross-legged in the chair sipping on her coffee, she observed his staring at her for a period of time, then he spoke and said Claudia, "I believe it's time for us to have a talk." Now looking directly at him her inner thoughts were, 'oh here it comes so just be patient you're going to know soon enough.' "Have a talk about what Charles, we really haven't talked in weeks because you've always been so busy?" "Look, I'm aware of the fact that I've been staying away from home a great deal, but I've been taking care of a lot of business." "Yes Charles, I'm sure you have." "Now what's that supposed to mean?" She just stared hard at him and said, "You figure it out, and what is it that you want to talk about?" "He looked at her for a brief minute and after clearing is throat said, "I'd like for you to give me more authority in the firm." "Oh really tell me Charles, why would you want more authority?" "Because I'll be in position to do more ." "To do more of what you've already been doing?" "What do you mean?" "I mean for instance, you've already exceeded your authority by transacting business and negotiating deals without Blake's or my prior approval. What you've been doing doesn't go unnoticed, but I'm waiting to see just how far you'll go, and why?" He suddenly stared at her and said," You've been talking to Blake and that private investigator haven't you?" "Yes I have and why? "Listen Claudia, why don't you just terminate Blake's services, he's becoming nothing but a meddling old man anyway." She abruptly uncrossed her legs and placed the coffee cup on the table beside her. Staring at him with anger in her eyes she said," How dare you refer to Blake in that manner and tone, perhaps you're not aware that in an Attorney client relationship, the death of my parents does not terminate the firm if my father had expressly agreed that Blake should conduct the proceedings to its conclusion. And as for the private investigator, he was specifically hired to find out why this situation with the firm began anyway. With a hard steady gaze into his eyes she asked?

"What's the matter Charles, is there something you don't want him to find out?" "I don't know what you're talking about." Claudia's assumption that he was up to something was correct, and was also apparent that he was becoming desperate. First, he attempted to manipulate her, and when that failed he tried coercion. It was quite obvious she was becoming an obstacle that stood between him and the power he sought. But she was going to make certain that he had nothing left. Abruptly standing up tossing the glass to the floor, and eyeing her with contempt he said, your old man's not here to protect you any more. I'm in control now, or soon will be." Giving him a stern look she asked, "Is that what you believe? Well, we'll just see who has control won't we?" He stared at her for a time, then quickly rushed out of the house. He didn't return that night.'

The following morning allowing him to get into his office, she telephoned Blake and apprised him of every detail. After hearing her out he said, "Listen Claudia Charles knows he's going to be found out and now, by all indications from what you've told me he's becoming very desperate. Now he realizes that we're no in the darkness about his involvement in the situation. There's one other puzzling thing, he said " "What is that she asked him?" "Yesterday. Brad telephoned me that he'd stopped by David's office of course; he had no way of knowing that you'd already cleared thing's out, but the point is- he walked in on a man who was trying to break in." "Say what? " "Yes it appears that Charles had paid the man to break into the office to steal the files and folders." "But Blake, that doesn't make sense, what could Charles possibly want with dad's files?" "Claudia I haven't the vaguest idea , and I haven't had the opportunity to sort through the files either, but I am going to now. Perhaps I'll come across something of interest that might give us a clue as to why he's so desperate to get his hands on them. In the mean time, I'm going to get in touch with Bradford and apprise him of the new development. " Blake was on the telephone with Bradford when he was interrupted by an urgent call from Robert the bookkeeper asking, if both he and Bradford *could possibly come to the office? Both men agreed to meet with him. After their arrival at his office and behind closed doors, Robert informed them that Charles had transferred a certain amount of the firm's funds to another account. Blake's immediate response to the information was "He did so without, prior approval from Claudia, or me." They were also apprised of the fact that Charles had collected funds and deposited them into his personal account. They'd finally gotten what was needed to implicate him in the business scandal. Looking at his wristwatch and noting the time, it was quite early so Blake's suggestion to Bradford was that they first obtain a subpoena even though he knew the bank manager, but considering the circumstances everything on their part should be handled legally.*

They arrived at the bank within a two-hour period. After the necessary formalities with the manager they had access to both of Charles's accounts. It was found that the amount of money in his personal account was substantially greater than the amount he's transferred from the firm's funds. This was an indication that he was getting a large kickback from someone., and Bradford had little trouble guessing who they were, but he also knew the facts would have to be substantiated. After completing their research everything was returned to the manager, with their appreciation. On their way back to the firm where Bradford had left his car parked, Blake stated that he believed with great certainty Charles was attempting to assume control of the firm. Staring at him for an instant Bradford asked, "What indications do you have to confirm your beliefs Blake?" Without hesitating, he began to apprise him of Claudia's telephone call to him earlier, and detailed the entire conversation to him, up to and including the verbal threats made to her. "And she said that he never returned home?" "That's correct. And I'm quite concerned because if pushed, he can be ruthless as well as arrogant and obnoxious. Bradford was silent for a moment then said, "I'm trying to figure out just why those files are so important that he's resort to having someone steal them?" "I don't know Brad, but I'm going to begin sorting through them when I return to my office."

Bradford returned to his office to complete the paper work he had started on when he was interrupted by Blake's telephone call. The two recent events were also added to the information he'd already obtained. He began lightly rubbing his eyes, and after noting the time, on his watch only then did he realize that he's spent nearly four hours compiling and analyzing his data. Now things were beginning to fall into place, but he knew there were still pieces unaccounted for. There was one thing for certain; it was time to bear down on the big cheese which, was going to be his next plan of action. He had accomplished quite a bit besides, he could certainly use the rest and sleep. Bradford had just unlocked the car door when suddenly, he heard a rustling noise from behind. Instinctively side stepping as he swirled around, he brought the right leg up and outward catching the assailant in the upper torso , he landed in the middle of the parking lot. Striding over to get a closer look at the unmoving form of a man, and immediately recognized him as being with Carrington. He was unaware of the fact that the man he's just knocked out was for hire to anyone willing to pay his price. What he really wanted to know was why had this man come after him? Yanking him upright and slapping his face a few times finally brought a response. He was being pinned down against the trunk of Bradford's car, and looking up into the tall man's face he knew he was in for big trouble. Bradford said," look fellow you guys are becoming a thorn in my side. What's your name?" There was a steady gaze on Bradford and a look of desperation on his face as if he was trying to find a way out of the deadly situation. Apparently realizing it was hopeless he said, "my name is Stacy Connors." "Alright Connors, why did you attempt to jump me?" He hesitated a few seconds and perhaps; recognizing his predicament he said, "I was hired by Mr. Carrington , he told me just to shake you up a bit so you'd back off." Looking at him suspiciously, Bradford asked him, "back off from what?" Shaking his head he said, "I don't know, guess it's whatever you're doing. Anyway, I didn't ask I just told him what it'd cost him he paid me, and that was that." Half grinning and shaking his head in annoyance he asked, "guys like you never seem to learn do you?" "What's that he asked?" Slowly and deliberately releasing his grip he said, "you figure it out." After staring at Connors for a brief time, he pushed him away from his car got in and drove home. His inner thought was 'the poor sap gave him the information he wanted there was no need for anything further.

The next morning he paid a special visit to one of the largest constructions companies and by the time he left the site, he'd obtained all of the information that was needed. It was as he previously suspected. Carrington was taking kickbacks from a number of larger companies like the on he'd just visited. Later that same morning, he went search of dear Charles and where ever he found him things were going to be much different than before. Because he'd grown tired of his games, it was now lesson time in acceptable behavior. After looking around he eventually located him out in the lumberyard and thinking to himself, there couldn't have been a more appropriate place.' Slowly approaching him he said Carrington, 'I want to have a talk with you." He didn't move, but staring at him said, "oh it's you again Maxwell. What'd you want this time, aren't you finished with harassing people?" "Is that what you call an investigation, he asked him?" "I believe I believe I warned you that you could count on seeing me again. Bradford didn't give him time to respond, but instead said, I have two questions to ask you Carrington, and I suggest that your answers are the correct ones because this is the last warning you'll ger from me. " While gazing steadily at Bradford he said, "all you've been doing is snooping around into something you know nothing about. " Little did Charles realize that his patience was wearing thin especially, since someone else had spoken nearly the same words. "Listen to me you slinky arrogant, belligerent jerk, why did you hire someone to break into Lansing's office to snatch his files?" "Who said I hired someone to break David's office?" "The one

I surprised that was trying to break in, and with a little persuasion he couldn't stop talking. What you didn't know was there were no files in the office to begin with so, your efforts were for nought. Everything had been removed earlier. Maintaining his focus on him Bradford saw the look of disappointment and perhaps; surprise that appeared on his face as he continued to speak. When that didn't work out, you paid a simple-minded monkey for hire to come after me, he also lost. Now I've come here after you."

In the meanwhile, Blake was having a conversation in his office with Barry Wilham an old acquaintance, and learned he was the source who informed Bradford of the bad blood that existed between David and Charles. Blake laughed and said, so that's how he knew about it. "Yes, I believe it was doing our second meeting. He said something that more or less in the form of a question." "What'd you mean, like what for instance?" "Well, it was his method of questioning and mannerism that really caught my attention when he said, 'so the situation developed soon after Lansing's death.' "What really hit home was when he said,' could something have happened previously that would create the present situation?" He was busy writing, and it was as if at the same time, the question was revolving in his mind, but out aloud." Blake sat back in his chair staring at Wilham smiling and said,," that's the way he is, go on." "It was about a week, or so after you and I had met for lunch when something began to nag at me. For the life of me I didn't know why until I remembered our conversation. Blake, I believe the son-in-law is out for revenge." Slowly coming forward in the chair this time this time with eyes squinted, and focused directly on Wilham he asked revenge," Why do you believe that Barry?" Blake, you and I both know that David Lansing used his influential power to get what ever he wanted, and by whatever means necessary." "That's true, Blake agreed, but it still doesn't answer the question why revenge, and against whom? David and Claudette are both dead, but that leaves only Claudia, and you. Wilham interjected." "Let's take a minute to look at the situation this way Blake." "Now Charles was already involved with a young woman who worked in the office building across the street suddenly, he and Claudia becomes engaged and married in less than months. A couple of months later, I personally saw Lansing with the same woman at a luncheon on two separate occasions and there's something else. She and Charles have been seen together since the marriage." Inner thoughts were rapidly revolving around in Blake's head as he sat listening to the other man's scenario. "Blake, what if this was the rationale for the bad blood that had existed between the two of them?" You recall there was quite a bit of speculation rumored regarding the same thing, but no one really knew for certain." Blake sat quietly gazing into space for awhile. Then looking at Wilham he said, "Barry I believe I know which means of course; Bradford was correct in his assumption that something had transpired previously to have invoked the situation." "Oh, he asked, questionably?" "Shortly before the deaths, David came to my office he was infuriated with Charles to the point that he immediately minimized his authority in the firm, he didn't explain his actions and of course I didn't ask. Getting back to Charles, before Claudia left for her two weeks stay in Santa Barbara , she informed me of her suspicion regarding Charles and another woman. I attempted to allay her suspicion, but with little success, I'm afraid. Anyway, after she'd gone I decided to make an unexpected visit to the firm. I had just arrived in the parking lot and gotten out of the car when I observed Charles and a young woman getting into his car I recognized her immediately, as the woman I had seen previously with David. I had a sudden impulse to approach them, but after considering the concept I just continued on my way inside." Following a brief pause he said, "you've brought my attention back to the conversation Claudia and I just recently had. " "What's that he asked?" "Blake apprised him of their conversation when he'd finished speaking Barry stared at him with deep concern and said, "Blake I suggest that both you and Claudia be careful, he can become dangerous." Blake was also concerned and said, "Barry we're very much aware of this and believe me we've considered it, but the fact of the matter is he's not the only one involved in this nasty mess." "You mean to tell me that someone else is assisting him in this diabolical scheme?" "Precisely, and we know who, He's Steven Chatsworth, but only Bradford and I know Claudia Doesn't." "Chatsworth, what in tarnation could he possibly want out of this to get involved with Carrington?" "I don't know, but that my friend is what we're planning to find out. Bradford has already linked he and Charles together, and also had shall we say a chat with the man." Barry exclaimed, 'holy moly.' Blake you and I both are aware of how Chatsworth and his group feel about minorities and you're telling me that Maxwell has spoken with him?" Blake sat back in his chair and began laughing so hard that Barry just sat staring at him. Finally, he spoke and said, "Blake when I heard that he'd stirred up a 'hornets nest', it didn't occur to me at the time, that the hornet was Chatsworth. My word Blake, I've never met a man quite like him before." "Gazing into his eyes and a broad grin on his face he said, "and you never will again Barry he's one of a kind and a man that's difficult to forget, as Chatsworth and Charles will soon learn." Barry looked at him and on a more serious note said, "I'll tell you this much, according to the rumors that are going on around here I'd certainly hate to be in their places." Blake said nothing, but his inner thought was-so would I! Which reminds me. I haven't heard from him and with this new revelation we definitely need to talk." "Excuse me for a minute Barry, I'll have Jenny put in a call for me." Just as he went to pick the phone up it rang." Mr. Colwell excuse me sir, but I believe you should take this call, it's coming from the firm." "Thank you Jenny put them through please." "Yes sir." "Hello, this is Blake Colwell." "Blake this is Robert , man am I glad you're still in your office." Listening to his tone of voice Blake asked, Robert what's the problem?" "I think you should get here as quickly as you can. Bradford is beating the living tarnation out of Charles and his two hired bullies and I'm not about to intervene." "What, and just where is all of this taking place?" "Out back in the lumberyard, he told him>" "Thanks Robert, I'll get there just as quickly as I can."

Blake was staring at the phone for a minute then he began to laugh. Seeing the bewildered expression on Barry's face he stopped laughing long enough to say, ' the water is no longer calm'. "What'd you mean Blake?" That was Robert the bookkeeper who just informed me, that Bradford's at the firm out back in the lumberyard, and he's beating his words were, 'the living tarnation out of Charles and his two hired bullies.' I've got to get over there, care to come along?' Barry was laughing hard when he said, I'd consider it an insult if you hadn't asked me. It's about time that someone brought him down a couple of pegs. He's always been far too arrogant for me. " Blake readily agreed as they were driving away. While they were enroute to the firm, Blake called Claudia on his car phone apprising her of the situation and suggested that she should be there also. After hearing him out, she agreed to go.

When Blake and Barry arrived at the firm, they were met at the front entrance by Robert who was so excited that Blake noticed that his eye glasses were loped-sided on his face and began to grin at the sight. Robert realizing the comedy he was creating made a small grunt and immediately, corrected the situation. He proceeded to escort the two men to the rear of the building, as they approached the lumberyard, all three men abruptly stopped in their tracks. Barry Wilham was the first to speak saying, "my word, this place looks just like a tornado just came through here." Blake laughed out aloud and said, 'by the looks of thing's I'd say the tornado's name is Bradford T. Maxwell. I assure you, this is mild." Robert stared at him and said, "but Blake I've spoken with him on more than one occasion, he always appeared to be mild-mannered and composed." "He usually is until crossed, and I can tell you this much, gentlemen somebody just did! By this time, they'd arrived at the engineer's office at least what was left of it, and as the employee's saw them approaching they quickly moved aside mumbling among themselves. Blake's inner thoughts at that moment were of his friend. 'Even though he though he knew that he was quite capable of taking a life, but he'd never known him to do so unless, there was no other option.' Blake's awareness of Bradford's capabilities was the result of having received his comprehensive training as a commando. They walked through the doorway and saw Bradford sitting on the corner of a large desk with a half smile and arms folded across his broad chest, as he greeted them with, 'hi gentlemen.' The left shirtsleeve was ripped at the seam and one pocket on his trousers was ripped. That appeared to have been the extent of damage he'd sustained. Observing the other three was a different story altogether. Charles had suffered a broken nose that he was nursing, a swollen right eye that was discoloring, both lips were swollen and a lump at the right temple. Without asking, Blake assumed the two men sitting in the corner on the floor were the hired bullies who'd somehow thought they could perhaps ; rescue Charles. One had sustained a broken arm and the loss of two front teeth, the other a dislocated shoulder and broken wrist. After the medical team's evaluation, Blake thought, 'I would say all and all they'd been quite fortunate. ' Suddenly, Claudia asked, "what in the devil happened here?" Her eyes were focused directly on Charles. She'd probably just arrived because non one acknowledged her presence until Blake heard her voice from behind him. Abruptly turning around to face her and smiling he said, "we're just about to get to that." Turning to the side and focusing his eyes directly on him he said, "alright Bradford the weights on your shoulders. Precisely what did happen here?" Just as he'd begun to speak Blake interrupted saying, 'hold up a minute Brad.' Addressing the employee's who were still milling around the area, all of you who are assigned elsewhere can return to your perspective positions. As for you who work directly in this area do what clean up that you can for now thank you! Turning back to him,' he apologized for interruption and said, proceed Brad. " 'This time, the attention was focused on Charles and in a subtle tone he said,"first of all; I came here to ask this jerk why he'd hired someone to break into Lansing's office to steal the files. When that failed, he hired a would-be assassin to come after me." Simultaneously, Claudia and Blake exclaimed what! Then Blake asked," where and when

71

did this take place?" " In the underground parking lot at my office building, last night. I had been working late in my office and when I went down to get into my car, he was waiting for me. I don't know how long he'd been there and I certainly wasted no time in asking him. He wasn't at all cooperative until after a little encouragement, then he couldn't stop talking. His name is Stacy Connors and he said he'd been hired by Carrington to shake me up a bit so I'd back off. I asked him to back off from What? He didn't know from what, he wasn't told and naturally, he didn't ask. This sap paid him to do the job and according to him, that was that! Claudia gave Charles a disgusting look and asked him, are all these things Bradford is saying true?" Still whimpering and pampering his injured nose he said, "he's crazy you know that? Look at what he's done to me!" "You're not answering my question. Is what he's telling us true?" He said Claudia," he's lying I don't know what he's talking about, and I sure don't know this Connors guy he mentioned." Bradford stared directly into his eyes and said," "You're lying through your teeth Carrington. I saw you with him in the rear parking about a week ago, and last it occurred to me where I'd seen him before. I assume that's when you were making arrangements to eliminate me, but you can forget about it because I'm in it for the long haul. These two idiots that you hired here focusing his attention on the two men in the corner thought they could do your dirty work and place the blame on someone else, but it didn't work. Claudia stared hard at Bradford and then at Blake with questioning eyes. Blake looked at her then at Bradford and asked, "Brad what do you think?" "Looking at Charles and the other two men he said , "I was on my way to check out something else when this little episode occurred so, give me a couple of days to see what else I come up with. Blake when I feel the time is right, I'll call to schedule a meeting with you and Claudia in your office. Is this acceptable to the both of you ?" They both looked at him and said, yes." Then he turned and said, "In the meanwhile, I don't know what your plans are for these three, referring to Charles and the other two men. I'll be in touch." Chatsworth was in a meeting when he was summoned to the door by three of his men who apprised him of the incident at the firm. At first, he was silent and after a brief look around to make sure the doors behind him were closed and they were alone he quietly said, I knew that young idiot Carrington was going to foul things up. Now what I want you three to do is go out there and what else you can find out. Report back to me as soon as you have something and the next time, telephone me instead of coming here, is that clear?" "Yes sir, the three of them replied in unison." Watching them as they left, he finally turned and started to walk back towards the still closed door. And his inner thought was- 'I knew Maxwell was going to be big trouble the minute I laid eyes on him, his kind always are.'

In the meanwhile, Bradford had gone home taken a quick shower changed clothes, and went to his office. Spread out on the desk in on front of him were folders, files, and a note pad. He'd stopped and grabbed a 'take-out' dinner and soft drink on the way. Now he had the opportunity to complete his documentation yo to and including the most recent events. But something was still disturbing him inside though and he didn't care for the feeling of it at all. He was hoping to get through everything this time without any interruptions. He was constantly organizing, compiling and analyzing his notes for any discrepancies, or inconsistencies . All of the information he'd obtained had indirectly, or directly implicated the firm in one way or another. It had already been established that Carrington wasn't the only one involved in the situation. He might have been instrumental in bringing it about, but he definitely wasn't the brain behind it, and the only one who had the guts and the ingenuity enough to create something of that magnitude was Chatsworth. According to Robert, the firm is being ripped of that would account for one, of Carrington's accounts, but even the contractors who admitted to paying a kickback could only afford to pay just so much, if they planned to remain in business. His personal account contained a substantially greater amount that would indicate the money is coming from some place else. So, where is it coming from and what benefactor can afford to disperse out that kind of money and why would they? "Unless, they're expecting a greater reward in return. " Sitting back from the desk looking down at the papers and note pads in front of him, events were revolving around in his head and there was one thing that stood out above all else, the situation developed after Lansing's death. Why? So far, there are only two established major players, Chatsworth and Carrington. Then something hit hi like a brick. Could this possibly be some sort of revenge perhaps 'not necessarily against Claudia per say, but against the firm because it represented Lansing himself? If this is the case, then something had to have transpired before his death that would invoke the situation to this degree. It's been stated numerous times that David Lansing had a sordid reputation and kind words were few, far and between. There appears to be two major issues here. Charles's minimized authority in the firm, but what if there was more to it than that and why was he so desperate to get his hands on Lansing's files? Perhaps there is! Then there's Chatsworth, who was Lansing's silent partner and close friend. I'd trust a scorpion before I would him! He was sitting upright and focusing his eyes on the note pad, 'wait a minute he said to himself but out aloud, 'what if he's funding Carrington for his own agenda?' Claudia told Blake that he would soon be in control, and what if by some mad measure Chatsworth is using that little egotistical idiot to ruin the firm? That would mean he had a vendetta against Lansing and the questions are what and why? 'my word.' He's leading Carrington to do his dirty work for him, and when things come to a head, his hands will appear to remain clean leaving unsuspecting Carrington to bear the burden. The snake! Well, we'll just see about that. "Blake, this is Bradford. "Hello Brad, don't tell me you're still working?" "Yes, and I believe I've found something of great interest, but first, have you had the opportunity to start on the files yet? " "I was just beginning to when you telephoned, but why do you ask?" I went through the files in Lansing's personal safe and found nothing pertaining to Carrington, but if you're looking through the ones from the office safe, there might be something in them that will explain why he's so desperate to get hands on them. Blake, perhaps it's something that he doesn't want anyone else to know." "You know you just might be right and I'll go through them first. If I happen to find anything I'll telephone you." "That'll be great Blake and thanks." "You're welcome, now what have you come up with?" He laughed and asked would you believe revenge?" What! Revenge?" "Yes, he said." "For what if I may be so bold to ask?" "This is what we're about to find out. Tomorrow, now I'm going to have a serious chat with Chatsworth and I'll get back with you." Blake hesitated for a minute then said Brad, watch yourself; he's getting cornered and that can become very dangerous." "Yes, I know, but he's the Big snake in this whole situation, not Charles, he's merely trying to be." "Brad are you quite positive about this?" "Yes, I am and if you cut the head off, the snake dies." "That's true, but keep in touch." "Will do, he said." He didn't go into details with Blake, that time would come when they met in his office. Taking a last look at the notes, his next move was going after Chatsworth in a big way especially, since he was so good at playing hard ball. In the meanwhile, he decided to close shop and go home for a nice relaxing night.

The following morning Blake arrived at his office a bit earlier than his usual time. He felt that going through Lansing's files and sorting them out definitely had top priority. He was also anxious to find out just what information they contained. As he began to read through them his inner thoughts reverted to the conversation he and Bradford had the previous evening and the questions that were raised. What really came as a surprise, and never entered his thoughts was the possibility that Chatsworth could be the one at the head of the situation. But what reason would he have he and David were close friends as well as his silent partner in the firm? If what Bradford suspects is, true that something had transpired between he and David prior to the deaths then that in itself could be the motive. Which at this point is still speculation. And why ruin the firm? On the other side of the coin, Charles only wants to *control both Claudia and the firm. And where he's concerned, the only thing we have so far, is the minimized authority. There had to be more to the jigsaw puzzle than what they had. And realizing the complexity of the whole situation he shook his head and returned to the task of sorting through the files. Blake had gone through two cartons of files and in to the third one when came upon an envelope addressed to him marked, 'personal and confidential'. Written by David Lansing and sealed. Moving the other papers aside, he stared at the envelope for a couple of minutes wondering what it could possibly contain before finally opening it? He began to read and suddenly, exclaimed out aloud, "my word David." The information in the letter confirmed his suspicion regarding Claudia's marriage to Charles, and then some. Then as if in disbelief and shock, he slowly sat back in his chair wondering 'how could he have allowed that to happen?' Although he was convinced Claudia had no knowledge that David had orchestrated her marriage. At that time, there was a lot of speculation by those who knew them, but no one ever knew for certain. As he continued to read he realized it was an apologetic letter of sort. David Lansing told of the role he'd played in the marriage (of course he withheld his true motive for the interference). It appears that David was very much aware of Charles's avariciousness. In many ways, he reminded him of himself, and knowing of his profound passion for wealth, it was easy and he knew precisely how to do it. He'd offered him the hand of his daughter in marriage, assuring him that as his son-in-law, there would be certain benefits. He made him a partnership offer and one-fourth share in the firm. However, there would be two speculations that he would have to agree to. Claudia was never to learn of the agreement and e was to, severe all ties with his present relationship. The letter stated that it wasn't important how Charles resolved the relationship just as long as it was done before the marriage was scheduled to to take place. David made the offer and Charles accepted it without hesitation. Of course he had no way of knowing that was the opportunity Charles had been seeking. As Blake continued to read his inner thoughts on the matter were-*

'my gracious' I knew David was cruel and without scruples, but how could he have done this to Claudia? The more he read the more furious he became, but he continued to rea anyway because it hadn't become clear as to the rationale for Charles's desperate attempt at getting his hands on the files. Apparently, David had learned the relationship wasn't resolved but continued even after, the marriage. He'd spoken to him regarding the matter and when there was a lack of compliance the contingency plan that he'd made was put into effect by immediately, terminating their agreement. That also included the promise of one-fourth share in the firm, which he never did he only made it appear to Charles that his intention was to do so. Leaning back in his chair staring down at the letter on his desk he said, 'well, well, Bradford was right on the mark. All of this is about retribution, and this letter explains why he was so interested in getting his hands on the files, but what had he planned to do with them? Suddenly, a shocking question entered his thoughts, 'surely he wasn't planning to show this to Claudia? 'I've got to get in touch with Brad immediately.' He was just about to pick up the telephone when it began to ring, answering the call that Jenny had put through to him. It was the broker informing him that Charles had been in his office attempting to transfer some shares from the firm. After receiving this information he telephoned Bradford who was unavailable at the time, and left an urgent message to contact him ASAP. Now Blake's inner thoughts were perhaps; David's rescission of the secret compromise was an indirect form of regret for his unwarranted behavior. And an opportunity for self-satisfaction against Charles because that was his last and final action. Sometime later, Charles telephoned Chatsworth unaware that he'd been informed of the incident at the firm. After listening to him, Chatsworth told him that it was because of his stupidity that the situation had taken an adverse turn, and that wasn't the way he'd planned it. Abruptly, Charles asked him, "what do you mean, it's not the way you planned it?" "What do you think I mean you idiot?" "Do you seriously believe all of this was your idea? You've only played a part in it, from the beginning. Charles my boy, you're

like the size of your brain, you think too small." Before he had a chance to respond to Chatsworth's statement there was a click, and then nothing but complete silence.

Bradford was on his way to pay Chatsworth a call. And while driving his inner thoughts were-his demeanor towards non-whites was a reminder of the fact that some individuals in a certain segment of society still judge a person by their appearance, or skin color while choosing to disregard the content of their character. He wasn't going to allow the bigotry and hypocrisy of some poor soul to deter him in any way from accomplishing the job he was being paid to do. Being of black origin he was accustomed to those kinds of attitudes as contributing factors of ignorance. Just as he turned onto the long cobbled-stoned driveway leading up to Chatsworth's residence, he spotted two extra cars. 'Company I see'. Thinking to himself. He was preparing himself for whatever came his way, because he'd grown weary of the cat and mouse game.' It was time to get serious. As a precautionary measure, he parked behind the last car, and as he was getting out of his car he saw Chatsworth and three of his henchmen coming out of the door. Included among them was the one called 'Joker', because he acquired a bad reputation for playing jokes on people. They began to approach him, but stopped short of the second car. Then he came face to face with the bigot Chatsworth, and his disparaging comments. Bradford gazed at the three of them for a brief minute and with a half smile directed his attention on Chatsworth saying" Chatsworth, you're a difficult man to catch up with." "Who's been trying he asked in a tone that was anything but pleasant?" Bradford said, "I have." "Well, you've found me Maxwell, what do you want this time?" "I'd like to speak with you regarding the firm, Charles Carrington and yourself." He stared at him for a time, before speaking then with a crooked smile said, "people in hell would like to have ice water too." "I wouldn't happen to know about that since I've never experienced it," Bradford told him in the same tone of voice. "Look Maxwell, I don't know just whom you think you are to me you're nothing but a castaway because you still lack individuality, and originality." Bradford stared directly into his eyes began to laugh and in a mild tone said, "Chatsworth , I do believe you're suffering from 'negrophobia'. Instinctively changing his focus to the other three, it was quite obvious that they had no concept of what it meant, but didn't care for the sound of it because they began to change their positions. And as for Chatsworth, he never uttered a word, but had become the color of a lobster in boiling water. While carefully observing their movements his inner thoughts were-'oh oh'. Here we go as he stood there without moving. The one with the broken nose just stood back watching as the other two began advancing towards him. In the meantime, Chatsworth had moved aside and away from them. Then the battle began. One was out cold in less than five minutes and as for Joker who was now coming towards him he said, "you little weasel, what do you think you're going to do? You're nothing but a four bit counterfeit flunky. Come on, remember the advice I gave you the last time we met?" When he approached, Bradford sent him in the direction of Chatsworth skidding right between his legs knocking him off balance. As Chatsworth was attempting to push Joker off him, Bradford was staring down at him and smiling he said, 'now the joke's on you weasel." Never taking his eyes off Chatsworth, he took a couple steps backward allowing the man to get up. As he finally managed to get to his feet, brushing himself off and gazing at Bradford he said," "alright that's enough, I don't want my men killed." Looking directly at him Bradford said, that's more like it, I didn't come seeking trouble only some answers from you." Moving away from him and leaning against the side of the car he asked Bradford,' just what is it that you're interested in learning? " Positioning himself on the trunk of the next car and facing Chatsworth directly, while keeping a watchful eye on the other three he began saying, "Carrington didn't plan this thing alone, he doesn't have the brains or the experience to execute such a diabolical scheme such as this." For the first time, Bradford thought he saw the glimpse of a sinister grin appear on the mas's face when he replied by saying," right, but how did you figure that out?" "You see Chatsworth I am an individualist. It took awhile believe me, but when everything started pointing back at the firm and I discovered that the rumors were valid, I knew I knew there had to be something more than just a business scandal . I saw you and two of your men leaving through the rear of the firm after you'd denied having any business dealing's with them. Still gazing at him he said, 'go on. 'Let's just say when your men began their harassment and making threatening overtones to try and impede my investigation, I became suspicious and thought why?" Chatsworth never interrupted, and Bradford continued. When I learned of Lansing's shifty background and saw you talking with Carrington in the firm's parking lot, I knew there was something much more significant involved in the situation, but I still didn't know exactly what and I really began to question the whole making of the situation when I learned that you were Lansing's silent partner. I also wondered why would you allow yourself to become involved with his son-in-law unless you had an agenda of your own. He finally interrupted him by asking, 'and you do now?" Bradford stared at him without blinking an eye and Chatsworth saw the certainty in his eyes as he replied yes, I finally figured it out. "Go on, he told him." This situation only developed after the deaths of the Lansing's, then I began to backtrack by asking, 'why after the deaths and not before?' Something had to have occurred previously, and it wasn't just the bad blood that had existed between Lansing and Carrington that would've created something of this magnitude. Then we learned that Carrington was ripping off the firm by taking kickbacks from the larger companies, but when his bank records were seen, there was one that stood out particularly. As it turned out even with the kickbacks there's no way he could have obtained that amount of money. Which meant he was being funnelded by someone else, a benefactor who could afford it, and that meant you. You were using Carrington as a scapegoat and insisted on remaining in the background in this situation because when it comes down to it, your hands will appear clean and he'll be the one to bite the bullet. Bradford's resourcefulness and determination paid dividends when he learned the underlying cause for the business scandal. Chatsworth you only used that young egotistical and ambitious sap as a ploy in your scheme. The business scandal was nothing more than a smoke screen because it had everybody at each other's throats to divert attention away from your true motive. With a stern blazing look in his eyes he said incidentally, after some searching I finally located Phillip Brandt the dispatcher. Why didn't you just have those goons of yours kill him? As the poor soul is now, he'll never be able to walk again, but that's up to the authorities. Two of your men were identified as the one's who drove him away from his apartment building ." Chatsworth abruptly turned and stared at the three who were standing a short distance away, and speaking in a tone that made them look at each other in fear said, "my orders to you were to put him on a plane out of the country and nothing more. As far as I'm concerned, the authorities can have all three of you. Now get out of my sight and stay out." Bradford was observing was observing them as Chatsworth was speaking and noticed a sneaky grin appear on Joker's face, he was up to something, he was certain of it." After they had driven off, and focusing his attention back on the man standing in front of him he said Chatsworth, "your motive for whole incident was revenge, and my question is why?" Chatsworth stared at him for awhile then looked in the direction of his home and said Maxwell, for the most part of your scenario is correct with one exception. Carrington came to me with a deal soon after the Lansing's deaths.". 'What was the deal , he asked him?" "He wanted me to help him gain control of the firm." "And just how did he think he could do that?" "By trying to persuade Claudia to terminate Blake Colwell's position. He thought if he could get him out of the picture, he'd stand a better chance of manipulating he into giving him more authority in the firm. Since both parents are deceased there would be no one else to oppose him. But what that stupid idiot didn't realize is the fact, that an agreement was made years ago between Colwell and the Lansing's ." 'And what was that agreement, he asked him?" "As long as Claudia remain principal owner of the firm Colwell will be the Attorney to complete the business to its end.." "That is no one else could do anything except you, since you were the silent partner." "Yes, except me. And that's when the opportunity came for me to accomplish what I've been planning to do for years, I was only waiting for the right moment to present itself. I have only two regrets in this whole thing." Bradford gave him a hard stare then asked," What are they Chatsworth?" He gazed at him with a half smile and said,' for one, Claudia is caught in the middle of it all, and two, David Lansing's not here to witness its happening now which is the greatest of the two. Bradford was staring hard at him and asking, "he's not here to witness what Chatsworth?" He almost smiled, but stopped short when he said," the destruction of the Lansing Contractor's firm, that imbecile Charles only wanted to ruin it in hopes of gaining control, but I want it destroyed." Just what is your rationale for wanting it destroyed?" "Because its representative of David Lansing, himself. Years ago, I watched him destroy Claudette's father by taking control of the firm from him, after he'd become seriously ill. At that time, he also became involved with y younger sister. That's when he had begun taking frequent out-of-town trips. Claudette knew he was involved with another woman, but she never knew just who she was and, neither did I. That is until one day when I received an urgent telephone call, asking me to come to Santa Cruiz. When I arrived there, se apprised me of everything up to and including the fact that she'd become pregnant by him. When she told him about the pregnancy, he told her to get rid of it because he had no intentions of seeing her again. Three days later, I received the horrible news that she'd committed suicide and that's when I vowed that he'd pay. He never knew she'd told me. " "And all these years he assumed you were friends?" "Yes, including Claudette. I knew she never cared for me and for a very good reason not to. Because I was the one who was with Lansing at the time, he tricked her father into giving him power of Attorney. My hatred of him grew as I watched hoe he connived and manipulated other people. And I would've succeeded if you hadn't come into the picture."

Bradford gazed at him for awhile and said, so you're the 'Head Huncho'? Ma, you've really got it bad! Bitterness is one thing, but hatred will destroy you. "Well, I've got the answers that I've been seeking. Taking a long hard look at him, he said good bye, Chatsworth." Bradford left him standing in the same spot, but looking in the rear view mirror as he was driving away, he observed him slowly walking back towards the house with his head lowered.

On the way to his office, Bradford thought he'd stop by the Construction Company to inform Haskell of Brandt's whereabouts. He'd just entered the site and was parking his car when he spotted him coming out of the door. Two men were behind him. They appeared to have been worker's on the site gathering from the hard hats they were wearing and their appearance. Haskell upon seeing him told the men that he'd be around to see them later. He began to approach Bradford who was standing beside his car. "Hey Maxwell, how's the investigation coming along?" He looked at the man's rugged face for a couple of seconds then said, "Haskell, I regret having to be the bearer of unpleasant news." Bradford appreciated the fact that he'd asked him a direct question when he asked, "what is it now Maxwell?" "Haskell after some searching I located Phillip Brandt and he won't be coming back to work for you, or anyone else, and according to the doctors prognosis, he's permanently paralyzed from the waist down." Gazing steadily into his eyes he asked Bradford, "how did this happen Maxwell?" "To make a long story short, Chatsworth and his goons are responsible." "Are you sure, he asked in an uncertain tone?" "Yes, I'm positive. As a matter-of-fact, I just left Chatsworth's residence. He paused, and Haskell said, go on man." "Well as it turned out, Steven Chatsworth was the' head huncho' behind everything that's been happening. Carrington was only a ploy in his sinister scheme, and as for Brandt, he told his men that their orders were to put him on a plane out of the country and nothing more. They decided to take matters into their own hands instead. I informed him that the authorities had been notified. He told them that they could have all *three of them and to get out of his sight and stay out. The scandal was a diversion to conceal the real motive.." "And just what was his motive Maxwell ?" 'Secret Revenge' was the catalyst for the 'Business Scandal'. Haskell looked at him in bewilderment and asked, "revenge against whom and for what?" Bradford gazed directly at him for a couple of seconds then said, listen Haskell, I've still got a few loose ends to tie up before this thing can be resolved, but I can tell you this much if it'll be of any consolation to you. Chatsworth's revenge wasn't directed at any of you. All of you were only pawns in his plan, and when this is concluded, I'll get back with you. You have my word Kendall. Haskell shook his hand saying, "that's good enough for me Bradford.." They both grinned because that was the first time that he'd referred to him as Bradford. Before leaving, he wrote down the address where Brandt was andgave it o him, smiled and nodded his head. While driving to the office his inner thoughts were-it had been quite an eventful day, one in which he was very pleased.' Stopping briefly to pick a lunch order he'd placed earlier, he continued on his way.*

After he arrived at the office, he began checking for messages. There was an urgent call from Blake Colwell. He's ahead of me thinking to himself; He'd planned to call him after settling down a bit. But after snatching a couple of quick bites and washing it down with a soft

drink he decided to telephone him then especially; since he'd stated it was urgent. Upon hearing his voice, Blake responded with excitement." Brad, are you alright, I've been concerned since I hadn't heard from you?" Chuckling loudly almost to the point of chocking he finally said" yes Blake, I'm fine. Thanks for your concern, but what's the excitement all about?" "Brad, I went through David's files and came upon a letter that he'd addressed to me marked 'personal and confidential' '. Now I can understand why Charles was so desperate to get his hands on the files.." "Are you serious Blake?" "I couldn't possibly be any more serious at this point Brad." He wasn't quite prepared to discuss his most recent events of the day with him so. So he said, "look buddy. I've had a rather exciting day myself; and I'm sort of beat. How about my meeting with you in your office tomorrow, and I can bring you up to date on things?" "Brad that will be great. Are you certain you're all right?" Laughing heartily he said yes Blake, I'm quite certain, and I'll see you tomorrow."

After having ingested a hearty breakfast with O.J. And coffee Bradford was prepared to face the challenges of the day. He arrived at Blake's office around nine-thirty a.m. After a friendly good morning to Blake and Jenny, they entered Blake's private office closing the door behind them. They both seated themselves and after a brief minute, Blake looked at him with a smile asking, shall we get started?" Returning the smile, Bradford's reply was, "by all means let's do." Brad as I stated to you last evening that I that I came across a letter from David, now I understand Charles's desperation on getting his hands on these files. He was hoping to find the 'secret agreement' that was made between he and David. "Bradford looked at him in astonishment, but never interrupted him, allowing Blake to continue. According to his letter, David orchestrated the marriage between Claudia and Charles by offering him a partnership and one-fourth shares in the firm with two stipulations. Claudia must never learn of the agreement and he was to sever all ties with his present relationship. It wasn't important how he resolved it, just as long as it was accomplished before the marriage was scheduled to take place. David made the offer and Charles naturally accepted it. But apparently, he was unaware that was the opportunity Charles had undoubtedly, been seeking. However; there were two things Charles wasn't aware of. David had set up a contingency plan in the event, he reneged on the agreement. And he had him believe that his intention was to validate his share in the firm, which he never did. Somehow he learned that Charles's involvement with the other woman continued even after the marriage, and that was the rationale for the bad blood that was known to have existed between them. David minimized his authority to act in the capacity of representative for the firm. His last and final act was the termination of the secret agreement between the two of them. Bradford sat farther back in the chair and focused his eyes directly on Blake. After a brief period of silence trying to absorb everything he'd just heard he asked, "Blake what kind of man would bargain his daughter's life away?" "Brad, David Lansing was a vicious , manipulative and immoral man. He never stated in the letter why he acted in such a despicable manner, but I believe he was involved with the same woman, and with Charles out of the picture he'd have her all to himself." "Why do you believe that Blake?" "Do you recall when Claudia went to Santa Barbara for two weeks?" "Yes, I remember." "Well, the day she left I went to make an unannounced visit to the firm and as I was getting out of my car, I spotted Charles and this attractive young woman getting into his car. Brad, I recognized her as the same woman I'd seen with David on occasions. My first instinct was to approach them But I decided against it and continued on my way into the firm. And if that was the case, she was playing both ends against the middle." "Blake, I'm puzzled by all of this, what was Claudia and her mother's responses?" "Brad, I believe in my very being that Claudia was coerced, and manipulated into the marriage. David Lansing was a very demanding and authoritative man. I was present when Claudette confronted him on two occasions, but her plea was futile. When he wanted something to go his way, he could be very conniving and persuasive. And as for Charles's part in the plan, my perception is that he considered the possibility of shall we say, 'eat his cake and have it too.' With David's offer that really opened the door of opportunity for him, but things backfired on him, now he's seeking retribution of some sort. Just yesterday, I was apprised by the Broker that he'd been in his office attempting to transfer some shares from the firm. Claudia doesn't know about this letter, or any parts of it for that matter." Bradford looked away and then back at Blake saying, 'man, this is some heavy stuff and any way you look at it, Claudia's caught right in the middle and she has no concept of what has transpired.' "I know, and that's precisely what I'm afraid of Brad. "

There it was again, he had a distinct feeling that Blake was withholding from him, but that question would have to wait until later. Stretching out his long legs and grinning he asked all right, "are you ready for the rest of the puzzle?" Blake blinked at him and sat back in his chair saying, my gracious man by all means, bring me up to date. This has been a most distressing situation." "Blake, do you recall our conversation when you asked me what had I come up with , and I asked 'would you believe revenge?' Looking away and back at him he said yes I remember, and I also asked you, 'revenge for what?" " I told you that's, what we were about to find out because I was going to have a serious talk with Chatsworth the next day. Well, that's precisely what I did. When you telephoned the office I was at Chatsworth's residence." Blake sat up and with his eyes still focused on Bradford he asked, "Brad just what happened out there?" "When I arrived at his residence I informed him that I'd come to speak with him regarding the firm, Charles Carrington and himself. After a few snide remarks were made, two of the three goons that were present came towards me Afterwards, I sent one skidding right between his legs and he was down on the ground with them. I stood back allowing him to get on his feet and that's when he said, 'that was enough, he didn't want his men killed.' As he was speaking, Blake was steadily chuckling within himself. So, I agreed and told him that I hadn't come looking for trouble only some answers..' Blake continued to eye him as he spoke, but had a wide grin on his face. 'He asked me, just what was I interested in learning?' "I told him that Carrington didn't plan this thing alone, he doesn't have the brains or the experience to execute such a diabolic scheme as this. Blake, I saw a sinister grin appear on his face and such an air of superiority when he said, 'you're right, but how did you figure that out?' "I told him it took me awhile, and when I discovered the rumors were valid, I knew there had to be something more than a Business scandal." He appeared quite surprised when I told him that I had seen him and two of his men leaving through the rear door of the firm after, he'd denied having any business dealings. Then I really became suspicious when his men began their harassment and threating overtones. There was something someone didn't want me to find out because they were trying to impede my investigation, and I asked myself why?' I told him that later, I 'd learned of Lansing's shifty background and observed he and Carrington talking in the firm's rear parking lot. That's when I reached the conclusion that more was involved in the situation than just a business scandal, but I still didn't know specifically what?" "That's when he interrupted me by asking? 'and now you do?' "I said, yes I finally figured it out. The situation only developed after the deaths, and why? Which meant something had to have occurred previously, that would create something of this magnitude. Then I apprised him of Carrington's bank accounts and financial discrepancies. Which only indicated that he was being funneled money by a benefactor who could afford it. Finally, I told him that he'd only used Carrington as a ploy in his diabolical scheme. The business scandal was nothing more than a smoke screen used to divert attention away from his true motive." "He asked me, 'Just what would that be?' "I said revenge, and my question to him was why?" He paused for a brief minute, then continuing on he said Blake, I do believe you're going to be in for a big shock, when I tell you what came nest. Blake said nothing but leaned back in his chair with an intense expression on his face. "It appears that Charles's little stunt presented him the opportunity to accomplish what he'd been planning to do for years. "Looking at him inquisitively Blake asked, and just what was that Brad?" "He stated that he has only two regrets. Claudia is being caught in the middle of it all; and David Lansing's not here to witness it." "Gracious man, he's not here to witness what, Blake asked him?" "Would you believe the destruction of the Lansing's Contractors' firm?" "My goodness Brad, but why?" "Because its representative of David Lansing." "That just doesn't make sense Blake said, looking stunned. " "Neither did it to me at first, but listen to the rest of it. Apparently years ago; and this was before your time. Lansing had become involved with Chatsworth's younger sister she became pregnant, and when she informed him of the pregnancy; he told her to get rid of it because he had no intentions of seeing her again. Three days later, he received the horrible news that she'd committed suicide, and that's when he vowed that Lansing would pay. He never knew that she'd confided in him. Blake all those years he led Lansing to believe they were friends and at the same time, he was planning ways in which he would destroy him. His hatred of him was just that fixed. Finally, he told me in no uncertain terms that he would've succeeded if I hadn't the picture. I don't know whom he had the most hatred for, Lansing or me?" "Why do you believe that Brad?" "For two reasons, we know his perception of minorities and my investigation prevented him from fulfilling his plan of destruction. And David Lansing didn't live to witness any of it." Blake sat back staring at Bradford with disbelief in his eyes and asked, "so this whole nasty situation was about secret revenge on both, Charles and Chatsworth's part?" Bradford looked at him and said," I'm afraid so." I knew David Lansing was a despicable human being, but for this to have happened , there are no words that could possibly justify his actions Brad." "There was also; the matter of Phillip Brandt the dispatcher, from one of the Construction Companies who suddenly, disappeared after Charles had paid a visit to the site. Anyway, I informed Chatsworth that I had located him and he's permanently paralyzed. He was also taking kickbacks from Charles. From the description the apartment manager where he lived gave me, they were his men. As it turned out according to his words, he'd given them orders to put him on a plane out of the country not harm him, but they had other ideas. I told him that I'd notified the authorities. He said they could have all three of them. He ordered them to get out of his sight and stay out. But Blake, I was observing their expression as he was talking to them and as they were leaving, the one called Joker began to laugh, I don't trust him, he's sneaky." "Well Brad, once the authorities get their hands on them I don't believe he'll be laughing for a very long time. I'm quite sorry to hear about Brandt though." "Blake he was used along with the others. You know, since my first meeting with Chatsworth, Again; I've been reminded of the fact that blacks are indicative of the false assumption of appearance and regardless of one's accomplishments or status in life, minorities are still viewed as "Second-class" citizens by many in today's society, and that really angers me to the core man." Blake stared at him for awhile, and seeing the pain in his eyes also angered him because what he'd spoken nevertheless, was the truth. "Brad, you and I have been friends for many years and it disturbs me deeply that in spite of some changes that have been made, it still isn't enough. And as much as I dislike having to admit it, I'm afraid we're always going to have some Chatsworth's in a certain segment of our society. But you my friend know precisely how to communicate with them. And that is what's going to make a difference he said with a big smile. " Bradford returning his smile with a grin said, "Oh well, that's life for you isn't it?" "I believe so Buddy, Blake responded. " " Blake now that we've established a motive for the situation. There still remain a couple of loose ends, and you know that means going after Charles, the one who instigated this whole episode." "I know Brad and I was just thinking about Claudia. She's already gone through so much and now to learn that the very man she's married to is out to ruin her business." I realize that Blake, but I honestly believe she should be told at the very least; she'll know what to expect from him. That is if she isn't aware of it already. Claudia's a very brilliant young woman and she's already suspicious of him we've just got to figure out a way to prevent her from knowing the full details for now. Besides, since she's out of the country right now we have a little time before she returns And I believe there's a solution to our problem. "What do you have in mind Brad?" First, we get him in here and take it from there. Are you gamed?" "You bet I am, when do you suggest we start?" "Well, there's nothing like the present." "Then let's begin by calling him to come here."

As he stood knocking on the door a gruffy voice from within yelled," come on in its open ." "Hey Brad, have a chair I'll be with you in a minute" He sat quietly as the big burly man sitting behind the desk began placing papers in a number of folders then moving them to the side. The task finally completed and leaning back in his chair he looked at Bradford smiled and said, "I see you're back. Good news this time I hope." "I'm inclined to believe so he said, returning the smile." Kendall, during my last visit here I couldn't go into details with you because the investigation was ongoing." "Yes, something about some loose ends?" "Affirmative, he replied with a grin." "And the loose ends, they 're all tied up I presume." "Your presumption is correct. You see this whole episode was about secret revenge." "Secret revenge?" "Yes, with Carrington he was seeking control of Claudia and the business, and Steven Chatsworth had been planning for years how he would destroy Lansing as the result of something that had transpired years ago. When Carrington went to him for assistance in his little scheme it opened the door of opportunity that he'd been waiting for. By stirring up trouble between the Construction and Contractor's companies diverted attention away from the true motive, so no one would realize what was happening until it was too late, including Carrington himself. He was only using the young idiot to further his own personal agenda. Because of his greed, he only sought to gain control of the firm, whereas, Chatsworth wanted it destroyed." "But why would he want to destroy the firm?" "His words were- it represented David Lansing himself." "But Brad, I always assumed he and Lansing to have been close friends, and so did everyone else around here." "That's the ironic part about it Kendall, he planned it that way so he would be above suspicion if his plan had been successful." "Shakespeare's beard he exclaimed, what's going to happen now that it's over?" "Well, I wouldn't worry about Carrington getting into any more mischief, and as for Chatsworth, he paused, then said, with a man like him it's difficult to say. Maybe now, everyone has learned a valuable lesson from all of this, he said with a broad grin." "Man, I for one certainly have. From now on I'm going to initiate a thorough background check on all my perspective employees." They both laughed. Then Bradford's expression changed to a more serious one when he asked, "Kendall have you had the opportunity to visit Brandt?" "Yes, as a matter-of-fact, I was there last night, he's doing about as well as can be expected under the circumstances. He's going to be placed in a nursing care facility and the guys including mine have volunteered to set up a financial fund to help defray some of the medical expenses." "Kendall, I think that's just great." By the way, a meeting was held for all the companies who wanted to attend both small and large. You opened our eye's to what it really means by fair competition, and we owe you a big debt of gratitude for which we can never repay Brad," Bradford stood on his feet, so did Kendall and said, "I'm only glad to have been of help." He looked at him smiled and said, "and you have been, thanks Brad." Returning the smile he said, you're more than welcome Kendall." As they were shaking hands. After he'd driven a short distance away from the construction site his car phone rang. Answering he said, "This is Maxwell." The voice on the other end said, "Brad this is Blake I've been trying to reach you." "What's the matter Blake?" "The authorities are out at Chatsworth's residence. It appears he's been shot several times." "What, when did this happen Blake?" "From what I've been able to learn so far, it was around the time, of our meeting ere in the office." "Did they say how he was shot and by whom?" "No, they're speaking with his housekeeper now, and from what I've been able to understand, she heard something and called the authorities." "This is terrible even for a man like him. At this stage you're probably not going to get much information, but continue to see what else you can learn." And after a short pause he said, "look Blake, I'll be in your office shortly. While still driving Bradford was recalling the previous day's event at Chatsworth's residence and said, something's not right about this. I wonder if my suspicion about Joker is correct?"

Bradford arrived at Blake's office within half an hour after their conversation, and was immediately apprised of the latest information on Steven Chatsworth. As they sat in his office watching a special, news cast on television announcing the recent developments in the

Chatsworth's case. Bradford wondered to himself if his suspicion was warranted. Since the investigation was ongoing there was certain information being withheld. A hospital spokesman for the medical team stated that his condition was guarded and would be up-dated periodically as warranted . A short time later, a spokesman for the Santa Monica police department made a brief statement saying, they were searching for three of Chatsworth's employees for questioning in the matter. Blake turned the set off and leaned back in his chair then asked, "Brad, could what could have possibly happened out there?" His direct response to Blake's question was-"I don't know Blake, but there's one thing for certain, it was violent enough for Chatsworth to end up in the hospital seriously wounded." "The authorities never gave the names of the three employees, but I'll bet you a ten dollar gold piece I can give you the name of one." Blake looked at him for a full minute then asked, "Brad, just what do you mean?" He was all too familiar with facial expression when Bradford leaned forward and said,"during my last meeting with Chatsworth, I informed him that the authorities had been notified regarding the assault against Phillip Brandt by his men. Do you recall my telling you that I observed the expression on their faces when he ordered them out of his sight and to stay out, the one in particular called Joker had a sneaky grin on his face?" "Yes, I do recall your telling me and you also said with great certainty that he was up to something." "Wait a minute, are you implying that he could be one of the three involved in this incident?" "Blake, I honestly believe so. Now this shooting has presented another problem for us as well," With deep concern Blake asked him, "How is that Brad?" "Blake, just consider this for a minute. Chatsworth was behind the Business Scandal. And since he was Lansing's silent partner in the firm, he still has ties with it. Therefore; the case can't be fully resolved until we can speak with him and find out just what his position is going to be?" Blake stared at him in recognition of what he'd spoken and said, "you know you're right, I hadn't thought of it in those terms Brad. So, what are we to do now?" "Well, for the time being there's nothing we can do, but wait until his condition hopefully, improves enough for us to have a talk with him." Blake gazed into his eyes and seeing the concern in them said, "you've got a point there Brad. And just when we thought you could close the case.' Bradford looked at him and said, "At this stage Blake, not a chance." There was a brief period of silence then Blake asked, "Brad, I'm rather curious about all of this." "Just what could be the motive behind the shooting?" Bradford gazed into his eyes and said, I honestly don't know Blake, but there's one thing for certain, they're not going to stick around waiting for the authorities to get their hands on them. Blake said, "Then I'm afraid they will become fugitives from justice." Blake had barely finished speaking when the telephone on his desk rang. Immediately picking up the receiver he said, "Yes Jenny?" "Mr. Colwell, excuse me sir, but a detective name Jacob Skylar with the Santa Monica police department is on the other line and wishes to speak with you." "Thank you Jenny, please put him through." Looking directly at Bradford questioningly, he said, "This is Attorney Blake Colwell speaking." "Attorney Colwell, my name is Jacob Skylar I'm with the Santa Monica department. I've been assigned as investigator in the Chatsworth case." "How can I be of assistance to you Detective?" "I understand you know Mr. Chatsworth?" "Yes that is correct." There was a short pause then he asked, "Attorney Colwell there are a few questions I'd like to ask you if I may. Would it inconvenience you if I come to your office today?" "No, not at all! What time will you be prepared to come?" Apparently looking at the time, he spoke and said," it's now ten fifteen, how about around eleven?" "Eleven o'clock will be just fine. Do you know where my office is located?" "Yes, I do and thank you for taking the time to speak with me." "You're welcome Detective." He looked at Bradford and said, he wants to ask me some questions regarding Steven Chatsworth." Bradford smiled and said, "that's great perhaps; we can learn something else. In the meanwhile, I've a couple of errands to run so, I'll get back with you later. You know how you can reach me if anything else comes up." "yes, I do."

"Yes Jenny?" Detective Skylar is here to see you sir." "Thank you Jenny, please send him in." "yes sir." Blake was standing up behind his desk closing some folders when the Detective entered the door. He looked up at the man as he came towards him with an extended hand and introducing himself. Blake shook his hand and asked him to have a seat. "Now, what is it that you would like to know Detective?" "Attorney Blake, I'm going to come straight to the point. How long have you known Mr. Chatsworth?" "I really appreciate that Detective and to answer your question I've known him for many years." "And how long have you represented the Lansing Contractors' firm?" "I've been their attorney for over thirty years." "I see. Now Blake's inner thoughts were 'what was he leading up to?' "The firm has been involved in a Business scandal since the deaths of owners, am I correct?" "Yes, you're quite correct." "Was Mr. Chatsworth associated with the firm in any way?" Blake stared at the man for an instant before speaking then he asked Detective Skylar, just what is this line of questioning leading up to?" "Attorney Colwell, I'm investigating an attempted murder case here and that entails covering all bases." "I understand your position perfectly well, but what I fail to see is what has the Chatsworth incident to do with the firm, or myself?" "Oh, I just thought perhaps; if he was somehow associated with the firm, you might have an idea of why he might have been assaulted?" "Well, I'm afraid I can't help you there Detective, I'm rather curious why the incident occurred myself. But have you had the opportunity to question Mr. Chatsworth's position regarding the Contractors' firm?" He looked at Blake then said, "No, I haven't." "Then I believe that is a question best answered by Chatsworth himself." Skylar gave him a sullen look and said, " I see." He looked directly at Blake and asked, "the daughter inherited the business after her folks deaths didn't she?" "yes, she did." At that moment, Blake knew he was changing in mid-stream and smiled inwardly. "Isn't she married?" "yes she is. "What about the husband?" "What about him?" "Does he share in any of the business?" "No, he doesn't he's the structural engineer in the firm and that is it." "I see, he said resolutely. Incidentally, I understand *a private investigator was hired to look into the situation." "That's correct. His name is Bradford T. Maxwell." "Has he made any progress?" " I believe he has. Blake responded smiling. As a matter-of-fact, I believe it just might be advantageous for you to speak with him." He gave Blake a blank stare and asked," why do you believe that?" "Because he, might be in a position to assist you more than I." "Is that a fact?" "yes it is." "Where can I reach this Maxwell fellow?" He laughed and gave him a sheet of paper from his note pad with Bradford's name, address and telephone number written on it. He stood up and said, "thanks for your time, Attorney Colwell." "You're welcome Detective Skylar."*

He'd just gotten into his car when the phone rang and looking at the display he asked "hello Blake, what is it?" "Brad, Detective Skylar just left my office. I gave him your office telephone number and address. I believe you should expect a visit from him soon. Pausing for a brief minute and with a wide smile he asked him, "Oh, and why is that Blake?" "For two reasons Brad. Number one, he asked if Chatsworth is associated with the firm in any way?" "What did you tell him?" "I asked him if he'd had the opportunity to question him regarding his position in the firm and he said no. Then I told him I believe that is a question best answered by Chatsworth himself." "And number two, he asked?" He's aware that you're investigating the situation involving the firm and asked if you've made any progress?" I merely told him that I believe so. As a matter-of-fact, I assured him that it might be advantageous for him to speak with you." "Oh you did, did you, he asked laughing?" "Look Brad, we know Chatsworth was the master-mind behind the whole incident, but I believe it's up to you to inform him of how much of it you want him to know right now. Besides if your assessment of the incident that occurred at Chatsworth's home is correct, he can probably use your assistance in this present matter." "You just might be right Buddy, but we'll see what develops when he comes to see me. I'm on my way back to the office anyway. So, I'll be in touch with you later. "In the meanwhile, Blake was still sitting behind his desk, and his thoughts were of Chatsworth and his ties with the firm which was, publicly known. That was the agreement between he and David Lansing years ago; and before he came to the firm. Since things had taken such a dramatic change including his having masterminded the whole incident, he wondered to himself what decision he would be making after his recovery? As of the moment, Claudia still wasn't aware of the role he'd played in the pickle situation, nor the full extent of Charles's involvement in all of it. She'll be returning from abroad in a few days. Perhaps; by the time she does return here things will be completely resolved at least; I hope they will be. '

Maxwell was sitting behind his desk going over some paperwork when he heard a knock on is door. Looking up in the direction of the sound he said, "come in it's open." While slowly moving back away from the desk. Just as he stood up a man nearly as tall as he was coming through the door. The man appeared to be in his early forties and a tan that might have indicated he was an avid surfer with reddish brown hair and grey eyes. Suddenly, they both began laughing. Apparently he was sizing Maxwell up as well. Finally, he said, "I'm Detective Jacob Skylar with the Santa Monica police department." "And I'm Bradford T. Maxwell." They shook hands and Maxwell asked him to have a seat. "Now, what can I do for you Detective Skylar?" "I've been assigned to investigate an attempted murder case. I spoke with Attorney Blake Colwell this morning and his suggestion was that it would be to my advantage if I spoke with you. To be perfectly honest with you, I was somewhat skeptical of his suggestion until I reported to my supervisor informing him that I was on my way to see you. Then he told me under no uncertain terms that I should have contacted you first." "And why is that?" "He informed me that you're the man who notified the department of an assault on a man by the three men who is employed by Steven Chatsworth, the case I'm investigating." "The first part of your statement is correct." "What'd you mean by the first part? "At the time of the assault they were in his employ, but when I Informed him of what happened he point blank told the three to get out of his sight and stay out." Upon hearing that statement, a puzzled expression appeared on Skylar's face. He asked, "How did you know they worked for Chatsworth anyway?" "I was investigating a case when the victim suddenly disappeared from his assigned post." "What do you mean?" "He worked as a dispatcher for one of the larger Construction companies." "How did you learn about his disappearance?" "I was in the office with his employer when he called the dispatch office. When there was no response he sent one of his men to search for him, and when he returned there was no dispatcher with him and all of the records were missing as well." By this time, Detective Skylar appeared to be more comfortable talking with him. Maxwell leaned back in his chair for comfort as well. "Well Maxwell, what happened after that?" "I asked the owner a few questions about the missing man. Then I asked if he had a current address on him? He wrote it down on a piece of paper and gave it to me and I gave him my word that I would make an effort to locate the missing man. Early the following morning I went to the address that he'd given me. He lived in an apartment complex across town. I went to the apartment number that was supposed to have been his. When there was no response from him I located the manager and upon questioning him, he told me that he'd left the previous day and was in such a hurry that he left no forwarding address to receive his deposit. Then I asked if he'd left alone? 'He said, 'as a matter-of-fact, two men had accompanied him. From the description he gave me, I knew they were Chatsworth's men." "Tell me, how could you have been so certain they were his men?" "Because I had met them on three previous occasions. Two of them were involved in incidents of harassment." "Against whom he asked?" Maxwell looked at him smiled and said, "Against me! "But why you?" "I suppose they thought it would intimidate me." "O really, Skylar asked smiling?" "Anyway I found Phillip Brandt the dispatcher about a block away from the apartment complex and he'll never walk again." He gazed at Maxwell for a full minute and said, "wait a minute, this stuff is getting heavy Maxwell. What in the devil's name is going on here?" "It's a long story Skylar and the case I'm working o hasn't been resolved yet; now this situation with Chatsworth only complicate matters further. I had hoped to close it, but I'll have to wait until he's recovered from his injuries at least; enough for me to talk to him. " He exclaimed! Man, 'out of the frying pan into the fire." Looking directly into Maxwell's eyes he asked, Just what does Chatsworth have to do with any of this and your investigation?" "Listen Skylar, I'm not at liberty to divulge every detail at this time, but I can tell you this much and before I do, there are a few questions of my own I'd like to ask you." "Skylar stared at him for a brief time, then said, 'all right what are your questions?" "First of all, number one, according to the news report the shooting occurred at Chatsworh's residence is that correct?" "yes, that's correct." Number two, were there any witnesses to the actual shooting?" "No." "What about the housekeeper? "What about her?" "I understand she was questioned?" "Yes, she was." ""Where was she during this time and what account was she able to give the authorities regarding the incident?" He was hesitant for a couple of seconds then said, "she stated that she was in the kitchen and heard Chatsworth yell, ' I told you once to get out and stay out, and I meant it. Now what are you doing back here?' "Then she heard another man say, I want everything you owe me now! Then he yelled,' get out of here! The next thing she heard were shots being fired. "The poor woman was so frightened that she locked herself in the pantry. And that's where she remained until she could hear nothing more and felt it was safe enough to come out. She stated that when she finally came out, the front door was standing wide open. Then she immediately went to the study and found Chatsworth lying on the floor bleeding. She called out his name, but there was no response. She thought he might have been dead and that' when she went to the phone and called the police." "The last question, how many times was he shot and what caliber of gun was used?" "He was shot once in the chest, twice in the abdomen and once in the arm. Ballistic reports it as having been a small thirty-caliber revolver.

Why do you ask Maxwell? I'll lay you odds ten to one I can tell you who fired those shots." " can you be so certain of this?" "Because the last time I was out there. I had a run in with the three o them, but only one carried a gun, a man name 'Joker'. "How do you know this?" Because when I sent him skidding between Chatsworth's legs it hit the ground not more than two feet away from him, and it was a thirty-eight caliber special." He leaned forward towards Maxwell and asked exactly, when did this take place?" "A day before the shooting occurred." "Why are you so certain he's the shooter?" "The other two are whimps and don't have the nerve. I saw the on their faces when he ordered them to get out and stay out. This Joker had a sneaky grin on his face and I had a 'gut' feeling as I watched them that he'd be up to something sinister." "After hearing all of this, you just might be right and if you are, I'll guarantee you they're going to be on the run, that is if they haven't fled already, because it's been all of the news and television stations that they're wanted for questioning." "Listen, I'm still puzzled by something.' "What is it, Maxwell asked him? " "Why did Chatsworth's men snatch that fellow anyway?" "They were supposed to have been following his orders." With a bewildered expression on his face he repeated, "Following his orders?" "Yes, you see they were instructed to put him on a plane out of the country not har him, but decided to do things their own way instead and by so doing, it cost all of them their job. That's why he fired them, after learning what they had done. According to Chatsworth, they disobeyed his orders and that wasn't something he would tolerate." "But why did he want him out of the country in the first place?" As a coverup for what he was doing." "You mean to tell me that he's involved in something else?" "Up to his neck in it." "So this is why that sly old fox sicced me on you! He smiled and said, "Well, Blake Colwell does have a strange way of doing things sometimes." "This case you're working on, it's the Contractors' firm situation isn't it?" "Yes it is." "Listen something's occurred to me during our conversation." "What is it, Maxwell asked him:" "I could really use some outside help on this and perhaps; it will also help to solve your dilemma." Looking down for a brief minute then up again he asked, "How do you see that? "Well, as you've stated more or less, you really can't resolve the firm's situation until Chatsworth's recovered right?" "Yes, that's true." "Maxwell, I'm going to be up front with you." "I would appreciate I would appreciate that very much he said, half smiling." "When I learned that you're the investigator in the firm's business scandal I wanted to know something about the man I'll be interviewing. I did some background checking on my own and I must admit, I'm very impressed at what I've learned." Smiling, Bradford gazed at him and asked, "is that fact?" Skylar returned the smile answering, "yes, it is " I'm speaking of the man as well as a well-known private investigator with a reputation for not only getting the job done, But you're honest and have integrity, This is something I've always in a person." Maxwell, I've been on the force nearly twelve years now and I've seen my share of those who've somehow; lost this quality along the way. And this meeting with you has been validated through our conversation," "Skylar, people are who they are it doesn't matter what profession they're in, or where they come from." "You've got a point there and I fully agree with you. And back to my question, will you at least give is some consideration?" Maxwell gazed into his eyes and said, "yes, I might just do that!"

Suddenly, the telephone on his desk began to ring and looking in Skylar's direction nodding his head apparently, asking to excuse him while answering. "Hello! This is Bradford T. Maxwell," "Hello Brad, this is Blake." "Blake what's wrong?" "Have you seen the most recent news report?" "No I haven't. I've been rather busy this afternoon. What news report are you speaking of?" "Brad, one of Chatsworth's men was found bleeding to death, but get this, before he died he told the police that he'd been shot by Freddy Sinclaire". "What! "When and where did this shooting take place?" "Apparently about an hour ago near the Santa Monica pier." "All right Blake, I'm tied up right now, but I'll get back with you and thanks for the info." After replacing the receiver he looked at Skylar and said, "Joker's gone wild. Skylar stared at him in total bewilderment and asked, "What's this Maxwell?" Maxwell said, "that was Blake Colwell on the phone. About an hour ago near the Santa Monica pier, one of Chatsworth's men was found critically wounded, but before he died he told the police that he'd been shot by ,Freddy Sinclaire 'the Joker'"My word! "Who's going to die next at the hands of this maniac?" Skylar asked, if he might use the telephone? "By all means," He knew Skylar was most likely to be calling into the station after all, that was his case. He spoke with his supervisor and received an up-dated report on the incident and Maxwell knew the case had now developed a new twist. When the murder occurred, it became a homicide and would then be turned over to the homicide division for further investigation. Skylar thanked him for the use of the phone and asked," What do you say now Maxwell, will you help us catch those maniacs? "Looking directly into Skylar's eyes he asked," What is your suggestion Skylar?" He answered and said, "Chatsworth's hospitalized and you're the only one who knows what any of those guys look like. I spoke with my supervisor and he's agreed for you to go to the crime scene to make a positive identification. This way we'll know which ones to be looking for, will you do it?" He stared at Skylar for a brief second then said, "Yes, I'll go with you." "Thanks man. " "You're welcome, I want to see the remaining two off the streets as well." "Then let's go to it, Skylar said smiling". They departed from the underground parking structure each in their own car.

Skylar arrived at the crime scene shortly ahead of Maxwell who parked his car a short distance away. Observing the draped form on the ground it was obvious that the coroner hadn't yet arrived. Sometimes, it takes hours before they make to the scene because they're so busy and for the most part, understaffed. The crime scene was constantly being monitored by assigned police personnel. People were still mulling around and occasionally, one of the officers would tell them to step back away from the tape. Understandably this was being done to preserve the crime scene. 'It never ceased to amaze him why some people would want to stand sometimes, for hours staring down upon the lifeless form of another human being.' While observing all of the activities , Maxwell hadn't noticed that Skylar was attempting to get his attention. Suddenly, he was making his appearance towards him. He spoke and said, 'Maxwell, the information that I received is the guy who shot once in the chest and twice in the back. From all indications the way his body is positioned. It appears that he was trying to escape from his assailant. I spoke with mu supervisor only explaining that you've had a run-in with the three while working on a case, and perhaps; you can identify which one of the three he is. At least; we'll have a name. He's agreed for you to come inside the perimeter." "Thanks, let's go I'm curious to see which one he was. " That's something he never felt quite comfortable with looking at the still, lifeless form of another human being. They reached the area and signaled to proceed on beneath the tape. As they approached the scene he was introduced to the supervisor in charge who shook his hand and escorted him to where the body was lying. Lifting the yellow plastic sheeting, 'he asked him if he could identify the body? "Looking down into the face of the lifeless man he replied, "Yes, his name was Jason Stevenson an ex-employee of Steven Chatsworth." After replacing the sheeting stepped aside and the supervisor said," I also understand you're familiar with the remaining two we're now searching for? "That is correct." "Maxwell frankly, we don't know their identity, but you do. Would you mind going down to the station and meet with our 'sketch artist'?" "No, I wouldn't mind at all." " Thank you and welcome aboard. We can certainly use your expertise in this case. And yes, I know who you are he said smiling. " Maxwell returned the smile and after speaking briefly with Skylar returned to his car and left the area. While enroute to thepolice station he called Blake on his car phone and informed him of everything including the deceased man's name. Blake said, "Brad, that means the other two are possibly still some place in the surrounding area." "Oh, I don't know about that Blake." "What do you mean?: "Look at it this way, if you've just killed a man would you stick around knowing the authorities are already searching for you?" "No, I would not." "That's precisely my point. Joker might be wild Blake, but he is far from stupid. I don't know what happened to provoke the shooting down there, but he's up to something I'm certain of it. I'll be in touch." "Stay safe buddy." "Will do, he replied".

Maxwell walked up to the front desk at the Santa Monica police department and upon giving his name, was immediately escorted back to the sketch artist who was a tall slender green-eyed brunette with a captivating smile and deep dimples carrying a large sketch pad in her hand. After introducing herself she asked him to have a seat and the task began. Within an hour's time, there were faces on the two suspects. In his description of them were their weight, height, build and distinguishably marks that he'd noted on them. As he was leaving the station Maxwell thought to himself; man she's really good.' Suddenly, remembering Chatsworth's demeanor he spoke out aloud, 'that old buzzard's too mean and onery to die.' Musing to himself! Within an hour's time, the duo's description was being distributed through the surrounding areas including television and the news media. Things were rapidly changing for the Santa Monica police department. Now they had a homicide case on their hands, but they also had the identity of the two suspects, which wasn't available to them before. Since the victim was shot in the upper torso both front and back, it was uncertain if more than one weapon was used in the shooting and that meant waiting for the coroner's and ballistic report. As he was returning to the crime scene, he observed the coroner's vehicle leaving the area. Parking his car nearby, he searched for Skylar and after a few minutes he spotted him having a conversation with two other men. They were also dressed in plain clothes and being familiar with policy he was certain they were the ones that had been assigned to the case. Skylar looked in his direction smiled, excused himself from the two and walked over to Maxwell. "I see you made your way back huh?" "Yes, it took much less time than I'd anticipated. You know she's really good Skylar." "Yes she is and *from the report I received you did a tremendous job which will make it much easier for all of us." "Glad to have been of help, he said with a wide grin." "Now it's just a matter of time before they're caught. "Maxwell gave him a steady gaze and Said, I don't know Skylar." "Oh, oh what are you thinking Maxwell?" "I have a 'gut' feeling that Joker's up to something else, because he hasn't accomplished whatever it is that he's planned to do." "Why do you believe there's something else, Skylar asked?" "All right, we have two shooting's that he's been implicated in and one resulted in death. According to the housekeeper's statement, Chatsworth was told by one of them that' he wanted everything that he owed him am I correct?" "Yes, that's correct." "As of this minute we have no concept of what he meant by that statement. The only thing we can be certain o is the fact that Chathworth was shot as the result of it." "yes, that's correct." "And just what provoked the second shooting and why kill one, of his men? Maxwell, you know you're raising some valid questions and we don't have any answers to any of them, I'd say this situation is becoming pretty sticky." "My point precisely! But apprehending them isn't going to be an easy task either." "Why do you believe that?" "Because he's wild, not stupid! "He's going to take every precaution to prevent getting caught before he gets whatever it is he's after. And right now, no one has figured out just what that might be." Giving Maxwell a long hard gaze he said," ?" "Oh well, the case has been reassigned to someone else anyway. You saw those two men I was talking with?" "Yes, I did and if my guess is correct they're the ones that have been assigned to the case since the status of it has changed." "You're quite correct, they're with the homicide division." "Maxwell smiled at him and said, this is only a reminder of how quickly a situation can develop into a new twist." "Man you said it." "I only hope they're caught before we have another report that he's killed someone else." "A-man to that! "Well, what are you planning to do now Skylar?" "First, I'm going to check in with my supervisor and find out how he wants to play this out. I'll probably be assigned to another though." "What about you Maxwell, what are you going to do, or need I ask?"*

"Now just what do you mean by that question, Skylar?" "You have something up your sleeve so, to speak." He gave him a broad grin and said," I think I'm going to do a little scouting around on my own and see what I can come up with." "That's precisely what I thought you were going to say." "Oh you did, did you?" "Yes, and be careful these guys are facing attempted murder and murder charges, They've gone this far, and who can say what they're going to do next?" "Your point is well taken. If I do happen to come across something I'll give you a call." Shaking hands, Skylar said, that's fair enough." They each turned and walked away in opposite directions.

Maxwell sat in his car for a few minutes then looking at his wristwatch decided to grab a bite to eat. Thinking to himself, Joker's not stupid he's not going to stick around after what he's done, and I've got a hunch he's about to put his plan into effect, but the question remain the same what and how does he go about implementing it?" In the meanwhile, Skylar returned to the station. Since the suspects had been positively identified he began to run a background search for any known criminal history and found nothing on Flint Bishop, not even a traffic violation. Freddy Sinclaire was a different story. Two years prior, he'd been charged in a felonious assault case. The report stated that the incident resulted in the victim having sustained bodily injury requiring hospitalization. But for some unknown reason the case never made it t trial and the charge was dismissed based upon insufficient evidence. There was no record of any family or relatives for either one. Since a composite of the duo was being distributed, the opportunity to move in and about unnoticed was becoming very slim. A dragnet was set up in and about the surrounding areas. It appeared that Maxwell's earlier assessment of the two were correct. That they hadn't stuck around after the shooting. But left the immediate area. However, at that time, the authorities were not yet aware of this.

Approximately four hours later, Joker's 1992 red mustang convertible was found abandoned just two blocks away from the crime scene on a side street. The information was called in to the station by a unit patrol that happened to be patrolling that area.

Maxwell had just gotten into his car when the phone rang. Looking at the display he said, :hello Skylar this is Maxwell, what have you learned?" "How did you know?' "He gave a hearty laugh and said, just a lucky guess." "yeah, like I believe that one he said, laughing. Anyway, I did some background investigation on our two suspects and guess what came up?" "Surprise me, he said." "There's no police record anywhere on Flint Bishop, not even a traffic violation, but interrupted Joke has a record?" "you said it man! And it appears you've been right about him all along." "How's that? "He gave him all of the information that was obtained, Maxwell said," considering the source I can't say that I'm at all surprised." Then, Skylar informed him that Joker's mustang was found abandoned just two blocks away from the crime scene. "What do you think Maxwell?" "Number one, I didn't expect them to stick around after the shooting, and number two, I'm trying to figure out why he shot the other fellow and three, I believe he's working on his next plan of action," "Something's wrong with this picture." Skylar said, "you sound troubled what is it?" Something's not right about this situation." "Listen, I'm going to check something out, where can you be reached?" He immediately gave him his desk number and cellular phone number. Maxwell asked himself; 'just what was the issue with Chatsworth and Joker resulting in his having been shot?' "I don't believe it had anything to do with the three of them having been fired. His instincts led him to believe there was much more to the incident than what appear obvious."

"Joker where are we headed now, Bishop asked him?" Joke said, "We can't go back to my ride so, we'll just have to get one somewhere." "What'd you mean get one, from where and how Bishop nervously asked?" Joker said, "Look stupid, just what do you think I mean, we need a ride out of here pronto and nobody's going to up and give us one. Bishop's stomach was churning inside, but the way Joker was behaving he didn't want him to go off on him! There was *already an all points bulletin out on the duo. Now the car jacking and assault with a deadly weapon would also be added to the other charges alleged against them. Bishop stared at Joker and hesitantly asked, "Where are we going now, you know the cops are going to be looking for this car?" "Without taking his eyes off the traffic he said, "We're going to Arleta, I have a cousin there, besides he owe me a favor anyway. "Bishop wanted to ask Joker what was the beef between he and Chatsworth because it had been in his thoughts since the first incident occurred? He soon realized that it was best to leave well enough alone, knowing first-hand what he was capable of doing. Bishop didn't want to be his next victim, so he remained silent. Suddenly, without warning, he exclaimed "Drats!" Narrowly missing a rear end collision he abruptly drove into the outer lane and took the first available exit off the freeway. "Joker what's wrong with you man, you nearly caused an accident back there?" He looked at Bishop and said, "I saw the highway patrol stopping traffic just ahead of us. We'll have to go another way now. "Bishop's inner thoughts were-"Jeeps, why did I get tied up with this lunatic?" "I knew he was nuts, now I'm tied up in a murder rap and car jacking and just because I was with him, that makes me an accessory to the crimes. "Oh God, I hope there's no more killing. "Joker was having thoughts of his own. 'we've got to get rid of this car, maybe that's why the cop was stopping traffic. All I ca say is, they were lucky I saw them first, because I don't plan on getting caught!'*

Maxwell was on his way to check out a tip he'd received regarding the two suspects. Suddenly, the radio station announced there had been a recent car jacking incident by two already sought after suspects. "What in heaven's name are they going to do next, he asked himself?" He immediately dialed Skyla's desk telephone number at he Santa Monica police station. "Hello, this is Detective Jacob Skylar. " "Skylar this Maxwell, I just heard the news bulletin of a car jacking on the radio. " "Yes, that's correct Maxwell. According to the description given by the victim, it was definitely our two suspects." "Was anyone injured?" "No, thank God for that! The sixty-seven year old man was just frightened half to death because he states that he thought the one holding the gun to his head was going to shoot him." "That would have been Joker, Maxwell stated." "Listen Skylar, I received a tip from a source and was on my way to check it out perhaps; it will lead to some type of clue as to what those two might be up to. I'll be in touch later." Suddenly, his car phone rang and looking down at the display he said, "hello Blake, what can I do for you?' "And hello to you Brad. I saw the news bulletin on car jacking incident implicating those two suspects, have they positively identified them as the one's who are responsible?" "Blake, according to the description given the authorities by the victim, I'm afraid they're the same two." He exclaimed, "Great Caesar's ghost Brad, what are those lunatics going to do next?" "It's difficult to say at this point, they're on the run from the authorities and becoming desperate. Blake I've been doing some scooping around. No one's really saying anything, but I believe Chatsworth's getting shot far exceeds the speculation that it was the result of Joker having been fired." "Oh, and why do you believe that Brad?" "Because, my instincts are telling me there's more involved in this Chatsworth incident than an angry disgruntled ex-employee. " "And just what might that be pray tell?" "Number one, before the shooting occurred, the housekeeper stated that she heard the other man tell Chatsworth 'I want everything that's mine now! And from all indications the odds are we're assuming that was Joker, and it didn't sound as he was just speaking of back payment. Number two, what had he promised Stevenson and Bishop that would influence them to follow him back to the residence. Certainly it couldn't have been just about that, and kill one of them?" After a brief silence Blake said," I honestly don't know Brad and you've raised some valid questions here. It appears that this incident is deeper than first perceived." "None of this is making any sense Blake, Something's missing here and I have a feeling when we locate the source of the situation the answers will be there because it revolves around Chatsworth himself." "How and in what way Brad?" "Right now I really don't know. I'm going to check something out." "I gather you have something specifically in mind, Blake asked?" "Yes I do, and when I find something out, I'll give you a call. "Blake said now, with this Chatsworth incident the firm's situation still exists, because he's in the final phase of it Brad." "Yes I know Blake. As of right now, I'm on my way to check something out, it just might lead to some kind of clue. I'll get back with you later." "I appreciate that Brad, please be careful." "As always, he said smiling.

Approximately three hours later after the car jacking incident, Joker drove inside a Mobil Home {Park. Just beyond the entrance way, he spotted a pay telephone and after quickly looking around the area, "he told Bishop to sit tight and keep his eyes opened as he was getting out of the car." He returned to the car and told Bishop, 'we're in luck he's home. " A few minutes later, they were pulling into a space that was occupied by a blue late model pick-up truck that was parked beside a large Mobil Home. As they were getting out of the car a man came out of the door and began walking towards them, as he approached Bishop gasped and did a double-take. Looking first at Joker then the other man he said, "good gracious Joker you two look like twins." They both let out hearty laughs and Bishop thought to himself ' I wonder if he's as loony as Joker?' After hugging each other Joker introduced Bishop to his cousin John D. who acknowledged him, then hurriedly ushered them inside the house. The three of them were sitting at the table sipping their cooler lights when John D. looked at Joker with a concerned expression on his face and asked, "how long are you planning to stay, you know you've made 'head- line' news '. For the first time, Bishop observed a seriousness about Joker he had never seen before that was in his tone of voice and facial expression as he looked directly at John D and said, "not long man just until night. I don't want to get you and Lizzie involved. By the way, where is she I didn't see her car when we pulled in?" "She's been in Santa Maria for a few days visiting her mother and she's coming back tomorrow. You know if she finds you here there's going to be the devil to pay." Joker laughed and said, 'Don't worry we'll be long gone before she comes back." He stared hard at John D and said, "All I need is a little cash and a different ride, we've got to ditch this one pronto." "Man I hear what you're saying, I've got about a hundred and fifty bucks here and you're welcome to it." Joker gave him half a smile and said,, Thanks cousin you'll get back." John D gave him a long stare and said, "I'm not worried about the dough, I get paid in two days, but I am concerned about you, what are you planning to do?" Joker stood up pushing his chair back from the table and walked over to the window, which was partially opened. Standing there with his back to them while peeking through the blinds and in a smooth and sullen tone said, "John D. For your own welfare, I think it's best that you don' know. If by some chance the cops happen to trace us here, there won't be anything you can tell them and there's only one person out there who even knows you exist and he's in the hospital. " Bishop suddenly wide-eyed stared into the face of the man sitting at the table across from him, and as he turned his head, Joker was walking back towards them. Bishop saw an expression on his face that caused chills to run up his spine. As Joker was seating himself Bishop wondered, 'How could Chatsworth have known about John D. and no one else did, because Joker certainly never mentioned anything about having a family?' John D. Looked at Joker and asked," For my own peace of mind, just what did happen between you and the old man?" Joker gazed directly at John D. and said, "He had me do all of his dirty work and when it got too hot for him he fired me, can you believe that?" John D. stared at him and said, "wait a minute he can't fire you, you're not just someone who was working for him. Is that what the shooting was about?" In the meanwhile, as the two men were speaking, Bishop was in a state of total bewilderment and was slowly absorbing everything that was being said.

It was late in the afternoon when he entered the bar and chose a stool, a tall athletic -looking with salt and pepper hair and deep-set dark penetrating eyes stared at him briefly then asked," What 'd you have to drink?" Maxwell said, "I'll have a seltzer water if you *don't mind." The man looked at him and said," A seltzer it is." After serving him the drink he asked, if there was anything else?" Maxwell looked directly in his eyes and said, "Yes, as a matter-of-fact there is, I'm looking for a man called Big Mike." " The man eyed him for a full minute then said, "You've found him, I'm Big Mike." "My name is Bradford T. Maxwell. I'm a private investigator, Pete Sorenson said I should talk to you. Staring at him with a puzzled expression he asked," Talk to me about what?" Taking a brief glance at end of the bar, then focusing his attention back on Big Mike Maxwell asked, Is there some place where we can have this conversation without an audience?" With a steady gaze on Maxwell seeing the determined look I his eyes and his own curiosity he said," "Yeah, and called a man named Jake. "He instructed him to take charge of the bar for awhile." The man gave Maxwell a quick glance then asked, "Is everything all right boss?" Big Mike responded , "Yes Jake, everything is fine." Big Mike led them away from the bar and staring eyes. They walked about ten feet to the rear Then Big Mike stopped in front of a door with a black and gold embossed plaque that read Private. He reached inside his trouser pocket withdrew a small ring of keys, after fingering through them and finally selecting one, he unlocked the door and ushered Maxwell inside closing it behind them. He invited him to have a seat pointing to a small brown leather sofa that was positioned against the wall, which was the color of desert sand. Near the center of the room was a medium sized desk with a matching swivel chair and on the wall directly behind it stood a six-drawer brown metallic colored file cabinet. Maxwell observed another door and assumed it might have been his private restroom. Big Mike was the first to speak, "Now Maxwell, just what is it that you want to talk to me about?" Looking at him Maxwell replied, "Saying I understand Joker and his buddies spent a great deal of their leisure time here." Big Mike leaned forward placing both elbows on the desk interlacing his fingers and in a rather stern tone said," Maxwell I hope the cops catch that psychopath real soon. " "Oh, and why do you say that Big Mike. I get the impression that you don't particular care*

for him?" "You've got that right, he's a boastful bully and a lunatic."
"In what way, Maxwell asked him?" Suddenly, as if he'd just received
a shock wave, Big Mike lowered his arms to the desk and gazing into
Maxwell's eyes he asked, " wait a minute you said you're a private
investigator and Pete sent you here, there has to be a reason?" My
answer is yes on both counts, was his reply." Then he said, Big Mike
I'm investigating a case in which I strongly believe Joker is in some
way tied into it and I'm trying to get some information that will give
an indication as to where he might be headed." The man looked at
him and said Maxwell, as long as it's away from my business, but just
what exactly is it that you want to know?" "You stated earlier that he
was a boastful bully, how was he boasting?" "Oh he'd beat the guys at
the machines then he'd tell them that he could buy the machines and
pay them to work for him. " "I take he's created a few problems here?"
'That's putting it mildly' "oh, and in what way if I might ask?" Joker
first began coming here regularly a little over two years ago. He'd
have a few beers and play billiard with the guy's, but after awhile, I
guess it wasn't exciting enough for him because that's when he started
playing pranks on them and it seemed to have become a routine with
him." "Why do you say that, Maxwell asked? "Every time he came
he'd always pull some idiotic prank on one of them before he left here.
Finally, Big Mike spoke and Maxwell became acutely aware of the
change his tone of voice as he said, "I shouldn't have allowed him to
come back in here that was my mistake."

"Hello Kate, this is Jacob Skylar, I need a favor from you."
"Just what is it you need Jacob?" "I'd like for you to pull up some
information from the court files data base Kate, this is very important
and urgently needed." Skylar just what is the information that you
need?" "He said, around two years ago there was a felonious assault
case filed against a man named Freddy Sinclaire, but suddenly
disappeared just prior to that time, and the charge against him for
some unknown reason the case never made it to trial. It appears the
victim suddenly disappeared just prior to that time, and the charge

against him was subsequently dismissed based upon insufficient evidence." Kate abruptly asked, "Skylar, did you just say Freddy Sinclaire?" "Yes Kate, I did." "isn't he one of the guys the authorities are looking for in that Santa Monica murder case?" "Yes, he's the same man." She said, "Skylar that man has a very serious problem." He gave her hi cellular phone number. Approximately two hours later, Skylar's cell phone rang. "Skylar this is Kate it took awhile, but I believe this is all of the information that you want." He said, "Let's have it." The attorney who represented Sinclaire was Victor Atkins- he quickly interrupted her "What! "He was disbarred last year." "Oh well, he was the attorney on the case at the time." He asked her, "What's the next one?" A Mr. Steven Chatsworth put up the cash for his bail. " Skylar asked her, "Are you certain?" "According to the records yes." "Maxwell is not going to believe this." "What, she asked?" "Oh, I was just thinking out aloud and thanks a mil doll." "You're quite welcome and Jacob, next time, let the call be for a dinner date." He laughed and said, "It will be my pleasure Kate." Skylar was thinking to himself, Maxwell was certainly right about this case. There is something going on here with Chatsworth and Joker, why would he put up that kind of money for someone who is only working for him. Then, the same man turns around and assaults him?"

Bishop stared first Joker then John D. Mentally questioning "what did he mean when he said Chatsworth couldn't fire him?" He had no concept that the answer to his question was forth coming and much more until Joker said, "No John D. the shooting wasn't about his trying to fire me because he knew he couldn't. I went back for him to release my inheritance. I didn't go back there, with intentions to shoot him, but when he flatly told me to get out that's when I just lost it and shot him. John D. said, "Man I'm sorry it came to that, there should have been some way for you to remain with him after all; he is your uncle." "Suddenly, Bishop who been sitting silently by quickly gulped a swallow of liquid and began to gag. John D. quickly gave him a couple of quick smacks in the back then he was fine physically, but mentally he was becoming loose at the end. Joker stared at his flushed face and burst into laughter, but to Bishop nothing at that point was amusing and once he'd recouped he thought to himself; 'so that's why he was always trying to put Stevenson and me down, but he's the one who's nuts.' John D. said, "Cousin you're lucky the old man's not dead. But what I can't understand is why he didn't release it to you when you turned twenty-five?" Joker said, "we only discussed it once and he said, I should be patient, but a lot of his business I still don't know about." John D. stared at him for a minute or so before speaking then said, "Cousin you're probably not going to like what I'm about to say, but I'll tell you anyway. I don't think anyone else wanted the responsibility of having deal with you. You were spoiled and as the result, your folks were always bailing you out of one incident after another because you pulled those stupid pranks on people and laughed it off as a joke." Bishop thought to himself; (so that's why he's called Joker). "But no one was ever seriously hurt, Joker retorted." This time, John D. spoke in a different tone in fact, it was rather harsh when he said, "Look, it's time for you to grow up and assume responsibility for your own action. Has it ever occurred to you that just maybe the old man feel's you're not ready yet?" Joker yelled, "but it's my money." "yes that's true, but there was an agreement between he and your parents and he's abiding by their wishes, that's the only way I can figure it out." Joker gave him a steady gaze and asked, "Just what am I suppose to do in the meantime, John D. since you seem to have all the answers?" "You're wrong about that cousin, I don't have aa the answers, but this much I do know, you're in a lot of trouble right now and the only one who can straighten it out is you, and for once in your life, think about it! " Little did John D. realize that while he was talking, Joker was thinking, but his thoughts were of 'how to get transportation for he and Bishop out of there.'

Maxwell gazed steadily at Big Mike and said, from what you've said I get the impression that you regret having allowed Joker back into the bar, and in what way do feel it was a mistake, if I might ask?" "Maxwell, when he came in that time, a man was seriously injured he ended up in the hospital and Joker went to jail." "Maxwell asked, "What happened here for him to have been arrested?" "I was busy taking care of customers and didn't see the incident when it first occurred. But Jake saw it all because he was collecting the bottles and glasses at the time. From what I was told, Joker and one of the newer customers got into an argument over one of the pinball machines. Joker started laughing and before he could break it up he'd snatched up a beer bottle hitting the kid breaking his jaw. By that time, the music had stopped and I could hear Joker swearing telling Jake to take his hands off him. After I saw had actually happened I called an ambulance and the police, they handcuffed him and took him out yelling, I'll be out you're not going to keep me locked up. "And just what do you suppose he meant by that, Maxwell asked him?" "I really can't say for sure, maybe he does have the money that he was boasting about." Slowly gazing at him Maxwell asked, "How do you figure that?" Big Mike said, "Well he or someone else does because according to the rumor that was going on around here at the time, his bail was set pretty high and two days later he was back on the streets, but he never came back here." Maxwell there's something I never quite understood about the whole incident with him." "What is that, he asked him?" "A number of things. For one, I understand he was charged with felonious assault. Number two before he was to go to trial, the victim just happened to have mysteriously disappeared so it was rumored. And for about two weeks or more after that, the detectives came around asking if anyone had seen the fellow, or knew where he might be." "I'll tell you something, the whole thing seems rather strange to me." Maxwell leaned back crossed his legs and said, "you've got a point there, it does appear to be odd considering the charge alleged against him. Did you ever hear Joker mention anything about relatives that he might have?" Big Mike thought for a few seconds and said, "no, not that I can recall." Maxwell uncrossed his legs stood up and smiling said, "thank you for taking the time to have this conversation with me I appreciate it." At that point, Big Mike also standing walked around the desk and said, "You're welcome, I'm sorry that I couldn't have been of more help to you. I hope they catch those two soon though. "So do I Big Mike, he responded." After shaking hands and walking through the door Big Mike said, 'hey Maxwell, the next time you're this way, the Seltzer is on me" "Thanks, I'll be sure to remember that, he said as he began leaving out of the door."

He had just started the engine when the car phone rang and looking at the display he said, "hello Skylar this is Maxwell." "Say Maxwell, since our last our last conversation, I've been checking on a couple of thing's myself and you're not going to believe this." "Then how about surprising me, let's hear it." "The attorney who represented Joker in the case two years ago; was none other than Victor Atkins." Maxwell interrupted him with, "you don't say! Wasn't he disbarred from practicing law?" "Yes, he was, but that was just last year which was after he'd represented Joker." "I don't suppose you have an address for him available, he asked laughing?" "As a matter-of-fact I do." Skylar gave him the attorney's telephone and the address. Then Maxwell asked him, "What's next on your list?" "Steven Chatsworth put up the bail money." "Oh he did, did he?" "Yes, according to the information I received." "Skylar, if Chatsworth put up the cash for Joker's bail then fire him and who paid Atkins to represent him and from what I've heard his services didn't come cheap?" He was silent for a few seconds then Skylar said, "You've got a point there. Maxwell perhaps, you might be successful in getting some answers from Atkins himself; you can be quite persuasive you know?" "Only when necessary Skylar. Then he said, something has just occurred to me." " Skylar promptly asked, and what is that? "Something's fishy here, what if the victim was paid a large sum of money by someone to suddenly disappear from the scene before the trial date?" "Well what you're suggesting is plausible, but if proven as you well know, is called obstruction of justice also, it's been known to happen." "But who would dare to go such great lengths , just to keep Joker out of prison and what could possibly be the motive behind it, Skylar asked?" Maxwell said, "there it is again". Bewildered by his statement, Skylar asked," Maxwell what do you mean?" He quickly replied. "Skylar this is the third time, that the word motive has been applied in this situation. The first time, is when Chatsworth was shot, the second time, was the Stevenson shooting and now Joker's case." Skylar asked him, "What are you thinking now?" "Skylar, at this point, I'm thinking that Chatsworth is somehow involved in things much deeper than what has been speculated." "Why do you believe that?" "Because each time we strike with Joker, haven't you noticed that Steven Chatsworth's name comes up?" "Well I'll grant you, this is a baffling situation and all I can say is, go with your instincts pal." I'm not quite certain how the two of them are tied into this together just yet. Let's see what Atkins has to say, and thanks Skylar, I'll be in touch."

It was early afternoon when Maxwell and Atkins met in a quaint little coffee shop on Palos Verdes Blvd. Located in a somewhat elegant shopping center surrounded by a number of three-story office buildings that had been recommended by Atkins himself. Maxwell had barley gotten out of his car when Atkins pulled up beside him and parked. As he was getting out of his car, Maxwell was closely observing a man when who appeared to be in his mid -sixties with greying hair, of medium height and a stocky statue. Maxwell thought he might be meeting someone dressed in suit and tie, but instead he was casually dressed in a light blue cardigan sweater, white shirt and blue trousers. After a brief observation of the now filled to capacity parking lot and seeing no one else, he turned to Maxwell and said, "You're Bradford T. Maxwell I presume." Maxwell gazed at him, smiled and said, "Your presumption is correct and I believe you're Attorney Atkins. "With deep set grey penetrating eyes and thick eyebrows raising one slightly upward, he smiled while extending his hand out to Maxwell and said, "yes, I'm Victor Atkins. After shaking *hands they turned and walked inside the coffee shop. They saw only two unoccupied booth and Maxwell chose the one with its back against the wall and immediately took occupancy in that seat. He preferred to face the entrance. Atkins didn't appear to mind. However, he did mentally take notice of Maxwell's sitting position and smiled to himself and thinking "um, a very cautious man who doesn't easily present his back." He quickly sat down in the opposite seat. There were only four booths, two tables and the counter. Nearly every seat in the shop was occupied. A short while after seating themselves, a young red head waitress with a pleasant smile asked if they were ready to order? They each ordered club sandwiches on rye and coffee. Maxwell also ordered a slice of apple pie topped with a scoop of vanilla ice cream. While awaiting their orders Atkins focused his eyes directly on him and said, "Maxwell, I agreed to meet with you for two reasons." Slightly leaning back in the booth he asked, "Oh is that a fact?" Atkins replied, "Yes it is." Maxwell stared at him and smiling he asked?" And just what are your two reasons if I might ask?" Their orders arrived and they both remained silent until the waitress had left their table. Then Atkins said, "Number one, for the moment let's just say I'm rather curious to learn why a private investigator such as yourself would be interested in talking with me? And number two, I'm no longer permitted by law to practice my profession, as I'm quite certain you're well aware of." With his eyes slightly squinted and smiling Maxwell gazed at him and asked," Just how do you mean such as myself?" "Oh come now Maxwell, you don't have to be so modest." "I fail to see your point of inference Atkins, he responded." "Certainly you don't believe I would agree to talk with someone before learning something about them first, do you?" "I get your point, but you can't believe everything that you hear." "That's true, but after meeting you Maxwell in this case I must admit, your reputation is no mystery and I'm also aware of the fact, that you're the one who investigated the Lansing Contractors' firm scandal. And was quite successful in bringing a resolve." "See Atkins, this is precisely what I meant by you can't believe everything that you hear."*

"I don't understand, Maxwell." "What you've stated is correct in part." There was a sudden change in Atkins tone when he asked," What do you mean correct in part Maxwell? He took a sip of coffee leaned back and never taking his eyes off him he said, Atkins I don't know what you've heard, but the fact of the matter is the case Hasn't been completely resolved that is not yet anyway. You see there are still some loose ends that has to be tied up before there can be a resolve, oh we know who's responsible for creating the situation and why, but it's more complicated than that, I can assure you." Atkins gazed at him and said, "I'm not following you. Maxwell stared hard into the man's eyes and said, about two years ago; you represented a man who had been charged with a felonious assault, his name was Freddy Sinclaire. Does that ring a bell?" "Yes, I remember handling the case, but why do you ask?" "I'll answer your question after you've answered the two I'm going to ask you." "Just what are these two questions Maxwell?" "It's a known fact that your services didn't come cheap s, what I'd appreciate hearing from you is this, who hired you to represent Sinclaire and paid his attorney's fee?" "Maxwell, why is that important to you because it certainly appears to be?" "Listen Atkins, you haven't answered my question and don't give me that bunk about attorney and client's privilege because it doesn't apply in this case." At that point he knew Atkins was hedging and he wanted to know why? So he decided to go farther. "Atkins, let's stop playing the cat and mouse game here and get down to serious business." He retorted, "I don't know whatever you mean." "All right, since you're determined to have it this way, I'm going to lay it out for you." "By all means Maxwell, please do." "Your former client was charged felonious assault on another human being that happened to result in serious injury requiring hospitalization. His bail was set at such an exuberant amount that only someone with a lot of money could afford to pay, And Sinclaire was not known for possessing such wealth, and he certainly didn't earn that kind of money working for Chatsworth. Atkins you know what strike me as being odd? The case never made it to trial date, the victim suddenly and mysteriously *disappeared and has not been seen again." There was a brief period of silence and Maxwell was thinking to himself; he's concealing something and I'll bet he's trying to make a decision on how to respond. It appeared that his perception of Atkins was correct because he took a sip of coffee then, slowly setting the cup down he said, "Continue on Maxwell." "There's another disturbing fact that can be seen here. The case was dismissed on the basis of insufficient evidence and I certainly would consider that to be of a suspicious nature. Now the same man, is being sought by the authorities for murder and attempted murder, on his former employer Steven Chatsworth. And so far, no one has been able to come up with a motive as to why? However; I am certain of one thing, the shooting of Chatsworth had nothing what so ever, to do with Sinclaire having been terminated. Staring at him Atkins asked, "why do you believe that Maxwell, because it's a reality that these things are occurring incidents whether we like it or not." "Yes that's correct and it's said, but Sinclaire's case is different, he's after accomplishing something of importance to him." Maxwell planned to maintain his leverage by not divulging the information he'd obtained prior to their meeting. Atkins remained silent. He just leaned back letting his head rest on the booth, but his gaze on Maxwell never altered who incidentally, did seem to mind the waiting period besides, he was enjoying his dessert with the satisfaction of knowing that he'd given Atkins just enough ammunition for him to discharge. Maxwell began to observe an expression of deep sadness appear upon Atkins face and wondered why the abrupt change?" At that same moment, the answer to Maxwell's question was about to be revealed. He learned that Atkins had once been part of a lucrative Law Firm a short distance from where they were prior to having been disbarred. Maxwell had a feeling there was ore to the story, but he didn't press the matter. Atkins stared out of the window all of a few minutes when his gaze returned on him he said, "Maxwell, I was Steven Chatsworth's attorney, had been for years. He put up the money for Sinclaire's bail and also paid me to represent him in the case you spoke of. Of course, I advised him against it, but that was* the way he wanted it." "Maxwell said, "wait a minute Atkins' you're loosing me." "Why would Chatsworth put out that kind of money for a lunatic like Joker? Maxwell was certain that Chatsworth had played an integral role I Sinclaire's case and he was definitely wanted to know how and why?" The answers could not come from Chatsworth himself, but Atkins was definitely in a position to oblige him with the information he was seeking. He had no concept that the answers to both questions were forth coming and much more.

Joker, how long do you think it'll be before the cops find the car, Bishop asked him?" "I would imagine when they open the place up in the morning, was his response." "I sure wish we could've found a different kind of transportation to get back , because we're going to be smelling just like these chickens." Joker snarled at Bishop and said, "I figured this would be the best way, the cops aren't going to be looking for us in the back of a truck loaded with live poultry, so stop your whimpering will you?" "I'm just glad we left before John D.'s old lady got there, she might've called the cops on us, she never had much liking for me anyway. " "Yeah, me too, Bishop agreed." Joker still had the gun and Bishop was silently praying that they wouldn't be stopped and the truck searched by the cops. He was fed up with all o the shooting, but kept his concerns to himself, knowing quite well that if he expressed his feelings Joker would be all over him in a minute. He was already agitated anyway, but he wasn't responsible for the predicament they were in. They'd encountered a roadblock. Bishop was silently praying, "Lord please don't let them find us, I don't want to see any more shooting." Joker had taken the gun out and was pointing it directly at the truck's large door. What seemingly to have been a long few minutes they heard voices outside, then the truck began to move again and Bishop gave a deep sigh of relief saying, "thank you Lord." Joker never uttered a word just returned the gun to its place of concealment.

Maxwell said, "You stated that you advised Chatsworth against paying out the money for Sinclaire's bail and defense, why was that?"

"I personally felt that he should have faced the consequences of his actions by assuming responsibility for the crime he committed. " "Wouldn't that have been a conflict of interest on your part?" "Oh I would have recommended someone shall we say, with less experience in criminal strategy. " It happens more frequently than most people realize Maxwell." "You have yet to answer my question as to why and don't tell me it was out of the kindness f your heart." "I believe I can say just that Maxwell you see, with Steven it was the matter of making a personal choice. "At that point, Maxwell was beginning to grow weary of Atkins's hedging, it was time to change tactics. Maxwell gave him a stern gaze and asked," What do you mean it was the matter of making a personal choice Atkins, how personal and I prefer to hear all of it." Before allowing him to answer, Maxwell decided to sprinkle mor cinnamon on Atkins's toast. Sitting upright, moving the dish aside, and staring directly into his eyes he said, "Atkins the lunatic you reluctantly defended regardless of your personal motive, is the same one who is responsible for a murder and the condition Chatsworth is in. And I'm not quite certain right now what it is, but my gut is telling me that he's planning something else." "Why do you believe he's planning something else when the authorities are searching every place for him Maxwell?" "For one thing he's wild not stupid, he could very easily have killed Chatsworth, but he seriously wounded him instead which leave me to believe he wasn't thinking rationally and for some reason, he lost self-control now, I'm curious to now why?" "Maxwell, I'm afraid I can't answer that question, I don't know if anyone can except Sinclaire himself." "And Chatsworth, but he's in the hospital and no visitor's are allowed as of right now, Maxwell interjected." There was a brief period of silence then Maxwell observed Atkins staring what appeared to be blankly into space .Suddenly, and to his astonishment, Atkins focused his eyes directly on him and said, "Maxwell, I've been sitting here listening to your scenario and thinking . Enough injustice has been done and I'm growing tired of it all. Mind you no actual facts have been found to substantiate this, but what if your assumption is correct

that Sinclaire is planning something and as of right now, no one has any concept of what that might be?" Leaning back in the booth and folding his arms across his broad chest Maxwell said, "go on, I'm listening." "Considering Sinclaire's state of mind whatever that is and the possibilities, I now feel compelled to answer your question regarding Chatsworth's personal choice. To begin with, Freddy Sinclaire is Steven Chatsworth's nephew."At that revelation, Maxwell sat straight up and staring into Atkins eyes exclaimed what!" "That is correct. Freddy is Steven's nephew and there's more to follow." " I'm only conveying this to you because I'm concerned for Steven's well being and perhaps it will be of some use in determining what Freddy might be planning to do. My fee and also the bail money were taken out of his Trust Fund. You see, Steven is Freddy's legal guardian until the age of twenty-five, or at his discretion after that." "You mean to tell me that Sinclaire has that kind of money?" "Yes, I'm afraid he has. " Maxwell said, "what I fail to comprehend is why would he prefer to keep the relationship a secret, and why the pretext of firing him along with the others?" "When was this Maxwell?" "Just prior to the shooting, he told them to get out of his sight and stay out." Atkins gave him a puzzled look and asked," where did this take place?" "At his residence, he replied." With apparent astonishment upon hearing the answer he gazed at Maxwell for a brief instant then asked him, "you went to Steven Chatsworth's residence uninvited?" "Yes I did because what I had to tell him there was no rationale to feel I needed an invitation." (At that, and seeing the expression on Atkins face, he could only imagine what he might have been thinking, but made no further reference to the matter). Atkins said, "The only explanation I can possibly think of is Chatsworth didn't want the others t know he's Freddy's uncle and I can't give you an answer as to why he preferred to have it that way. Steven Chatsworth is a very complicated and sometimes, difficult man to understand and I never questioned his rationale for it." Maxwell asked, "Does Sinclaire have any siblings?" "No, he was an only child and from what I've come to learn and see, he's been spoiled rotten. I believe Chatsworth was their last recourse" In reference to your statement regarding Sinclaire's age, which I believe was twenty-five, or at his uncle's discretion what did you mean by that?" Taking a deep sigh and leaning back in the booth with a steady gaze on him he said, "Well, Steven was to teach him the business and a sense of responsibility of how to use the money to become established in a lucrative business of his own. But from what I've seen, he 's still being irresponsible and I'm quite certain this is why the money is still being held in trust because he reached age twenty-five last year." Maxwell was mentally asking himself; could this be the motive for the shooting? He asked Atkins, "as to your knowledge has Sinclaire asked Chatsworth for the money?" "Yes, as a matter-of-fact he has, why do you ask?" "What was Chatsworth's response when he asked for the money?" "Steven told him that he wasn't going to get a cent until he'd proven to him that he was sincere in learning the business and willing to assume the responsibility of ownership.

Oh he became angry and belligerent, but that was the extent of it." Maxwell said, I'm not quite so certain of that." Atkins stared hard at him and asked, "why what do you mean?" Maxwell said, Atkins, we've been searching for a motive that would somehow explain Sinclaire's state of mind for his actions and I believe you just gave it." "Wait a minute Maxwell, are you implying that Freddy shot Steven because he refused to give him the money?" "yes, I am implying just that, can you think of any other motivating force that explain his wild irrational behavior?" "No, I'm afraid I can't Maxwell. I'd say all things having been considered, there's a strong possibility that your perception is correct." "I've a very strong hunch that he's planning something." "But what Maxwell, considering Chatsworth is still hospitalized?" Atkins, I don't know it's difficult to say because as of now, we've an irrational man who is completely out of control." Looking at his wristwatch and noting the time, he gazed at Atkins smiled and said, this has been a most rewarding afternoon. You've filled in the missing pieces to this end of the puzzle and I appreciate *your cooperation Atkins, thank you." He stared hard into Maxwell's eyes smiled and said, it's been quite sometime, since I've had the opportunity to spend such an enjoyable afternoon in the company of a man who's professional and tactful. I'm pleased with the outcome of this meeting Maxwell and to have met you." Maxwell gave him a wide smile and said, "the feeling is mutual Atkins. I'll be in touch." "I'd like that very much Maxwell, he responded."*

Maxwell was enroute to his office when the car phone rang and taking a quick glance at the display he said, "hello Skylar, what are you up to this time, laughing heartly?" "And hello to you Maxwell, you remember the car jacking incident by our fugitives. we've just been notified that the vehicle was found abandoned at a car wash up in Arleta. They ran the plates and immediately called us." "Well, well it appears they've been doing some moving, wouldn't you say?" Skylar laughed and said, "yes I would Maxwell." "Most car washes open up early in the morning don't they, Maxwell asked him?" "Yes, I believe they do, but why do you ask?" "Skylar, if you were being sought atter by the authorities and knew the car you're driving is hot, what and where would you consider to be the best time and place to get rid of it?" He thought for a moment and said, "I see where you're coming from. Naturally, I'd wait until it's dark and no one's around to see me, then I would make certain it'll be some place where it won't be discovered until the next day and by that time, I'd be long gone to where ever, that might be." "My point precisely, Maxwell stated." Skylar said, "since the car was found in their jurisdiction, they're doing their own investigation, we'll just have to wait and see what they come up with, if anything at all." Maxwell laughed and asked, "What's the matter Skylar, I sense a note of skepticism?" "I just don' think they will succeed in producing anything Maxwell. And those two, certainly wouldn't stick around after ditching the car. But it would be very interesting to learn where they went after that and how?" Maxwell said, wherever, they're headed has been under the cloak of darkness. There's less noticeable traffic and one thing for certain, they're still on the run and are somehow managing to elude the authorities."

Skylar asked, "Oh by the way Maxwell, how did your meeting with Atkins go?" Suddenly, something hit hi like a lightening bolt and he said, "Listen Skylar, I'm enroute back to my office, something just occurred to me when you were asking about the meeting with Atkins. Are you going to be available within the next hour?" Skylar replied, "Yes, I'm on evenings this week what is it Maxwell?" "We just might have a break in this situation after all Skylar, I'll be in touch."

Maxwell arrived at his office a short time later and immediately began to mentally focus on the conversation he and Atkins had earlier. Thinking out aloud he said, "this situation with Chatsworth and Joker has more twists than a spinning tp. As for Chatsworth I find him to be quite a strange and unpredictable man, to say the least. "I wonder how long had he planned to keep the relationship a secret and what is the point of it? He's allowed everyone with the exception of Atkins, to believe Joker was just employee and yet, when he said they were all terminated he was the only one who retaliated and that's because Joker knew something that the others didn't. Atkins stated that he's Joker's legal guardian over his Trust Fund and he'd refused to give him the money when he asked for it. Now I suspect that is why he went back to Chatsworth's residence and if that's the case, his motive for shooting him would have been the money, there's no other logical explanation for his having gone off the deep end." He was mentally compiling all of the information into stages when the telephone on his desk rang and looking at the caller ID he said, "hello Blake I wasn't aware that you're e.s.p. Blake responded," hello to you Brad and what is this about e.s.p.?" "Well old buddy, it's as if you were reading my thoughts because I was just about to call you." Blake chuckled and said," "Oh I see, well what have you learned regarding the Chatsworth situation?" Maxwell gave him a hearty laugh and asked Blake if he was sitting down comfortably?" "He responded, I am now and from your tone of voice, I expect whatever it is that you're willing to tell me is going to be interesting." "Blake, I believe what I am about to bring you up to date on, you're going to find quite interesting." "Oh, oh , please continue Brad. " "I was following upon a lead that had supplied me with information regarding Joker. As it turned out, I met with Victor Atkins." On that note, Blake immediately interrupted him and asked, Victor Atkins was disbarred Brad, what does he have to do with Joker?" "I hope you're ready for this, Maxwell said. Two years ago, Joker was charged with felonious assault against another young man in a bar fight. But the case never made to trial because the victim suddenly and mysteriously disappeared prior to the trial date and as the result, the charge against him was subsequently dismissed based upon insufficient evidence." Blake exclaimed what!" "That sounds rather suspicious to me and no one ever followed up on the case?" Maxwell said, "My sentiments exactly, but that is only a part of it, guess who the attorney handling the case was?" "Not Victor Atkins, Blake said." "One and the same, "Maxwell replied." "Wait a minute Brad, Victor Atkins was considered by some to have been a shrewd attorney who didn't come cheap so, working for Steven Chatsworth how in heaven's name could Joker have afforded his services?" Maxwell sad, I was interested in learning how and why was Chatsworth involved in Joker's case to begin with? According to Atkins, the bail money and his fee was paid out of Joker's Trust Fund. Blake, Steven Chatsworth is Freddy Sinclaire's uncle and legal guardian." Up until that time, Blake Colwell had been leaning back comfortably in his chair, but when he heard what Maxwell has just conveyed to him he sat straight up and asked, "did I hear you correctly Brad?" He responded, "Yes, you did Blake, Chatsworth is Joker's uncle. His mother was Chatsworth's older sister. And again according to Atkins, he was an only child and his parents left a substantial trust fund for him." Brad, I have two questions to ask," I believe the victim was paid off to disappear, but by whom and why on earth would he keep the relationship a secret?" Blake, I didn't push Atkins to admitting Chatsworth paid the victim to disappear and I'm certain he did because that would be his style of operation which would also mean, he was guilty of obstruction of justice . However, I did ask about the relationship part and his answer was and I quote, Steven Chatsworth is a very complicated and difficult man to understand. He wanted it that way and he certainly didn't question his rationale for it, unquote." "We've been seeking a motive for the Chatsworth shooting and I believe we have one, he said. 'Blake said, "I don't understand Brad. "I asked Atkins as far as he was aware of, had Joker asked Chatsworth for the money and his answer was yes. I asked him what was Chatsworth's reply? He said Chatsworth told him that he wasn't going to get a cent until he'd proven to him that he was serious about learning the business and willing to assume the responsibility of ownership. Apparently, his parents and Chatsworth had a verbal agreement pertaining to the trust. " Blake sighed and said," when you informed me that the information was going to be interesting, I'd say that, was an understatement." "You know Blake, everyone else has been speculating about a motive for the shooting, but I'll bet you a ten dollar gold piece Chatsworth knows the answer." "From everything you've conveyed to me, I'm inclined to agree with you Brad, he said." "Incidentally Brad, have you spoken with Detective Skylar recently?" His response was, "yes earlier as a matter-of-fact, I'm going to give him a ring next. It appears that the Arleta police department notified them, that the car taken by the two fugitives in the car jacking was found abandoned at a car wash there" "In Arleta, what in heaven's name were they doing there, Blake asked?" Maxwell said, "I haven't the vaguest concept Blake other than the fact that perhaps; he's trying to throw everyone off track." "Wait a minute you mean like planning to do something else, Blake asked?"

"My instincts are telling me yes they are, but at this I have no concept of what it is and it's annoying me to the utmost, he said. Listen Blake, I'm going to give Skylar a call I'll be in touch, he said."

"All dight Brad, just be safe." He laughed and said," I'll do my best buddy."

"Hello Skylar, this is Maxwell. Can you spare a few minutes?" the voice on the other end said, "hold on a sec. Hello Maxwell sorry about that, but I had to switch phones and yes, I'm free for the moment, he said." He came right to the point and said, "Skylar without going into all of the specifics right now, I believe we finally have a motive for the Chatsworth shooting incident." There was a brief silence then Skylar asked, "are you certain Maxwell?" His direct response was, "I'm quite certain, money was the motive. I'm not speaking of the speculated theory that the motive might been a disgruntled employee. it's greater than that." "Then what are you about to tell me Maxwell?" "Do You recall asking me earlier how the meeting with Atkins went?" "Yes and I remember your abrupt response was something had occurred to you when I asked about the meeting with Atkins. "He said, "Yes and I do apologize for that Skylar I would say the meeting was quite productive." "Oh really, just how productive Maxwell, he asked?" "Let's just say I learned a number of things that wasn't on the score board earlier. The information that you were able to obtain gave me the leverage I needed to shall we say, bolt Atkins down. We've been searching in all of the wrong places for answers to this dilemma. Listen to this, Steven Chatsworth is Freddy Sinclaire's uncle and legal guardian over a substantial Trust Fund left by his parents. And according to Atkins, Joker asked his

Uncle for the money, he refused to give it to him. "Skylar asked him, "Maxwell don't tell me you're serious about all of this?" His reply was, "I'm as serious as a throbbing toothache." "Did Atkins happen to say why Chatsworth refused to give Joker the money?" "Yes he did. It appears that the parents and Chatsworth had a verbal agreement." Before Maxwell could say more , Skylar asked him to hold for a second. He returned to the phone saying," I'm sorry about the interruption. We're a little short handed this evening. Now where were we he asked?" Maxwell said, "No apology is necessary I understand. "Apparently they felt Chatsworth could straighten him out." Skylar asked, you're saying that Chatsworth is still holding onto the money?" Maxwell said, precisely and I would venture to say when he ordered them off his property, Joker decided he wasn't leaving without first getting his money. Skylar, do you recall my telling you that I saw a sneaky grin on Joker's face when he told them to get out of his sight?" Skylar said, "Yes I remember so in other words Joker went back to collect and again, Chatsworth refused to give him the money?" Maxwell responded, "Yes and asked Skylar, remember the housekeeper's statement when she said, that the other man told Chatsworth he wanted all that he owed him?" Skylar thought for a moment and said,", that is true." Then he asked skylar,"can you think of a different, or stronger motive for the shooting?' Skylar said, "No and I'm inclined to agree with you, but there's still one thing I'm curious about." "What is that, Maxwell asked him?" He said, "the car was found abandoned in Arleta, where were they headed and why Maxwell?" Maxwell laughed and said, "I believe those are two questions, but here's my scenario. I believe they were headed for a particular place, it would've only been for a short period of time. In addition, perhaps that was the time, he needed to decide what his next move is going to be. Remember Joker is out of control and cunning not stupid, which makes him even more dangerous. He's managed to elude the authorities by moving under the cloak of darkness and what better way to throw them off track than to leave a false trail?" For a full minute Skylar said nothing then he asked Maxwell," Are you saying he's planning something else?" Maxwell laughed and said," Skylar I'll bet you a Sunday dinner he is, but I have no concept of what it might be. I believe the best we can hope for is he'll make his move soon." "Well, I hope you're right because the Arleta police haven't been able to come up with anything either, it's as if a ghost drove into town parked a stolen car and left, Skylar said." Maxwell said, "Yes, but we know it wasn't a ghost. I've some paper work to go over and tomorrow I plan to do some scouting around. I'll be n touch." "I'll be looking forward to it, Skylar said." Looking at his *wristwatch and noting the time, and thinking to himself; "gracious," there's no wonder I'm beginning to feel nauseous, it's been quite sometime since I ate anything . And on that note, he stopped at a nearby restaurant and ordered a full-course dinner and a large pepsi to take out. While driving the short distance to his office he thought," this case with Chatsworth and Joker is really getting under my skin. "Oh well for now, I'm just going to enjoy my dinner while completing the paper work, close up shop go home and take a warm relaxing shower and get a good night's sleep before another disruption occur.*

Joker, why are we hanging around here you want us to get caught by the cops, Bishop nervously asked him?" Joker gave him a hard stare and said, "be quiet stupid, I'm trying to figure out a way to get us a ride, there's nothing out here but trucks and how are we going to make it out of here in a truck?" Joker asked Bishop, "you see that dump truck parked over there by the building, pointing to a building about ten feet away from where they were standing?" Bishop looked in the direction he was pointing and said, "yeah I see it, but how are you going to drive it out of here Joker?" He looked at him and said, "just follow me and be quiet will you?" Joker took off running in the direction of the truck and Bishop was following closely behind him. Opening the door on the driver's side while taking a swift look around them and getting into the truck, he looked over at Bishop who was just standing there and asked, "are you getting in or not?" Without saying a word, he immediately complied by that time, Joker had already started the motor and as Bishop was closing the door, he was driving off. Bishop looked at him and said, "Joker, we're not getting out of here without being seen." At that point Joker said, "just watch me and see." Other trucks were coming in and going out beginning their routes. As a truck that was loaded with cement and a mixer drove out of the gate, so did Joker. When they'd gone a short distance away from the site, Bishop said, " I can't believe we just stole a big dump truck from a construction company. Boy, they're really going to be looking for us now." Joker started to laugh and said, "yeah, but not before we get to where we're going." Bishop was afraid to ask, but he did anyway. "Just where are we going Joker?" Where do you think stupid?" Bishop looked hard at him and his heart did a flip-flop because of the direction in which they were going he knew the answer, but he asked anyway, "not back to your uncle's place?" Joker laughed and said, he's still in the hospital and I know where the safe is, I'm going to get what is rightfully mine and that's that! Bishop thought to himself; he's really nuts, Lord, I wish there was some way I could get away from him before he gets the both of us killed. "What if the cops are waiting for us out there?" "I'd rather take my chances with them than this lunatic, he said." As they were getting near Chatsworth's residence, Bishop was becoming more nervous, but he didn't say anything and suddenly, Joker began to accelerate faster, he looked at him and said, "Oh Lord no!

In the meanwhile, Steven Chatsworth had made a personal telephone call to Victor Atkins asking him if he would be so kind as to come to the hospital, there were some personal matters that he wanted to discuss with him. He informed his nurse that he was expecting an important visitor and did not wish to be disturbed other than his physician, under any circumstances. Atkins arrived at the hospital within a half -hour's time, after receiving Chatsworth's call. Upon entering the room he was surprised to see Chatsworth sitting in a chair by the window. Looking at him for a brief second he asked, "how are you feeling Steven?" He gazed at Atkins smiled and said, "I feel as if I've been run over by a bulldozer." Atkins laughed and said, "oh well, you've always been a tough old buzzard anyway and its good to see you up again my friend." He smiled and said, "thanks, it certainly feels good to be up, but for awhile there I must confess the odds seemed to have been against me." Suddenly, looking into his eyes he said," Victor I asked you to come here because lying in this bed has given me an opportunity to face up to certain things." Atkins never interrupted, he just sat Quietly and allowed him to speak Chatsworth said," this shooting incident has allowed *me the chance to put things in their perspective order. First, and foremost, if I had taken the advice you were trying to give me when Freddy managed to get himself into trouble two years ago perhaps; my ending up in the hospital as the result of his having shot me, could have been averted. I realize that and bear the responsibility of ignorance as well. You see Victor you never asked, but I'm quite certain you knew that young man whom Freddy assaulted was paid handsomely by me, not to make his appearance in the courts. And that my friend, was a huge mistake on my part because I should have insisted that Freddy assumed responsibility for what he'd done. I only hoped he would realize the seriousness of his offense and straighten himself out. But I can clearly see now that was only a misconception on my part and now this. I refused to release the inheritance when he turned twenty-five solely because of the agreement between his parents and I. Even now, I don't believe he's really learned what it is to accept responsibility. He's gotten himself into a predicament that even I will not be able to get him out of." Atkins stared at him and said, "perhaps; this is just what he needed Steven, only much earlier, he said." "You might be correct on that point Victor." He paused for a moment and said, "incidentally, I've been following the news and I'm very much aware of what he's been doing. First, he kills that young man Stevenson and then he car jacks someone else. With deep sadness in his eyes he said, "Victor I'm afraid, Freddy's behavioral pattern began long before I agreed to become his legal guardian. According to his father, by the time he reached age fifteen, he literally had gone through three Boarding schools. The reports received from each of them stated that, he taunted and intimidated other students by pulling malicious pranks on them. From that time on through high school, they found themselves getting him out of one incident after another. Now I regret thing's haven't worked out the way they so desperately wanted." After looking into his eyes and seeing the great sadness, Atkins thought perhaps; some of it might have been contributed to his feeling's of guilt, which can sometimes become a heavy burden. "Steven, now there's something else that I feel compelled to convey to you" Chatsworth stared at him briefly and asked, "what is it Victor?" Bradford T. Maxwell a private investigator, Chatsworth snapped, "I know who he is, what about him?" Atkins said, "we had a meeting." Suddenly, Chatsworth said what! Then asked Atkins, "a meeting about what Victor?" At that point Atkins saw his face become flushed and said, "hold on Steven, don't get your dandruff up. Maxwell somehow learned that I was the attorney who represented Freddy in the assault case and asked about it?' You know as well as I that when the victim suddenly disappeared just before trial date, the aspect of it all was going to be questionable to say the least. He was more interested knowing how he could afford to pay bail that was set at such an exuberant amount while working for you. And of course, who paid the attorney fee?" 'And what did you tell him, Chatsworth asked?" "I told him the truth, you paid the bail and his attorney fees. But then he wanted to know why would you take on such a responsibility for an employee with no possible means of repaying you that amount of money?" I learned from him that, he was concerned about you as well as I under the circumstances. That is when I told him about the inheritance and your relationship with Freddy." In a rather staunch tone Chatsworth said, "that was none of his business and why was he questioning you about it anyway?" Atkins took a breath exhaled, and focusing his eyes directly on Chatsworth said, "Listen to me for once in your stubborn life Steven. Whether you like or not , and you must face the fact that Freddy's out of control. Maxwell as well as the authorities are seeking a motive for his having shot you in the first place, and strongly believe he's planning to do something else." Chatsworth stared hard at him and asked, like what for instance, I'm in the hospital and out of control or not, he's not foolish enough to come here?" Atkins replied," No one knows for certain, because he's very unpredictable. They've somehow, managed to elude the authorities even with all of the roadblocks." Chatsworth sighed and said, "Victor one of Freddy's problems is and I believe has always been, he was never encouraged to take responsibility for anything." Atkins said," Well steven, I'm afraid he will have to assume responsibility this time, he will have no choice." Chatsworth said, "I'm sorry about the young man Stevenson though, and what puzzles me the most is, why did Freddy kill him anyway? The three of them came to my residence together unless, he'd promised them something.*

I believe it is time, for me to try and make amends for my negligence." Atkins gazed at him smiled and asked, "what is it Steven, you know I will do whatever I can for you?" "I would very much like for you to contact someone for me. He lives in Arleta, Ca. I'll give you his full name, address and of course; the telephone number." Atkins asked him, "how soon do you wish me to contact this person?" Chatsworth smiled and said," I would say, at your most earliest convenience." He took the pad and pen off the bedside table and after, writing the information down, he gave it to Atkins who after reading it exclaimed 'JumpingJupiter, Steven"

Maxwell showered, shaved and ate a hearty breakfast which, he prepared himself, that consisted of crisp bacon, over-easy eggs, rye toast with jam, orange juice and coffee. After ingesting his delectable breakfast he drove to one of the Construction sites he'd visited during his investigation only this time, the reception was much different. It appeared that his arrival was well timed. Because he hadn't gotten out of his car when the man who warned him to leave the site and don't come back came rushing up to him and said, "Maxwell we just got a call from one of the other construction Companies that, one of their men had spotted that crazy Joker and Bishop jump off the back of a truck near the Santa Monica Off-ramp." Maxwell gazed at him and asked. "When was this?" The man thought for a minute and said,

"That was early this morning because we were just opening up the yard." Then Maxwell asked him," Did the fellow happen to say what kind of truck they jumped off?" "No, he just said that it looked like some kind of large white or grey company truck, he couldn't read the name on it and I sure hope they don't show up here." Maxwell

looked at him and said, "Thank you for the information at least; we know they're back in this area." He remained in his car watching the man as he slowly walked away. He picked up the phone and dialed Skylar's cell number hoping to contact him at home since he's on the evening shift this week. "Good morning Maxwell, what can I do for you this early?" "And a good morning to you Skylar, I happen to have some good news to share with you for a change." Skylar laughed and asked," Well man how long are you planning to keep me in suspense?" Maxwell said, Not long. I was just informed that our two suspects were seen getting out of the back of a truck near the Santa Monica off-ramp early this morning. The man could only describe the truck as being some large white or grey company truck he was unable to read the name on it." Skylar said, "Maxwell this means they're back in the area look, I'm going to notify the station with this information perhaps; this is the break we've been looking for." Maxwell said, we know they're in the area, but we still don't know what is going on in his mind right?" After thinking for a moment Skylar said," That's true, perhaps he'll make a move in our direction soon ,but

In the meanwhile, what are you planning to do, some more scouting around?" He gave him a hearty laugh and asked, "How did you know that Skylar?" "Because that's what you're good at doing Maxwell and some ways, I envy you." Maxwell asked him why?" "You have the freedom to do it and my position, I can't." He said, "Well my friend I suppose you have a point I can't argue with, I'll be in touch with you later."

Following a hunch on something he recalled earlier, Maxwell went to another Construction site he'd visited and as he arrived and was parking his car, he observed the gathering of a small group of workers and wondered to himself; what's going on here?" Little did he realize that the answer to his question was forthcoming, as he began walking towards them. They all turned to face him in unison and the Foreman approached him looking as if he'd seen a ghost. The man informed him that the du had been there earlier apparently, on one of their supply trucks. The Foreman stated that they looked as if they'd been in the swamp somewhere and smelled like a chicken yard, he went n to say, everyone knew what had happened and didn't want anything to do with either of them. "I must admit I did feel sorry for Bishop though . Maxwell looked at him and asked,' why is that?" He said, "because he looked as if you blew hard, he'd fall down. " Maxwell asked him, "what happened here?" He said, "Joker was trying desperately to get one of the guys to loan him his car." "And did he, Maxwell asked?" The fellow lied and told him that he was just getting ready to take his wife to the hospital. He was always coming out here playing jokes on the men until the boss finally got fed up with it and threatened to report him to Chatsworth. This is the first time, that we've seen them in about a couple of weeks. We heard that the police were looking for them in the Chatsworth shooting and the other guy and the other guy that was always with them. Is it true that he killed him?" Maxwell said, "Yes, that's true." "My gracious man, no wonder Joker was acting like a raving maniac when they showed up here." Maxwell asked the Foreman, "How do you mean?" "He kept yelling that Chatsworth owed him and he was going to get everything that belonged to him." Chatsworth is still in the hospital just how does he plan to get it, Maxwell questioned?" "that's the strange part about it. I don't know and he never said." Maxwell said , "I see. And what was Bishop saying while all of Joker's raving was going on? " His response was, "He never said anything, you could tell he's deathly afraid of Joker." "Where did they go when they left here?" "Man, I honestly don't have any idea where they might have gone, as long as it's away from here." The men just started walking away and the next thing anybody knew, they'd vanished." "No one saw them leave, he asked? "No everybody was too anxiously trying to get away from them as quickly as they possibly could. The boss wanted to call the police, but by the time he'd made up his mind, he was told by one of the guys they were gone and I guess he was thinking 'good riddance.' Finally Maxwell said I see, while musing to himself they didn't just walk out of here somehow, they had help.

Just as he was about to speak with the owner, a man came running towards them yelling,"Where's the boss?" The Foreman pointed in the direction of the office. He and Maxwell stared at each other in total bewilderment as the man quickly snatched open the door and ran inside. A few minutes had lapsed when the boss and the man came running in their direction. That time, it was the boss doing the yelling. "That crazy Joker and the imbecile with him has stolen one of my dump trucks." Maxwell stared at the three of them, then in a rather stern tone asked. "And no one around here saw them leave not to mention a heavy vehicle such as a dump truck?" The Foreman said, "We have equipment coming in and going out throughout the day, this is a construction company, remember?" Maxwell replied yes, I'm fully aware of that fact, but what puzzles me most is, how did they manage to get a vehicle that size without anyone having seen them?" The Foreman said, "if anyone did see the truck they probably assumed it was one of our drivers going out on his run, and paid no attention." Speaking to the driver who came yelling. "When did you first discover the truck was missing?" "The man said, "I was doing some paperwork in another building and when I came out to make my scheduled trip, It wasn't there." Maxwell looked at his wristwatch and estimated the time to have been around an hour to give or take a few minutes. The Foreman defensively said, "I explained that everyone was trying to get away from them, who would have ever thought they would be taking a big dump truck out of here?" Maxwell looked at him and said,"Yes, who indeed And I agree with you? Under the circumstances I don't blame them perhaps; it's a good thing no one did catch them in the act because he could have been another victim." Turning his attention to the owner he said," I'm going to notify the Santa Monica police department. They'll also need the identification information on your truck." Without hesitating the owner said, "sure come with me to my office." Following the owner into his office Maxwell asked permission to use his telephone. He replied. By all means please do so pointing to the phone on his desk. Man, I don't know where they could be going, but I sure hope they don't wreck my truck., then he walked across the room to a very large file cabinet." In the Meanwhile, Maxwell was making contact with Detective Skylar, who informed him that he was having the call transferred to the supervisor's office. Once the connection was made, he apprised them of everything that had transpired up to and including his present location. He also gave them the information on the stolen truck. Then he addressed Skylar specifically asking him, "Do you recall our conversation when I told you there was something not right about this situation? He replied, "Yes, I remember quite well." Then he repeated what the Foreman had told him regarding Joker's demeanor and the words. Skylar, number one, Chatsworth's still in the hospital so how in the world can he expect to collect anything from him?" Skylar's response was, "yes, that's correct." Number two, "What would you need with a big dump truck if you're just trying to escape from the authorities?' There was a brief pause then the supervisor's voice came in and he asked," Wait a minute Maxwell, are you telling us that those maniacs are planning to use that that truck to break into Chatsworth's residence?" His reply was, "Yes, I believe so. We're dealing with a man who's totally out of control and in his case, logic doesn't apply here." Then he said, "Now we know what his plan has been all along and how, he's going to accomplish it. "After hearing that statement, the supervisor exclaimed! "Oh my word." Maxwell asked in a concerned tone," where's the housekeeper right now?" Skylar said, "She's living in Hermosa Beach with relatives until Chatsworth's recovered enough to be discharged to his home." "That's good news, Maxwell said with a sigh of relief." The supervisor said listen Maxwell, "We're on top of this situation as we speak. I pray we can get to them before too much damage is done to the man's residence." Maxwell said, "so do I, but I don't know, from estimation they've got a fairly good head start." After a brief pause Skylar said, "Maxwell, " "Don't you fret Skylar, I'm quite familiar with departmental procedure. I'll remain away and allow you men to do your job." Thanks! "I'll be in touch with you when all of this has been resolved, no matter what!" "Fine by me, he said." Thinking to himself.

While waiting for the authorities to accomplish their task, his inner thoughts reverted to the duo.. "I don't believe they will have very much trouble out of Bishop that is if they can manage somehow, to separate him from Joker. And as far as he's concerned, that's an entirely different story because from all indication, he's like a person with 'tunnel vision', he's focused straight ahead on whatever it is that he's trying to accomplish. It doesn't matter to him who's involved, or who gets hurt and he's not going to give up without a fight. He's really gone off the deep end it's too bad if they can't resolve the situation without it resulting in his death and I'm certain they're going to do everything they reasonably can to prevent that happening. He's in dire need of learning that life is commodity and not a 'joke' after all! Finally, refocusing his attention he thought," I'd better telephone Blake and bring him up to date on the situation especially, since he's responsible for my having become involved in it to begin with, as he was smiling to himself."

Thank you very much, that is very pleasant news indeed." Blake had just completed his call to the hospital and was informed that Steven Chatsworth's condition has greatly improved. In fact, he would be allowed to have visitors for a short period of time. Then his thoughts reverted to Maxwell and with an amused grin on his face, he wondered how he and Detective Skylar had gotten along?' The telephone rang and Jenny informed him that, Mr. Maxwell was on the line. He asked her to put him through. "Hello Brad. I was wondering how you and Detective Skylar have been getting along he said, with a mischievous grin on his face?" "Yes, I'll bet you were, he said laughing." "Well I've got some very good news for you, Blake told him." "Oh, oh what is it this time, are you planning to sic someone else on me?" Laughing loudly he asked, "now why would I do something like that?" "Blake Colwell that's in your nature buddy." "Oh I see he said. Are you interested in hearing good news for a change, or

not?" "I certainly am, was his immediate reply to Blake's question."
"I was on the telephone with the hospital a short while ago, and
was informed that Chatsworth's condition has greatly improved. In
fact, his physician is allowing him to have visitors for short periods
of time." "Now that's what I consider to be good news. I knew the
old buzzard was too mean and onery to just give up that way." I'm
inclined to agree with you Brad. Perhaps; we can get this pickle
situation with the firm that has stalemated us for so long resolved."
"Now that, my friend is an enlightening concept and nothing would
please me more, he said." Maxwell apprised him of all the recent
events that had occurred. Blake laughed so hard that he gasped then
asked, "Do you mean to tell me that they allowed a big dump truck to
be taken from beneath their very noses?" "Yes, that is precisely what
happened. It appears that everyone was so preoccupied with trying to
escape from the pair that stealing a big truck never occurred to them."
"What influenced your belief that he two were going to Chatsworth's
residence?" "Blake when I began to backtrack the situation, number
one. The housekeeper stated that she overheard an argument in which
the other man told Chatsworth that he wanted everything that he
owed him. Somehow, I never paid into the speculation that Joker was
simply a disgruntled ex-employee who was just out to settle the score
for having been terminated by Chatsworth although these things do
happen, to me it just didn't apply in this case. Number two, when I
questioned the Foreman at the construction company he stated that
Joker was raving and ranting about Chatsworth owing him a lot
of money and he planned to collect it. Then I recalled the meeting
with Atkins, and the information that he conveyed to me regarding
the money and what had actually transpired between Chatsworth
and Joker, the motive had to be money. But since Chatsworth is still
hospitalized, how could he possibly collect anything from him. There
had to be something in his home that Joker felt he could get his hands
on and at that point, no one really knew only Joker himself and
perhaps, Bishop since he was still with him. And when the Foreman
stated that Joker had tried to get one of the men to let him use his

car. And when it was discovered that the truck had been stolen that's when it hit me like a neon light. I knew they'd had some sort of help in getting out of there unobserved; but taking a dump truck never occurred to me either. Not only were they using the truck as a means of transportation, but also to break into the man's home. " "Brad, are you saying they're going to use it as some sort of ramming vehicle?" "I believe so. He's gone wild and to him it doesn't matter how much damage is sustained." "Good gracious! Blake exclaimed. He really has lost it hasn't he?" "I'm afraid so Blake, but the ironic thing about this whole episode is unlike Joker, the fellow who is involved in it with him doesn't even have a police record that is, up until now." "What! Then how did he manage to get himself involved with a maniac like Joker?" "That's my sentiment exactly Blake. After going through all of this, I would imagine he will, be asking himself that same question. Perhaps; we'll get some answers from him when this is over." "So, what are you planning to do now, Blake asked him?" "For the moment nothing. I'm waiting for an opportunity to have a talk with Chatsworth and find out what position he prefer; to take in this situation. " "yes, I understand what you mean Brad and I'm in complete agreement with you on this." "Listen Blake, I'll get back with you later." "That will be fine with me Brad and thanks for the up-date." "As usual, you're welcome Blake." After the conversation with Blake ended, Maxwell went back to his office to complete some unfinished paperwork. And after spending a couple of hours there and feeling tension in his muscles, he decided to close shop and go down to the gym for a good work out. In the meanwhile, the authorities were enroute to Steven Chatsworth's residence they knew the two suspects had undoubtedly arrived there ahead of them according to Maxwell's information. They arrived cautiously because under the circumstances, they had no concept of what was transpiring, or for that matter, what to expect. However, it was a known fact that the duo was desperate and desperate people seldom think rationally. At that point, all they could was to remain alert. As they were slowly nearing the residence someone in the group exclaimed Man! Look at that place and where is the truck?"

The next morning as he was getting into his car the phone rang looking at the display he said, "Good morning Skylar and just what can I do for you this morning?" "Good morning to you Maxwell, have you had breakfast? "No, not yet, why?" "Skylar said, there's a quite little restaurant called the "Galaxy" near the station and their breakfast menu is superb." "Yes, I know the one you're speaking of, he said." "Then how about joining me there, Skylar asked him?" "What time, he asked him?" "How about now, I'm officially off duty until tomorrow morning?" "It's a deal and I'll see you in about twenty minutes." Mr. Blake Mrs. Carrington is on the line sir; please put her through Jenny, yes sir. "Claudia my dear what a pleasant surprise. When did you return from your trip, he asked her?" she replied, it's good to hear your voice too Blake. I arrived home late last night." Blake asked her, "How was your stay in Italy?" "Oh Blake it was just fabulous and I had a marvelous time." He said," that's wonderful and you sound great Claudia." "I feel great too. Blake what in the world has been going on in my absence?" "What do you mean my dear?" "Don't you dare my dear me, that is your way of avoiding my question as usual but not this time, you sly old fox. You know precisely what I mean! She said laughing." Early this morning I saw a special news report on television and it was reported that two of three men involved in the Chatsworth shooting was apprehended at his home last evening. Blake, they showed a big dump truck that had plowed through the man's home, it looked as if a tornado had been there. There was a confrontation with the police by one of the suspects(Blake instantly thought to himself, that would have been Joker) who sustained minor injuries and both are now in police custody for questioning. Blake how is Chatsworth and when did all of this, take place?" "Claudia to answer your first question, according to the hospital medical staff, his condition is improving and to answer question number two, all of this transpired within the past seventy-two hours. It's a long story I can assure you so, after you've gotten some rest how about coming into my office?" This way it will be easier for me to give you all of the details, he told her." She said, "Oh, all right. Are you available later this afternoon around two-thirty?" "Yes, that will be good timing. I'll see you then he told her."

After consuming a hearty breakfast Skylar and Maxwell sat back sipping on their coffee. Skylar said, "Man your assessment of those two suspects was correct, you were right on the mark." "What happened out there Skylar?" He looked at him and said," What first hit all of us in the face when we nearing the residence was this huge gapping opening in the front of the house, then one of the guys asked,' where's the truck?' Because none of us saw it that is, until we got closer There was this big dump truck that had gone through the front section of the building and stopped near the rear section of the house. Glass and lumber was still falling because the house had been compromised by the impact. Maxwell, it appeared as if a tornado had passed through there and the roof was still collapsing. A perimeter was set up around the entire estate, and after everyone was in their assigned positions of-course you're familiar with the procedure following that." Maxwell said, "yes, I am." "Mind you, there was still no sign of the two and no indication of just where they might have been. Man, do you know we were out there nearly four hours before there was any kind of response from the two. The supervisor in charge decided we were going to wait it out and let the make the first move. Finally, we spotted this figure crawling on top of all this rubble like a large cat along side of the house. Maxwell began to laugh and so did Skylar saying, then, about ten feet from the house he stood up raising both hands above his head. With the spotlight shinning on him we knew it was Flint Bishop. He was ordered to turn around and walk backward to us. As he was within reach and told to lie face down with both arms stretched out and while three of the guys had their weapons trainedon him he was cuffed, there was no resistance from him at all. In fact, he seemed glad to have been out there. He said that he had to get away somehow because Joker had flipped out, all he kept talking about was getting what was owed to him. He told the supervisor that when he last saw he was trying his best to break into Chatsworth's safe and that's when he saw his chance to escape. My guess is he looked around, didn't see Bishop and probably tried locate him and when he couldn't, he realized that he'd left him because suddenly, we heard this yelling coming from inside. "I still can't imagine what prompted him to come through the broken window yelling and banishing the gun in all directions, that's when he was ordered to drop it. , but instead he started firing. "He was wounded in the shoulder and leg by one of our sharp shooters. He'll recover to stand trial on these cases." "A-men Maxwell agreed. After a brief silence, Maxwell observed a puzzled expression appear on Skylar's face and asked him, "Skylar, is something wrong?" He gazed at him and said, "Maxwell there is one thing I can't figure out about those two." "And just what is that Skylar?" The both of them smelled as if they'd been hibernating with poultry. I mean the mere smell of them was nauseating." Maxwell looked at him for a minute recalling what the foreman at the construction site had said. Then he said, "Skylar it's strange that you should say that because when I was questioning the foreman at the construction site where they stole the truck from, he said they looked as if they'd been in a swamp somewhere and smelled like a poultry yard. Skylar said, "that's the description I would've given of them. Maxwell I wonder where they were after their disappearance from this area. And if I recall our conversation correctly, didn't you state that someone had seen them jump off some kind of company truck ?" "yes, that's correct Skylar and why was the stolen car found abandoned in Arleta?" Skylar said, "you know Maxwell, you've got a point there. He thought for a moment and said, "Skylar, this situation is becoming more complicated by the minute, there are still loopholes that need to be filled in order to bring a resolve." Skylar asked him, You're referring to the time lapse am I correct?" "Yes, I am, Maxwell replied." Skylar stared at him and said," I hadn't thought of it in those terms, but since you mentioned it perhaps; we have the answers to those questions right before our eyes. " Maxwell said, "man I'm ready, let's hear it." He said, "get this will you- Bishop was more than ready to talk! The interrogating officer in charge is Detective Stefon Hauser." First he asked Bishop why did the three of them go to Mr. Chatsworth's residence?" "That's when Bishop opened the valve and said, 'he wasn't about to become anybody's scapegoat and was ready to talk. "That's when I decided to get out of there and let them do their job. "In answer, to Det. Hauser's question, Bishop said, 'Joker told Stevenson and him that since Mr. Chatsworth had told them to get off his property and stay off, he owed him a lot of money and he wanted all of it! Then he was asked, 'why did the two of you go back there with him, after you were told to stay away? 'He said, because Joker said that he was going to split with us when he got the money.' And you believed him he was asked?' 'yes, both of us did.' "Tell us exactly what happened when you arrived there?' "Well, when we first got there, Joker rang the doorbell and Mr. Chatsworth came to the door and when he saw us, he looked at Joker and asked him, 'What do you want?' Then he turned his back and started walking away Joker followed him into the study. Stevenson and me, we stayed outside in the hallway.' 'What happened when they went into the study?' 'We heard Mr. Chatsworth yell and say, 'I told you once to get out and stay out, and I meant it!' 'Then he asked Joker now what are you doing back here?' Joker told him,' 'I want everything that's mine now! Mr. Chatsworth yelled again 'get out of here!' Joker looked at him and started laughing like crazy. Then all of a sudden, we saw him pull out his gun and that's when Stevenson and me took off and started running back to the car, that's when we heard the shots and I told Stevenson man, he's gone crazy we never should've come back here with him. 'Bishop was asked, 'about how many shots did you hear?' 'Man , I don't know maybe three or four I'm not sure, we just wanted to get out of there. The next thing we knew, Joker came running out the door still holding the gun and told us to get in the car *quick. Neither one of us asked him any questions because we knew what had happened, but we didn't know he was going to shoot the old man.' Det. Hauser asked him, why did Joker shoot Stevenson? ' Bishop said, 'we started walking down towards the pier and I guess Stevenson had enough because he asked Joker, why did he have to shoot the old man?' "Joker just looked at him and said, 'he brought it on himself, he should've given me the money.' 'I could tell Stevenson was really getting scared because he said, 'now you're going to have the cops looking for us all because you went crazy out there, and still didn't get any money. Then he told Joker,' 'you two can do whatever you want, but I'm leaving. 'Joker wouldn't hear of it and told him that, 'nobody was getting out, that's when he pulled out the gun and shot Stevenson. When he turned and tried to run away he shot him again in the back .By that time, I was too scared to say anything because he was laughing like crazy. He was asked, 'what did you do after Stevenson was shot?' Bishop said, ' I didn't do anything. I was so scared I guess I jut froze because the next thing I knew, Joker was yanking me by the arm saying, let's get out of here' and we started running. I didn't know where we were going and didn't care just as long as it was away from there and poor Stevenson.' "Tell me Bishop,' who's idea was it to car jack that man at the service station and why an old man?' 'It was Joker's idea. He said there was no way we could go back to his car because the cops would be looking for it, so we needed a ride to get out of here. what happened after that, Det. Hauser asked him, 'Bishop said, 'Joker jumped into the car yelling, 'hurry up and get in the car stupid.' "What did you do then, he was asked?' He said, 'I did what he said and got in the car, he was still holding the gun.' 'Bishop, I'm rather curious about something, where did you and Joker go after, you left the service station?' He replied, 'Joker said we had to get out of the area and fast, so we jumped on the '101' freeway I asked him where were we going because the cops were going to be looking for the car. He laughed, and said that he knew of a place where they wouldn't be looking for us. ' Det. Hauser asked him, 'where was this place Bishop?' "Look Det. Joker has hurt people.*

I don't want to be responsible for hurting anyone especially, since they had nothing to do with what he's done. 'Det. Hauser said, 'Bishop, whether you believe me or not is entirely up to you, but we're not out to deliberately hurt anyone, we're just trying to get to the bottom of the situation. 'It was quite obvious that he was becoming nervous and after a brief silence he said, 'We went to Joker's cousin's home in Arleta. Det. Hauser stared hard at him and asked, 'Did you say Joker's cousin's home?' Bishop said yeah, why do you ask?' After fingering through his notes he looked at Bishop again saying, 'there's nothing here in Joker's files stating he has relatives anywhere, are you speaking the truth about this, he asked him?' Staring directly into his eyes Bishop said, 'I'm telling you the truth. I didn't think he had any kin either because he never spoke about it, but when we finally arrived there, I learned that not only does he have a cousin he also has an uncle. The one he shot, Mr. Chatsworth.' With that revelation, Det. Hauser pushed his chair back stood up and exclaimed what! Bishop said, 'yeah that's right, Mr. Steven Chatsworth is Joker's blood uncle. I learned this during their conversation while we were there. Finally looking across the table at Bishop he asked him,' what is the name of Joker's cousin? He was somewhat hesitant at first, then he said, 'Joker only introduced him to me as John D. and that's all I ever heard.' Bishop how long were you at John D's home? Just until it became dark. We had to leave before his wife got home because I gathered she doesn't care very much for Joker.' Where did you go after leaving there?' 'Joker drove around until he spotted this car wash that was closed, he said that was a good place to leave the car because it wouldn't be opened up until the next morning besides, there was a rest area not far from there. We made our way to it and just as we got there a "poultry" truck was getting ready to pull out. Joker stopped him and paid the man fifty dollars to let us ride in the back of his truck. At first he looked at us kind of funny. Joker showed him the money, he looked at it then us just shrugged is shoulders, went to the back of the truck unlocked the doors and told us to get in. Suddenly, Det. Hauser burst out laughing and asked, 'so that's why the two of you smell like a poultry farm?' At that question, Bishop lowered his head and sheepishly replied, yes. 'Det. Hauser asked Bishop ,'where did you go after that?' He said, 'we got off the truck near the Santa Monica freeway off-ramp and hitched a ride to one of the construction companies where we used to hang out, the one tat Joker stole the dump truck from.' I think Joker wanted to destroy Mr. Chatsworth's home anyway. 'After his interrogation was completed he said, 'well that's all Bishop, you've been very helpful to us. Bishop looked at him and said, you're welcome Det. Hauser." Maxwell listened intensely as Det. Hauser gave his account of the interrogation, which confirmed the information that Atkins had conveyed to him earlier particularly, in reference to the relationship between Steven Chatsworth and the suspect, Freddy Sinclaire. Skylar said, "well there's no more speculation about the motive for both shootings." Maxwell said, "now we know why the car was found abandoned in Arleta and those two having the smell of poultry farm." Det. Hauser, what about Sinclaire as far as you're aware of, has any progress been made towards getting anything significant out of him?" He stared at Skylar laughed and asked, " is that just wishful thinking Det. Skylar?" From all indications, it appears that he's going to be transferred to the psycho ward pending a court hearing." "You know something has me puzzled, why has Mr. Chatsworth chosen to keep the relationship between he and Joker a secret all of this time?" "Man, I can' answer that question because I don't understand either." Maxwell said, perhaps; we 'll have some answers to a number of questions when he's well enough to receive visitors, if he doesn't have a relapse first. You know this whole episode has been in the news and if I'm any judge of character at this point, Steven Chatsworth is anything, but calm. "Skylar looked at Maxwell then Hauser and said, "Det. That is another part of this maze. Maxwell is doing some investigation that involves Steven Chatsworth and he's the private investigator who was at Chatsworth's residence the day of the firing." Det. Hauser stared at each of them and said, this situation is like a revolving door. Well, I'm finished for now, I've got a lot of paperwork to get *out. Thanks for the company gentlemen. He looked at Skylar smiled and said, "Unfortunately, /I'm still on duty." After Det. Hauser had gone Skylar gazed at Maxwell and said you know, This Chatsworth case is becoming more complex by the minute. Now I'm curious to know how this John D. fellow fit into all of this and what relation he is to Chatsworth? Maxwell, I wonder just what other secrets does Steven Chatsworth's closet conceal?" As if to be staring into space and focusing his eyes directly on Skylar he slowly said, "I don't know Skylar, but you can rest assured I'm going to find out and very soon. He spoke without reservation and Skylar knew he was determined to do just that! Maxwell smiled and said, "now getting back to my question before we were interrupted. What are you going to do next Detective?" "I'm a crime investigator remember, he asked returning the smile?" Incidentally Bradford, "what about your case now?" "Well, that depends on a number of things Jacob as you know, there are still some unanswered questions pertaining to Chatsworth that need to be addressed before I can bring this situation to a resolve. And from all indications, I'd say, the case is far from being resolved. I haven't checked in with Blake Colwell yet, but I believe the owner, Claudia Carrington should have returned from her trip abroad by this time. At that moment, Maxwell's cell phone rang he checked the number, looked at Skylar and with a broad smile on his face said, " "hello Blake, what a pleasant surprise I had planned to telephone you later this morning. You sound awful, what's the problem? "Chatsworth telephoned you awhile ago, what did he say?" Oh, oh I knew he was going to hit the ceiling when the news came out. Well, I'll give you a call later." He gazed at Skylar laughed and said, "as you heard, that was Blake Colwell informing me that Chatsworth telephoned him ranting about the incident at his home and get this, his condition has improved and his physicians are allowing him to receive visitors now. And that my friend, is the break I've been waiting for he said." "However, there's another problem in this situation. Claudia isn't aware that Chatsworth and her own husband is responsible the Business scandal that developed." What, Jacob* asked?' "Yes that's right. Chatsworth masterminded the whole situation with a little assistance from Charles who was just a ploy in his diabolical scheme to ruin the firm." This time, it was Jacob who leaned back and gazing directly into Bradford's eyes he said, "good grief man, why would he want to ruin the business?" "It was a vendetta Jacob, he told him." "Against whom for crying out loud?" "Would you believe David Lansing himself?" "But, the man's dead so what could he possibly expect to accomplish?" "Listen my friend, first you'd have to understand this man's way of thinking. In his eyes, the firm is representative of Lansing. He point blank told me that he has only two regrets, and when I asked what they might be? Guess what his reply was? "I can't begin to imagine." "One, Claudia is caught in the middle of it all and two, Lansing isn't alive to witness it happening." Skylar gazed at him for a time, and said, "he didn't succeed because you came on the scene." Precisely! "Bradford, I would say he had a grudge." "It was more than that, it was something that had been festering in him for many years. " "How does he live with that kind of hatred, Skylar asked him?" "It appears that some people thrive off it." "May be, but for myself, I can't imagine ever living like that." "Neither will I Jacob." "Well, the breakfast was great and thanks for the treat. Next time, it's on me." "You got it Bradford. They smiled at each other fondly, a common bond had formed between them that wasn't there before. "I'm headed for the station, enjoy your day off." "I plan to do just that believe me. I'm going surfing Jacob said smiling." Bradford's inner thought was- I was correct, he is s surfer."

Atkins sat slowly and deliberately back down in his chair never taking his focus off Chatsworth and gazing into his eyes said, "Steven Chatsworth, we've known each other for a great many years. I've always assumed we were more than Attorney and client, but friends as well. How could you of all people, be this deceptive with me?" Chatsworth lifted his head and stared out the window for a few seconds then looking into Atkins eyes he saw the hurt and perhaps *disappointment in them. That apparently stirred something in him that he thought was completely lost. Gazing into his eyes he said. " Victor it happened years ago; a young woman and I were attending college together, it began with occasional dates then we started seeing each other more frequently. After about a year later, we both realized that we were in love with each other, but there was a problem. While I was struggling my way through college, her folks were taking trips abroad and for sometime. They didn't know about us because she resided on campus as well as I. She and I had I had discussed getting married after graduating college, but then her parents learned of our relationship and didn't approve of it. I knew something wasn't just right because after her parent's last trip abroad about two weeks prior to that, she didn't appear to be as happy as she had been. I asked her if something was wrong? She just looked at me and her eyes began to swell with tears, then she said Steven, my parent's doesn't want us to see each other any more. She started to cry and said after college, they wanted her to marry one of her father's friend's son who had just graduated from medical school. Naturally, I said what! Then she told me that she loved me and always will. That night, we stayed off campus and went to a motel. We saw each other for about two months after that night. Then one day when I telephoned her Dorm, I was told that her parent's had checked her out and she was gone. I called her home and each time, I would ask to speak with her I was told that she wasn't there. Finally, I got fed up with it, so one day I drove out there which was about two weeks later, and that's when I received the shock of my young life. Victor, they had moved lot stock and barrel. I was devastated at the prospect of not ever seeing er again. Then one day just before graduating, I received a message that I had a visitor waiting in the lobby. I didn't know whom it was or what to expect. As I entered the lobby, I saw this handsomely dressed tall slender salt and pepper hair woman. Her smile was warm and captivating as she looked at me. She introduced herself to me and said she was Cynthia's aunt. Man, you could have blown me over with a feather. As I sat in a chair directly facing her she said, I'm here on the behalf of my niece and your son. She undoubtedly thought I was going to college because she began to laugh and I suddenly realized that my mouth was wide open. And her laughter was the same as Cynthia's. After quickly gaining control of myself I asked her, you did say Cynthia and my son" She laughed again and said yes Steven. And I regret to inform you that I'm the bearer of both sad and good news. My niece passed away last year, she died of pneumonia and complications, but before she died, I had to make her a promise that I would raise John D. and try to locate you and give you the explanation that she could not. Victor, as the strange woman sat there speaking to me in her soft voice, all I could think about was Cynthia and remembering how much we loved each other. Then it dawned on me that she'd said I had, or shall I say, have a son. She explained that when Cynthia's parent's learned of her pregnancy, that is when they took her out of school and moved out of state, forbidding her to ever contact me again. They became furious with he because she refused to consent to a marriage with someone whom she didn't love and she'd become pregnant to boot. However, they allowed her to keep her baby and he was her pride and joy in life and I remained the love of her life. She also told me that she never had the opportunity to tell me that I was going to be a father. In fact, she didn't know herself until much later. She said, when her parents moved abroad, she and your son came to live with me. I respected this woman and admired her for her courage. After she'd finished speaking, I asked her where was my son? She told me that he was being cared for by her housekeeper while she was with me and would I care to see him? I joyfully told her that I certainly would. Two days later, I saw my son for the first time, and I couldn't withhold the tears because he has his mother's smile and her eyes. I remained with them for two days because it was time for graduation, I had to get back, but I definitely wanted to stay longer. After getting my degree, I went to work for a large construction company. I sent them a check each month and every two weeks, I went to visit them. She passed away during his freshman fear in college. Victor gazed at him and asked, how is your relationship with him Steven?" He thought for a moment and said, You know, it's strange that you should ask me that question." Victor asked him, Why is It strange Steven?" "Because lying here in the hospital I suddenly realized that I alienated my own son, the same way his grand parent's did his mother. Victor stared at him and recognized the sadness that appeared in his eyes and asked, "What did you do Steven?" "I wanted him to complete college, but in his junior year, he chose to go into the Military instead. He was in there four years and doing that time, we didn't communicate very often. You didn't mention it, but I saw the news and how that lunatic nephew of mine wrecked my home. I can't imagine what he thought he was doing because all he did was compile the charges that are already pending against him. But I'll tell you this, where he's going, maybe they will give him the medical help that he needs. And now this incident with Freddy, I feel that I should've shown more interest in my own son. He has a stubborn streak just like his old man so, I'm making the first move and hope, it's not too late. I would like to know whenever, I do start having grand children he said with a smile. "Finally he said, "I apologize for not having confided in you earlier Victor, I ask if you can forgive me?" "Of course I forgive you Steven, I believe you have learned a great lesson by all of this he said with a smile. Incidentally, how long has it been since you last spoke with your son?" "Around a month ago, I believe," All right Steven. I'll see what I can do." "Thank you Victor." "you're welcome".*

Just as he entered through the front door of the police station, the W.C. was coming toward the front desk, he looked in Maxwell's direction and said, "You finally made it I see. " "Yes, I understand you want to have a talk with me." "That's correct, will you accompany me back to my office please?" "Yes, of course. After closing the door behind them. "Maxwell, first of all, I'd like to congratulate you on the assistance in the apprehension of those two suspects. Without your information, I'm afraid the time span of our catching them would have been much greater. " Maxwell smiled and said, "I'm glad that I was able to help. " "Oh by the way, I paid a visit to Chatsworth at the hospital and he asked if I would give you a mesasage?" "Oh, he asked?" "Yes, he said something quite strange and I still don't understand for the lifeof me, what he meant!" " What was that, if I might ask?" "After I explained everything to him including your participation he said, 'I knew Maxwell was going to be trouble from the first time I aw him!' Then he said we have something to settle., would you ask him to come to the hospital at his earliest convenience?' Maxwell grinned and asked, "Oh he did, did he? Well this is certainly good news. And I will most definitely honor his request." Now standing and smiling he said, "thank you Commander for your interest and the message." "You're more than welcome Maxwell, and if you should ever need this department's assistance in anyway, please don't hesitate to let us know. I'm pleased to have met you. Again, thank you. " "The same here Commander, he responded with a broad smile."

"Mr. Colwell Mr. Maxwell is o the line sir." "Thank you Jenny please put him through." "Hello Brad, I'm pleased you called, Claudia is back home and she's aware of the incident involving Chatsworth. She' coming into the office for all of the details, but what are we going to tell her about the situation, since both Chatsworth and Charles was involved?" He said Blake, "I understand your concern, we're going to have to inform her eventually, but I was hoping to get the opportunity to speak with Chatsworth first, there are a number of things that should be clarified by him. Since the incident with Joker occurred there have been new developments in this bizarre situation. And I can't resolve it until everything has been cleared up and there are no more opened holes." "You're absolutely correct and I agree with you. How are things with the department?" "Oh things are just fine Blake." "Well, what have you got this time, not another stolen dump truck I hope! "No not this time, he said laughing. However, it does appear that since the incident with Chatsworth and his men have been resolved by the authorities, I was given a message that he wants me to visit him in the hospital. His words were-'we have something

to settle.' " Blake, this is the opportunity I've been anxiously waiting for perhaps; we can get the situation with firm resolved." "You want me to accompany you, am I correct?" "Yes, you're the Attorney for the firm and I'm the investigator hired to search out the truth and bring a resolve. We need to know what his position is going to be in this matter before speaking with Claudia." "Brad, you've got a logical point there and I agree with you. When do you wish to visit him?" "When is it convenient for you Blake?" "The only thing that is scheduled for today is Claudia's visit at two-thirty this afternoon. " "It's one o'clock now, this should give us enough time to visit him and return to your office before she arrives."

"Mr. Chatsworth, you have two more visitor's sir." "Good, please send them in nurse." Blake entered the room first followed by Maxwell. There were two other people who were also present in his room, they recognized Atkins, but not the young man who was sitting beside Chatsworth's bed. As they approached Maxwell stopped in his tracks. 'thinking no this can't be, Joker's locked up I'm certain of it.' Suddenly, he recalled the description of Joker's cousin that Bishop had given Det. Hauser. They acknowledged the other men, then Blake turned his attention to Chatsworth and asked, "hello Steven how are you feeling? "Staring at Blake then Maxwell he responded, "I've certainly felt better Blake, but thanks for asking. "Then turning his attention to Maxwell he said, "Maxwell, I see you received my message." "Yes I did Chatsworth." Gazing steadily at him Maxwell asked, "What is it that you would like to settle?" Chatsworth said "First, before we begin I'd like to introduce my son, John D. Chatsworth." Bradford and Blake stared at each other, Atkins, John D. and back to Chatsworth. Then suddenly, they all began to laugh because of their facial expressions. Atkins said, "you should've seen my face when he first told me. " Blake said, I've known you for many years Steven and I realize you're a very personal and complicated man to understand, but you've never so much as indicated that you have a son." He looked directly into Blake's eyes ," nor, did I *acknowledge that Freddy s my nephew. You know, lying here in this bed gave me a chance to look at things as they really and put them in their perspective order. Perhaps; the shooting incident was a wake -call to reality for me. I believe so anyway. " Turning his attention to Bradford he said,"Maxwell I realize you've probably got a few questions to ask me., but first, there are two main issues to settle."*

"And what might they be pray, tell?" Chatsworth repositioned himself in the hospital bed then spoke and said, "number one, I haven't changed my mind about you I knew you were going to be trouble from the first time I saw you. He smiled and asked, "what is issue, number two?" "I was given detailed information on what you did and I don't say anything that I don't mean." Then unexpectedly to everyone including Bradford, he extended his hand and said, "I thank you for the courage in what you did Maxwell." He shook his hand and said, "You're more than welcome." Chastsworth's gesture, brought smiles to everyone's face and even his own. And with a broad grin Bradford Asked him, "do you recall when I told you that I'm an individualist?' He replied. Yes I do, and I must admit without reservation you are Maxwell." Then he gazed at him for a second or two before saying "I'm quite curious about a number of things Maxwell." "Tell me how did you know that the shooting at my residence didn't occur as the result of the firing?" "Bradford said, " to begin with, he didn't try to kill you, because he very well could have. Then I began to question why did they return to your residence after you'd ordered them off your property. But I had a feeling that Joker was going to do something because I saw each of their expressions when you told them to get out and stay out. He had a sneaky grin on his face and the 'gut' feeling had about him followed me. For him to return whatever the reason, it had to be very important to him and when he didn't succeed in getting whatever it was that he wanted, he just went crazy and started shooting. From the beginning, there was speculation that he had been fired as being a motive for the shooting, but I just couldn't accept that, I knew there had to e something else involved. That's when I began inquiring about him because at that

point, he'd gone wild with the second shooting. I knew he wasn't going to come here he was wild not stupid and because he was too busy eluding the authorities until he could put his plan into action what ever it was. When Atkins and I met, is when I realized his motive for shooting you was the inheritance and of course, he's your nephew. There was no knowledge of your son until after they were apprehended. When the authorities found the car that was taken in the car jacking incident abandoned in Arleta. I first believed he was leaving a false trail to throw the authorities off track. Until the interrogating officer in charge of the case gave an account of Bishop's statement, and that's when I realized he had gone there to assimilate his plan without having to worry about the authorities, because no one here knew of John D's existence I had a 'gut 'feeling that he was planning t do something else, but I couldn't be specific as to wat and that had become an annoyance to me. I decided to visit one of the Construction sites and while I was there, a call came in that he and Bishop had been seen getting off a truck near the Santa Monica freeway off ramp . Which meant they had eluded the authorities again and returned to this area. After leaving there, I went to another Construction company, and had only missed them by minutes. According to the Foreman, they had hitched a ride there and were trying to get someone to loan them a car. He stated that Joker was raving and ranting that you owed him a lot of money and he was going to collect it. I reminded him that you're in the hospital so, how had he planned to collect anything?" He stated that he didn't know and didn't ask, they just wanted them to leave. While we were talking one of the drivers came yelling and asking for the boss? The Foreman and I stated at each because at that time, we had no way of knowing why e was so excited until, the owner and he came out of the office screaming that Joker and his imbecile friend had stolen his dump truck. At that revelation, everyone in the room began to laugh. Maxwell said, "I asked how could they take a big dump truck out of there and no one saw them?" That's when it dawned on me what he was planning to do. He didn't care how much damage that he was going to do to your residence. I alerted the authorities and informed them of what had transpired and my assessment of the whole situation. I'm sorry there was no advance indication of what he was actually going to do. " Chatsworth gazed hard at him smiled and said, "Had it not been for your persistence in the matter, I'm afraid things might have been much worse, so don't allow it to disturb you further Maxwell. 'Then he said, "No one knew of my relationship with Freddy because I didn't want him going about bragging to the other men. That is why I made no difference in them. ' Maxwell said, "Now I understand your position in that area and you've answered my question." As if to be thinking he suddenly turned his attention to Blake Colwell and said, "You're the firm's Attorney and you know there was an agreement between Lansing and I years ago; as I would become the silent partner in the firm. I believe these are the papers that you were holding over his head when you threatened him prior to ,Claudia's marriage. Both Blake and Bradford stared at him in total surprise. Chatsworth smiled at him and said yes Blake, I know all about it Lansing told me about the threat that you had made. Claudia isn't aware of it nor; was Claudette. That young lady has suffered enough because of something that she had nothing to do with. And I really don't know how you're going to solve the problem with that idiot husband of hers, but I'm officially terminating my partnership from the firm, effective as of today Blake and you may destroy those papers that are in your files. Thereby, drawing a stare from Bradford. Staring directly into his eyes and with a broad smile he said, incidentally Chatsworth, the next time we meet I hope it will be under a different circumstance." "Looking at him and returning the smile Chatsworth said, "I believe I'd like that Maxwell . " After leaving the hospital Blake and Bradford headed for Blake's office for the meeting with Claudia. It was two fifteen p.m. The lengthily meeting with Chatsworth had thrown them off schedule. There was just barely enough time, for them to discuss the situation between themselves before her arrival., because she always believed in being punctual. Blake's inner concern was Claudia's reaction regarding everything, including Chatsworth and

Charles's involvement in the whole nasty mess. Bradford's thoughts were of Chatsworth and he wondered what actually influenced his decision to terminate the partnership. Then recalling the old adage that A 'leopard' doesn't change his spots." But in Chatsworth's case he might have to disagree, that is to a certain extent, smiling to himself.

The both of them arrived at Blake's office about the same time, and takin a brief look at his wristwatch, Blake said, 'we have just about enough time to discuss this before she arrive. Bradford stared at him and saw the grave concern on Blake's face and his instincts once again returned that led him back to his first observation. Blake was concealing something from him and why was he so protective of Claudia? Oh well, first things, first. The present situation had priority over his instincts. Blake informed Jenny, to send Claudia in as soon as she arrived and to hold all calls. He and Bradford went into his office to discuss the situation. Claudia arrived punctually at two-thirty p.m. And upon entering Blake's office she was greeted by both Blake and Bradford. After they were seated, Blake began by saying Claudia my dear, I believe we can finally bring this situation with the firm to a closure. " Now this is what I consider to be a wonderful home-coming present, she said smiling. "Bradford is going to bring you up to date with a detailed report of his investigation and findings. "She stared at them and said, first I would like to know what has happened during my absence, I saw the early morning news and Chatsworth's home looked as if a tornado had gone through there and they showed a big dump truck stuck inside it? They glanced at each other, Blake nodded his head as if to say, 'you might as well tell her now! Bradford " said Claudia, while you were absent Chatsworth was shot by his nephew. She stared at him and asked, "did you just say his nephew Brad? "Yes I did. You see, according to Chatsworth's explanation as to why no one knew of the relationship, he didn't want him bragging to the other men who worked for him. So as far as they and everyone else were aware of, he was just another employee. Chatsworth is the legal guardian over his inheritance. They disobeyed an order he'd given so, he fired them and told them to stay away, but later they went back to his residence. Apparently Joker, (the nephew) decided that since he'd been fired he wanted his inheritance and when he asked his uncle for it he refused, that's when Joker went wild with anger and shot him. He was the one who was shot by the authorities because he gave them a hard time, and refused to surrender." She asked, "but Brad why did he run into the residence with a huge dump truck?" "Claudia you must understand, he was completely out of control and my guess is, he didn't care how much damage was incurred. Bishop the other suspect stated that' when he last saw him, he was attempting to get into the safe still yelling, ' I want all of my money'. "How is Chatsworth doing now, she asked him? "Oh he's improving in fact, I would say quite well." Bradford said" Claudia, as you know, I was hired to search out the truth and bring a resolve. The investigation was more extensive and complex than both, Blake and I could have ever anticipated because the situation had developed so many twists and turns that an early resolve was, virtually impossible. We were expecting to find the allegations made against the firm to be false. But after all of the inquiries and close observations, I had to conclude that they were valid after all. "Claudia, do you recall our conversation when we first met, and I told you that I was going to go deeper inside the firm?" "Yes Brad, I do recall your words and I told you to go ahead with the investigation I wouldn't interfere in any way." "He said, "every turn I made led me directly back to the firm itself. That's when I became certain that the trouble was coming from within. A number of people were directly and some, indirectly involved in the scandal and unfortunately, not all of them were by choice. " She interrupted and asked him, "What do you mean Brad, they were not all by choice?" "Well let's just say, most of them were being used as pawns in a ploy to divert attention away from the true motive." Staring at him curiously she asked, "and just what was the true motive Brad?" He said, to seek control of the firm, and to completely ruin it." She looked at Blake and back to him exclaiming what!" He sat back crossing his legs and gazing directly into her eyes said, "that's right control and to ruin the firm Claudia." She asked him, but by whom and why, for pete's sake Brad?" He looked at Blake who nodded his head in agreement to tell her all of it. Chatsworth and your husband were behind the whole business scandal Claudia. As a matter-of-fact, they were directly responsible for it in the first place." She stared at the both of them in total bewilderment, and asked, Charles and Chatsworth together, why?" "Claudia, do you recall telling Blake of the confrontation you had with Charles in your home, and he told you that soon he would be in control?" "Yes, I remember." "Well, that was one of the things he was speaking of because in fact, that was precisely what his intentions were. But first and foremost, he had to somehow, eliminate Blake then he would have no problem in coercion you into giving him the control he was seeking." She asked him, "then what was Chatsworth's interest in it, and why?" "Claudia, his was for an entirely different rationale. To begin with, from the information Chatsworth gave me, Charles went to him. Apparently, he was disgruntled by the fact that your father had minimized his authority in the firm. And since they're gone and Blake no longer in the picture that would leave no one but him. What better way to gain an ally than someone who had no vested interest in the firm?" Number one, what dear Charles didn't know was the man he'd gone to assist him in his little scheme that was just the opportunity he'd been seeking for years. Number two, neither did he know Chatsworth was your father's silent partner in the firm. Upon hearing that statement, Claudia sat directly up in her chair looked at both Bradford and Blake in wild astonishment and asked Bradford, am I hearing you correctly?" "I'm "I'm afraid you are Claudia. Chatsworth was your father's silent partner long before you were born." She stared at Blake and asked him, Blake, did you know about this?" He replied, "yes I did Claudia. However, I wasn't aware of it when I first came in to the firm, but learned of it later. Since I'm the firm's Attorney your father thought I should at least; know about that. The agreement was made between the two following the firm's name changed to what it is now." "Did my mother know about this, she asked him?" "No, Chatsworth stated that she was never informed of the agreement between the two of them. Blake looked at her and said," Brad and I visited Chatsworth at the hospital this afternoon Claudia, and he's terminated his partnership in the firm effective as of today." "Oh, he has, has he, she asked in a tone that was completely unlike her?" Blake replied, "yes, he has Claudia". She looked away for a minute or two then asked, "why the sudden change of heart, and just why was he trying to ruin the firm anyway?" Bradford stared at Blake and knew he was just shadowing around what was inevitable so, he began. "Claudia for all it's worth, I honestly don't believe his gesture was sudden. Chatsworth's statement to Blake and me was he feels that you've suffered enough. As his rationale for attempting to ruin the firm had absolutely nothing what so ever to do with you. That was something he'd been contemplating for years. Charles only opened the door of opportunity for him to carry out his plan. You see, something occurred years ago that had involved your father, and Chatsworth vowed to exact revenge against your father for what had happened. And in his eyes since your father is no longer here, the firm is representative of him and that's why he was determined to ruin it. It was nothing but an illogical concept of a man with hatred in his heart." She shifted her eyes to the floor for a few seconds then gazed into his eyes and while steadily focusing on him asked, "Brad, just why did Chatsworth harbor such hatred for my father?" He stared at her briefly and said Claudia," She immediately halted him before he could continue and said, "I'm not a child and you don't have to protect my feelings. I'm not the hysterical type and I want the whole truth. His focus shifted to Blake who was apparently as shocked as he, at her question, but said nothing just nodded his head in submission. He asked her, "are you certain about this?" She held her focus on him and replied. "Yes, I'm certain, all of it! According to Chatsworth's statement, it happened years ago, when your father first took over the business. He had begun to take frequent trips out of the city. Your mother was taking notice of it as well, but as far as he knew, she never said anything at least, in his presence anyway. Then one day, he received an urgent telephone call from his younger sister who lived in another city, a short distance away. She told him that it was important and could he come to see her? He told her yes, he would be there. When he arrived there, she explained everything to him including her pregnancy and of course the father's name. He was aware of the fact, that your father was seeing other women and so was your mother, but he said he never had the slightest indication that he was involved with his sister. She told him that when she informed him of the pregnancy, he flatly told her to get rid of it because he wasn't going to see her any more anyway. A few days after that, he received another telephone call informing him that his sister had committed suicide. He never said anything to your mother nor; your father. But vowed that one day, he would make sure that he paid for what he'd done. Everyone thought they were good friends including your mother because he planned it that way. .So no one, would become suspicious of his plan." She was quiet for a short time then said this, man was my father. Her voice held a bitter connotation when she finally said," How revolting! Brad looked at Blake then said, "Claudia I'm very sorry." She said, "don't be Brad I asked you for the truth." Bradford said, "As for your husband's participation in all of this, I'm afraid that's something you must decide for yourself. Claudia, the job that I was hired to do has finally been resolved. As of now, this case is officially closed. I have to file everything away and I'll be around for a few days, but if you or, Blake should need me for anything further, you know how to reach me." Claudia looked away for a moment then said," Blake, Brad I asked you for the whole truth, but I had no concept that all of those things were involved. As for Charles's part in all of this, I've got a very strong feeling there is more where he's concerned. I haven't made up my mind as to how I'm going to deal with him at this point just yet, I truly thank you for everything you've done and you've opened my eyes to many things." Looking directly at him, "she said Blake I'm going to spend a few days away to sort things out in my mind. By the time, I do return my decision will have been made. " He looked at her for a moment, and said, "Claudia my dear, I'm very sorry things turned out this way. But take all the time you need." She stood faced them and said, "I love you both and I'll let you know my decision when I return.' After she had departed, Blake and Bradford sat in silence for a few minutes neither said anything Finally Blake said, "Brad I'm quite concerned about her, She has already gone through so much now this situation with Charles isn't going to help matters any especially when she learns that he conspired with David in their marriage." He looked at him and said, "Blake she's going to make a decision that's right for her and all we can do is, respect it. I don't know when you'd planned to inform her of the deception, but I believe she has a right to know perhaps; this will help her decision making regarding him. There's one thing for certain I'm afraid if you don't tell her, she's going to resent you for not having done so. At that point, we don't know just what her decision is going to be and frankly, neither does she. But I believe all of the cards should be laid out on the table as an option for her. That's why she's made the choice to think about it for awhile, because whatever decision she does make, I'm certain will have an ever lasting effect on her life." Blake sat silent for a few seconds then looking at Bradford he said, 'You know, you just might be correct Brad. My concern is that Charles is so unpredictable there's no way of knowing how he's going to react if her decision doesn't satisfy him." "Yes, that's true, but I'm afraid he'll have to reconcile himself to the fact that the ball's no longer in his court, but hers this time, and his options are going to be minimum to say the least." Blake appeared to be mulling over that statement. Bradford stood up and said, "Well Buddy, in the meanwhile I'm going back to my office to finalize my paperwork. This case is finally closed. If you should need me for anything further, you know how to reach me. " Blake stood up walked around the desk smiling and said, "you know Brad a man can't ask for a stronger friendship than what we have. I thank you." With a wide grin he responded," Blake, the feelings mutual and I'll be in touch." After Bradford's departure, Blake returned to his desk taking

166

Chatsworth's advice, he immediately destroyed the written agreement that had existed between he and David Lansing for over thirty years. He retrieved the letter written to him by David Lansing from his personal files and after reading through it for the second time, he reverted to the numerous speculations that he'd been involved in the marriage of his daughter having taken place when it did. BY his own admission in the letter confirmed the speculations as having merit. David Lansing had orchestrated the marriage between she and Charles Carrington, the motive for performing such a despicable act was unknown, but he made Charles an offer and naturally, he'd accepted it. As if suddenly realizing something for the very first time. He thought 'my gracious' Claudia wanted to know the truth, but this information is something that was totally unexpected. She's aware of everything else regarding David, and now having to be told that Charles conspired with David in the orchestration of their marriage is entirely different. Brad and I didn't go this far during the meeting because we(rather I) wanted to spare her from further humiliation . There's no way to predict what her reaction is going to be when she's informed that her marriage had been orchestrated by her own father from the very beginning. Perhaps; Brad is correct in his statement, I'm definitely going to have the unpleasant task of telling her. He sighed and said Speaking of-"from the frying pan into the fire." Bradford had just left Blake's office when he suddenly, remembered he'd promised Jacob Skylar that he would bring him up to date on the meeting with Chatsworth. Looking at his wristwatch and noting the time, he'd forgotten that Jacob was off duty. So he decided to go on into his office and complete the paperwork on the Business scandal and officially mark the case closed. He spent a few hours there then decided to close shop and call it a day. He was feeling a bit tired anyway and thought night's rest would do him good.

After taking a long ride along the ocean side, he thought it would be a good time to telephone Skylar after recalling he had been scheduled to work the night shift. "Hello, this is Det. Skylar." "Jacob

*this is Bradford, when does your shift end?" "Hello Bradford," I was
wondering how long I'd have to wait before hearing from you again.
My shift ends in about half an hour. Where are you now?" "I'm about
two blocks away from the station." "Good! How about our meeting
at the restaurant, we can have an early lunch there if that's agreeable
with you?" "That sounds great. I've been up since dawn this morning
and I'm getting kind of hungry anyway. I'll get the table." "I'll see
you there then, besides, I'm anxious to hear how your meeting with
Chatsworth turned out." "Man, all I can tell you now is you've got a
big surprise coming, he said laughing." Jacob said, now I can hardly
wait! As he was driving to the restaurant, Bradford's thoughts reverted
to his friend, Blake Colwell. And thinking to himself; 'something's
not all together with Blake, I know I know he's concealing something,
but the point is, I can't put my finger on it right now. It's one thing
to e concerned for someone, but another to become over-protective
in such a way that it's beginning to effect his better judgement in
logical reasoning. From the beginning when he spoke of her, I sensed
something that to me, was more than just the concern about what
Charles was involved in. Now he's becoming genuinely frustrated,
and he's not even aware of it yet.' He arrived at the restaurant and
ordered coffee while awaiting Jacob's arrival. He'd consumed nearly
half a cup when he looked up and spotted him coming through the
front entrance. Jacob saw him instantly, and walked over to their
table. Seating himself he smiled and said," it's good to get out of there
and just relax for awhile. Would you believe I've been busy since
checking in. I didn't even get a chance to eat lunch unless, you would
consider half a sandwich and a glass of milk lunch?" Bradford gave
a hearty laugh and said, "Well that was something at least, which is
more than I've had he then he smiled and asked, shall we order before
the both of us pass out?' Jacob laughed and said, "yes we had better
because I believe we've had enough problems for awhile." He signaled
the waitress over to their table. He ordered broiled steak, mashed
potatoes, a green salad, rolls and a slice of Angel food cake. Bradford
ordered broiled chicken, rice, string beans, rolls and a slice of sweet*

potato pie. Their order also included milk and a fresh pot of coffee. After the waitress had taken their orders and left the table, they sat back in more relaxing positions. Skylar began by asking Bradford, "How did your meeting go with the W.C.?" He looked at him smiled and said, I think it went quite well as a matter-of-fact, he tried his best to recruit me into the force, but you know how I feel about that! I just thanked him for the consideration and that was it. However, he told me he'd gone to the hospital and spoken with Chatsworth and he asked him if he would give me a message?" "I asked, oh?" "He said yes, and he also said something quite strange that I still can't understand for the life of me, what he meant?" "I asked him what was that, if I might ask?" "He said, 'after he'd explained everything to him including my participation in the situation he said, 'I knew Maxwell was going to be trouble from the first time I saw him! Then he said, we have something to settle. Would he ask me to come to the hospital at my earliest convenience?' "I told the W.C. that was certainly good news and I would honor his request." Jacob gazed at him briefly and asked, "so he knew you were going to be trouble from the start, huh! Bradford smiled and said, "so he say! After leaving the station, I telephoned Blake Colwell and gave him the news. At that time, he informed me that Claudia had returned home from her trip and saw the early morning news. She wanted to know what had happened and he asked her if she could come to his office around two-thirty in the afternoon?" Their dinner arrived and was being serves so, they waited until the waitress had gone. Then as they were eating their meal Bradford continued. I explained to Blake that I believed that it would be to our advantage to have a talk with Chatsworth first, before our meeting with Claudia because we had to know precisely what his position was going to be regarding the situation with the firm. I gave him time, to get from his office and we met up at the hospital. We'd just assumed he was alone. Blake was ahead of me and when we entered his room, Jacob would you believe I stopped dead in my tracks. Jacob stared int his eyes for a couple of seconds then asked him, "just why did you stop Bradford?" "Do you recall Det.

Hauser's statement when he said during his interrogation Bishop stated that Joker and is cousin could pass for identical twins. And when he was asked the cousin's last name, he didn't know it because he was introduced to him only as John D. " "yes, I remember. Then Jacob asked wait a minute. you're getting ready to tell me that Joker's cousin is here? Bradford laughed and said, "that's only half of it my friend. Bishop's description of him was no exaggeration and when he told John D. there was only one other person who knew about him and he's in the hospital.. He was referring to none other than Steven Chatsworth himself whom; we already knew was Joker's uncle, but what we had no prior knowledge of is the fact that he's also John D's father. Jacob stopped eating gazed directly into Bradford's eyes and exclaimed what! " " He responded, that's right his name is John D. Chatsworth." Jacob said, "so that's why they went to Arleta in the first place." Bradford said, yes and to work out his plan as to what he was going to do next. Jacob said," Bradford tell me, what happened next?" "I gave him a detailed account of everything we covered. Then he asked me, 'how did I know they were going to his residence? "I told him I didn't , until the dump truck came up stolen. That's when I realized that had been his plan all along. I alerted the authorities and informed them of what had transpired and my assessment of the whole situation. Chatsworth said he was given detailed information on my participation

And he thought the day would never come when he would say it , but he was saying it then and he never said anything that he didn't mean. Then totally unexpected to everyone in the room including myself; he extended his hand to me and said, 'thank you for the courage in what you did.' Man now that really threw me for a loop. I expressed my regret to him that there was no advanced indication of what he was going to do. He just said, 'had it not been for my persistence in the matter, he was afraid things would have been much worse and I shouldn't allow it to disturb me further.' "I was going to ask him why he chose to keep his relationship with Joker a secret? But *before I could ask him, he said, 'he never told anyone because he didn't want him bragging to the other men. And as for his son, I assume he feels that is his personal affair, so I never bothered to ask him." Jacob asked him Brad, " I know you were concerned about wrapping up your case with the firm's situation and you were waiting to speak with Chatsworth first, did you get anywhere?" "As a matter-of-fact, Jacob we did. He gave some information that even I wasn't aware of. He spoke directly to Blake and said, 'since he's the firm's Attorney he knew there was an agreement between he and Lansing years ago, as he would become a silent partner in the firm. And he believed those were the papers that Blake was holding over Lansing's head when he threatened prior to Claudia's marriage. I believe Blake was as surprised as I when he smiled at him and said, 'he knew all about it Lansing had told him about the threat. He said Claudia isn't aware of it nor, was her mother. Then he said, 'that young lady has suffered enough because of something she had nothing to do with. He told us that he doesn't know how we're going to solve the problem with that idiot husband of hers, but he officially terminated his partnership from the firm, effective as of yesterday. And Blake could destroy those papers that were in his files, which up to that time, he wasn't even aware of. I plan to discuss that with Blake later. For a few minutes they were silent, then Jacob gazed into his eyes and asked Brad," did you learn specifically why he was determined to ruin the firm and harbored such hatred for David Lansing?' He looked at him and said," You're going to find this hard to believe Jacob. He said, "after all of what you've conveyed to me so far, try me!" I did promise to tell you when everything had been resolved. Now the case is officially closed. It began years ago, after David Lansing had taken control of the firm from his ailing father-in-law Claudia's grandfather. According to the account Chatsworth gave me, Lansing played around on his wife Claudette, Claudia's mother He said everyone knew about including her, but she never said anything to him about it at least, not that he was aware of. He was always taking frequent trips out of the city, but no one knew where he was going until one day, he received an urgent telephone from his younger sister who lived in another city not far away asking him if he could pay her a visit? He told her yes he would come. When he arrived there, she explained everything including her pregnancy and of course the father's name. He said he never had the slightest indication that Lansing was involved with his sister. She told him that when she informed him of the pregnancy, he flatly told her to get rid of it because he wasn't going to see her anymore anyway. A few days after that, he received another telephone call informing him that his sister had committed suicide. He never said anything to Claudette nor; Lansing, but he vowed that one day he would make sure that he paid for what he'd done. So at that point, he began to formulate his plan by letting everyone believe they were close friends that way, he would be above suspicion when things happened." Jacob just sat there staring at him in total awe. Then he asked, " does Claudia know about all of this Brad? He said, yes Jacob unfortunately, she does now. During our meeting with her, she wanted to know why Chatsworth had harbored such hatred for her father. I hesitated to tell her, but she insisted on knowing the whole truth about everything including Charles's part in bringing about the business scandal in the first place. " "How is she taking all of this Bradford?" "I believe she's going to be all right Jacob. She's a very strong young woman and she informed Blake and me that, she's going to take a few days off to think things through, and as for Charles well, we just don't know because she told us that she'd give her decision when she returns. But you know, I believe there are going to be some changes made in their marriage." "My goodness Bradford, how can one person endure so much disappointment and pain still manage to their sanity?" "I don't know Jacob, I guess the best way is not to give in, but to stand fast and persevere regardless of the odds, because they can always be changed if we become determined enough and think positively. Jacob looked at him smiled and said, "Man, you certainly do have some very interesting cases." He returned the smile and said, " this one was mild compared to some I've had to investigate and at least, I don't have to give a deposition in this one." "Well P.I. What are you going to do next, he asked him?" He replied, " I informed Blake and Claudia that I plan to stick around for a few days in the event they might need me for something else. And you know, I'm afraid they just might." Jacob stared into his eyes and asked," Bradford are you thinking that after Claudia has given her decision, she might incur problems with Charles?" "Yes Jacob, the prospect of it happening has occurred to me. You see I've had the opportunity of dealing with him during the investigation and all things considered, I believe he has a tendency to be quite ruthless if provoked enough. Claudia hasn't spoken it in so many words, but I believe she's aware of her husband's infidelity, and if that's the case, she just might make the decision to opt out of the marriage. And believe me, that's not going to set well with him at all. " I see where you're coming from Bradford and from what you've said, your instincts just might be correct and I'm inclined to agree with you. So now all you and attorney Colwell can do is wait until she returns with her decision. If you should happen to need any assistance for any reason, you know how to reach me." Smiling, he said, thanks Jacob, It's reassuring to know I have back up if it should ever come to that." "Well Jacob, how are things going with you since all of the excitement is over, he asked teasingly?" He stared at Bradford and said, "you've got to be kidding, there's always something else that has to be investigated in this business and unlike you, I don't have the luxury of choosing all my cases, he said returning the tease. By that time, they'd consumed their entire meal and just sat sipping on the coffee, until Jacob received a call from the station asking him to return. He gazed at Bradford laughed and asked, "see what I mean?" "he gave a hearty laugh and said, "have fun with this one. I'll be in touch." After Jacob left the restaurant, he sat there for a few minutes longer and decided to return to his office. Checking the messages, a call had come in from Blake Colwell asking him to give him a call, it was urgent. He questioned himself; 'I wonder what this is about while placing the call?" "Hello Blake, this is Brad, I've just returned to the office and got your message. What seems to be the* problem?" "Hello Brad, after you left my office yesterday, I was reading David's letter again and I believe in all fairness we should inform Claudia of it's contents regarding her marriage to Charles. Will it inconvenience you to come to the office this afternoon say around one-thirty?" "No Blake, it's not an inconvenience at all. I'm not doing anything at the present anyway. So I'll see you at one-thirty, was his reply." After the conversation with Blake was concluded, Bradford wondered to himself, 'what has influenced Blake's decision to divulge the information to Claudia now and not before? Something's seriously disturbing him and I plan to find out just what it is!

He arrived at Blake's office punctually at one-thirty p.m. As he entered the front office door, Blake was standing at the desk looking over some papers He turned around taking a brief look, at the clock smiled and said, "right on time as usual huh?" Bradford smiled back and said," you of all people Blake, know I detest being late arriving any place." "yes I do Brad. Shall we go into, my office?" Bradford noticed Jenny the secretary was absent from her desk which meant, she probably hadn't returned from her lunch break. Once inside his private office, Blake extended his hand pointing to the large chair directly in front of his desk. Gazing directly into his eyes, "He said Barad, after reading through David's letter yesterday for the second time, I'm convinced we should inform Claudia of it's contents. We don't know what her decision will be but at least, I believe she should have this information. As for my part I should have suggested doing just that when we had Our meeting with her. She asked for the truth, but a great deal of it was still withheld from her. At that time, I assumed that her not knowing everything especially about David was best, but since I've had time to think it through including your suggestion, I feel that I've done her a grave injustice. Bradford stared int his eyes and said, Blake, "I agree with your point that she should've been told all of it, but I you only thought you were protecting her from further humiliation. She's going to give us her decision when *she returns anyway and as now, we really don't know what that will b. However, whatever the case might be, I feel she should know what happened especially, since she's still married to Charles. Now according to what you've conveyed to me, she's already aware of his infidelity. And I'm certain that during her decision making she's also going to consider that as well as his betrayal in other areas, and I believe his having with David Lansing was the greatest of them all, Because it appears to have been a marriage of opportunity on both their parts. Blake said, "you just might be right Brad. " Suddenly, the telephone on his desk began to ring and promptly responding he said, this is Attorney Blake Colwell's office. The caller on the other end said, "Hello Blake this is Claudia." Looking at Bradford he said, "hello my dear, I didn't anticipate hearing from you until tomorrow." She asked. Is Brad there with you by any chance?' He said, "yes, he's right here. "She said, "good because the both of you to know that as of now, I've only made a decision to confront Charles regarding his involvement with Chatsworth in the business scandal that could very well have ruined the firm, had not Brad agreed to take the case. Blake stared at Bradford and asked," are you certain about this Claudia?" Without one moments hesitation she said, "yes Blake I'm certain it's time for me to do this and the sooner, the better. " He said, " if that is your decision then by all means, do it my dear. She said, "give Brad my love, I'll give you a call later." After replacing the receiver Blake gazed at Bradford and said,]" as of now, Claudia's only made a decision to confront Charles regarding his involvement with Chatsworth in the business scandal. Brad she's quite determined to confront him on that issue. " "You know Blake, I sort of expected that she would." "Oh really?" "yes I did, if you were she, wouldn't you be compelled to do the same?' "Yes, I imagine I would." And by the way, she send you her love." Bradford stared at him and asked," I wonder what his response is going to be when she does confront him.?" Blake lowed his eyes to the desk then, looking at Bradford he said, "at this point, I can't even begin to imagine Brad." He observed a shadow of deep concern appear on Blake's face. And again, his instincts began to telling him that something wasn't quite right. From the beginning the clues have been there, but difficult to pinpoint. And that was becoming an annoying factor with him. He believed with great certainty that, Blake was deliberately concealing something from him and it had very much to do with Claudia. Precisely what and why was becoming the million dollar question? Before confronting Blake with his suspicion regarding Claudia, he thought it best to just hold off until they knew what direction she was going to take with Charles. Suddenly, he said Blake, " I believe the best time to inform Claudia of the letter is after she's confronted Charles on the other issue. Perhaps by that time we'll have more to go on, depending on his reaction." "Blake looked at him and said, "you've got a valid point there Brad and I agree with you."*

She thought to herself that she'd procrastinated quite long enough, it was time to bring things out into the open. Claudia finally telephoned the firm, someone else answered the phone and when she asked to speak with Charles she was informed that he'd left the firm earlier in the day, on an out-of-town Business trip. Puzzled by the information she wondered to herself, 'where could he have gone and why?' During their last conversation, there was no discussion regarding any trip. Just what exactly, is he up to this time, asking herself?' She telephoned Blake's office and was immediately put through to him by hie secretary. "Claudia my dear, you sound upset, what seems to be the problem?" " Blake, the problem is Charles, she said." "What about Charles Claudia, he questioned curiously?" " I telephoned the firm a short while ago to speak with him and was informed that he'd left earlier in the day on an out -of -town Business trip. Have you any knowledge of this Blake?" "No, I haven't spoken with him recently. I can't imagine where he might have gone or why." "Neither can I. She said. Listen, I'll speak with you later." She had just ended the conversation with Blake when the telephone rang. Thinking it might have been Charles calling, she abruptly answered, but instead, she heard a strange voice on the other end. It was a recorded message from a hotel confirming the reservation scheduled for Mr. and Mrs. Charles Carrington at six p.m. Standing back with a fixed gaze on the silent instrument, she realized she had just intercepted a message that was meant for Charles. Obviously ,he hadn't expected her to be home. She began to think so this is something else he's been up to, further enhancing her suspicion that he's involved with another woman. I wonder just how long has he been playinghouse?' As she sat looking in particular, her eyes began to swell with tears, but blinking a few times, she refused to allow them to come and because of him not a chance, she thought to herself'. Thinking to herself; 'whether you realize it or not Charles, you've just made the next decision easier for me.' Claudia had no concept that when she'd asked for the truth only a small portion of it was conveyed to her. But in a short period of time her life would be forever changed, because she was in for an awakening that she would never have dreamed of in a million years!

In the meanwhile, Charles and Regina were having dinner at the Hilton hotel. While he was out romancing Regina he had no concept that Claudia had returned home and was trying to reach him. Neither was he aware that she had intercepted an important telephone call that was obviously meant for him. One might very well wonder having his choice of many other restaurants what was Charles's rationale for his selection of this particular one when Claudia, her family and friends dined there as well? It appeared that even His actions were not being unobserved by a number of other patrons who were also dining there. After Regina was uncomfortable in the surrounding. Was it that he'd become so complacent in his relationship with he that no one else mattered? His actions were not being unobserved by a number of other patrons who were also dining there. After leaving the dining area they checked into the over-night suite that was reserved for them. Regina expressed an inward sigh of relief as they entered the room and wished he had chosen some other place other than this hotel. She disliked having been stared at, but said nothing to Charles. Early the following morning they checked out of the hotel and drove back to the firm's parking lot. Regina went to her job and Charles went into the firm.

After filing some papers away Bradford returned to his desk. Something was knowing at his insides as he thought of Blake and Claudia he was becoming very precarious of Blake's motive regarding her. They had known each other for many years and he could read him like a book. Recalling their earlier conversation when he casually asked Blake, 'I sense there's something exceptional about this case, what's your stake in all of this?' His response at that time was, let's just say, at this point we're uncertain about him. Referring to Charles's loyalty. Even then, he felt there was something more, but he didn't press the issue. There had been instances when Blake's seemingly over protectiveness of her was quite apparent. Now that the situation with the firm had been resolved, he decided it was about time to have a talk with him. Blake was sitting at his desk when the telephone rang. It was his secretary informing him that, Mr. Maxwell is on the line sir." "Please put him through Jenny." "yes sir, she replied." "Hello Brad. It's good to hear your voice." "Is that so, he asked with a chuckle?" "Yes, and I'm pleased that you called because there's something else that's transpired." "Oh, what is it Blake?" "Claudia telephoned me a second time. The information was much different from the first call." "In what way, Bradford asked him?" "Apparently she called the firm to speak with Charles and was informed that he had left earlier in the day on an out-of-town Business trip. She asked if I had any prior knowledge of such a trip?" " I said no, I haven't spoken with him and couldn't imagine where he might have gone or why. Brad, I'm afraid he's up to something else, but what? I haven't any idea." "'taking his history of the past into account." "What did Claudia say to your response?" "She was up set and said she would call me later." "Blake as you stated awhile back, Charles is quite unpredictable, and there's no telling what he might be up to this time. In the meanwhile, I suggest we just wait until Claudia telephone you again. " "you just might be right Brad at this point, all we can do is await her call."

Bradford thought to himself; there it is again, Blake is sounding very nervous. There's something definitely going on here! Suddenly, he thought to himself; this just might not be the right time to question him at least not until, I've had an opportunity to speak with Claudia first. Then to Blake's bewilderment he said, listen Blake something has just occurred to me and I'd better check into. I'll get back with you later. " He responded, "that will be fine Brad," He had no intentions of letting Blake know what his thoughts were at that time. He decided to telephone Claudia and find out what he could learn from their conversation. "Hello Claudia this is Bradford, are you free say in about an hour?' "Hi Brad, yes I am, but why do you ask?" "I would like to speak with you about something, he replied." "Oh, shall I come to your office?" "Oh I'm not at the office, as a matter-of-fact, I'm only a short distance away from your place. What about meeting me at the coffee shop just down the block from you?" "That will be just fine, I'll see you there then." "Good, and thanks! "Thank you, I need to get out of here for awhile anyway, she said." Bradford arrived at the coffee shop shortly ahead of Claudia. After ordering a cup of coffee he walked over to an empty booth and seated himself. As he sat there sipping the coffee waiting upon her arrival he thought to himself something's wrong, she didn't sound her usual pleasant self.

As she entered the door he stood acknowledging her presence and as she began walking in his direction, he gazed upon her face. His instincts were correct, something was wrong. After they were both seated he asked her, "would you care to join me with a cup of coffee?" "yes thank you, I can certainly use one, was her reply." Bradford had a refill and they sat sipping on their coffee in silence for awhile. Only an occasional look away did he take his eyes off her. Finally he asked, "do you want to talk about it?" She looked hard at him and asked, It's that obvious huh?" "Yes it is Claudia." "Brad have you spoken with Blake "Yes, I have earlier." "Did he tell you why I telephoned him?" "As a matter-of-fact he did, and told me that you made another call to him. The first one ,I was with him when *you called. She took another sip of coffee and sat the cup down on the table, then she gazed at him and said, after I'd spoken with him the second time, we had just completed our conversation when the telephone rang. I assumed it was Charles calling, but that was by no means the case." He stared at her and asked," what do you mean Claudia?" "Brad, I intercepted a telephone message that was obviously meant for Charles since I knew nothing about it. " He saw her eyes began to swell with tears as she spoke. "Claudia just what was the message, if I might ask? " She looked away for a brief second then back at him saying," it was a recorded message from a hotel confirming the reservation for Mr. and Mrs. Charles Carrington at six p.m. " He leaned back against the booth and gazed directly into her eyes that revealed pain and anguish. "Claudia, are you certain the reservation wasn't made for the two of you?" "Yes Brad, I'm certain. How could it have been for the two of us when I've been away for two days and he had no way of knowing just when I'd return?" "Well, that is true, he replied. She continued, "then there's this out-of-town Business trip which Blake nor; I was ever aware of. And there was no discussion of any trip during our last conversation." "And just when was that, he asked her?" "Two days ago. I telephoned him from a friend's home." "Did he as you when you'll be returning home?" "No, and I didn't tell him!" "I see, he said. He gazed at her for a couple of minutes then asked,. "Claudia just what do you believe is going on with him?" "To be precise Bad, I honestly don't know, but I do know this much, he's up to something and it's not with me." "What do you mean?" "Charles is having an affair, I've been suspicious of him for quite sometime and that telephone call only confirmed my suspicions." ""How do you know for certain that he's involved with another woman Claudia?" "Brad, a wife can tell if her husband's involved with someone else, she doesn't have to see it to recognize the truth." He sat quietly for a minute and asked her," how often has he been taking these sudden business trips?" "Only a few times that I'm aware of, But I became suspicious when he always told me that he was spending so much time at the firm because there were thing's that he had to personally take of." "Has he ever told you what they were?" "Only that he would discuss it with me at another time which incidentally, never came and now this!" While she was speaking Bradford recalled Blake's words regarding Charles's infidelity. After she had finished speaking he asked her, "Claudia, would you happen to know which hotel called to confirm the reservation?" "Why yes, it was the "Hilton". "Would you happen to know which one, there are a number of them around you know?" "No, I'm afraid I don't Brad, why do you ask?" "Oh, I was just wondering was his reply." Abruptly changing the subject to avoid any further he asked," Incidentally, now that the situation with the firm has been resolved, how are things going now?" "Thanks to you, everything has begun to run smoothly again. A number of our former employees are back with us now and the atmosphere is again pleasant. There are no complaints and some have received bonuses." "Well, that is good news and I'm pleased to hear it." "Thank you she said, smiling." "You're welcome, returning her smile." Then on a more serious note he said, "Claudia I wouldn't be too concerned about what Charles is, or isn't doing. Time will tell the story. When he does return you can have your talk with him and give him your decision." She looked at him smiled and said, "you're right Brad, I've made my decision and that is that! "Good! He said look, I've got some errands to run before returning to the office, will you be all right?" "Yes, I'll be fine thank you. I'm just going to sit here for awhile longer and enjoy another cup of coffee." "If you should need to contact me, you know how I can be reached." "Yes, and again thanks!" "You're welcome." Bradford sat in his car for a short while. Recalling the conversation with Claudia his thoughts reverted to Charles and he wondered to himself; just how long has he been playing his little game and with whom?' First there was the situation with the firm, now he's playing house with another woman. 'Charles my dear fellow, it appears that you have a serious problem with priorities. 'Claudia doesn't deserve what she's getting and there's no charge for This one, were his inner thoughts as he finally pulled out into traffic. Bradford decided to take a drive along the ocean side. The panoramic view of the sky blue water was exhilarating and refreshing. Its rippling effect always appeared to help when he had troubling thoughts of uncertainty. The situation with the Business scandal had been resolved and yet, his instincts led him to believe there was still something more and that disturbed him greatly!*

Charles Carrington wasn't the only problem, there was also Blake and Claudia's relationship that had appeared to disturb him the most. Suddenly, he recalled what Matthew Crawford had conveyed to him in an earlier conversation regarding Lansing and Carrington that involved a young woman. Regina Casper was the name given to him during the conversation with Crawford the previous day also, and where she was employed which was directly across the street from the Lansing Constructions' firm. Thinking to himself, 'how convenient for dear Charles!' He chose a spot that gave him the best view of both buildings. Taking a brief glance at his wristwatch he'd only been there for half an hour when Charles came out of the door. As he was obviously looking over the parking lot, a small two-door black Caprice pulled up in front of him with appeared to be a slender brunette behind the steering wheel. After taking a brief glance around the passenger door opened and he abruptly got in the car. Bradford waited until they were out of the parking lot before driving out himself. Wanting to know where they were going he, remained at least two car lengths behind them. Four blocks later, they pulled into the parking lot of a restaurant on Devernshire Blvd. And parked. They sat in the car for a few minutes before Charles was observed getting out, then walked around the car and opened the driver's door as he assisted her in getting out of the car. Watching them walk with arms around each other Bradford remembered Claudia's words of certainty as she spoke of Charles's involvement with another woman. Thinking to himself, 'well Charles, this is strike number one!' Approximately an hour later, they left the restaurant. Charles went inside the Contractors' firm and Regina went into the parking lot directly across the street. He wondered if she is the woman that is occupying so much of Charles's time, when he was supposedly to have been working at the office? Recalling his conversation with Crawford, Regina Casper is the same woman he'd observed in the presence of David Lansing on several occasions. Asking himself,' What is it, with this woman?' He was determined to learn as much as he could about her, including her association with the two men. Later that afternoon he met with a couple of sources and learned that Regina Casper was not only involved with Charles, but had been involved with David Lansing as well. It was apparent to him that Claudia was the only person who wasn't aware of what was really happening. Yes, she was certain o Charles's involvement with another woman, but not with her father as well. Perhaps she was the rationale for the bad blood that was known to have existed between the two. Well, well, this appears to give credence to the speculation regarding Claudia's sudden marriage to Charles. Considering Lansing's history was his motive was to get Charles out of the picture so he'd have her all to himself? If that was the case then she had been playing the both of them. Now Lansing's dead and she's still involved with Charles. According to one source who empathetically stated that she'd been Lansing's mistress for nearly two years, which meant Charles had to have known about it, but how did he get the two of them, to cooperate with him in his scheme? 'I've definitely got to have a talk with Blake.' "Excuse me Mr. Colwell, but Mr. Maxwell is on the line sir." "Thank you Jenny, please put him through." "yes sir." "Hello Brad, what are you up to now, he asked laughing?" "Blake are you going to be free within the next thirty minutes?" "Why yes, why do you ask Brad?" "I'll give it all to you when I arrive at your office." "All right, I'll be expecting you." There's something going on that, has Bradford T. Maxwell stirred up and I wonder just what it could be? "

When Bradford arrived at Blake's office one half hour later, he was standing at the front desk and looking around he smiled and said, "You made it I see." "Surely, you didn't think I would disappoint you did you, he asked him smiling?" "Not the Maxwell I'm familiar with, no." "Jenny would you hold all calls for e please?" "yes, sir." He ushered Bradford into his private office closing the door behind them. "Have a seat Brad, what's on your mind?" Sitting back in the chair, crossing his long legs and gazing directly at Blake , he said, "I believe it's time, to inform Claudia of the information in Lansing's letter." "Oh, Blake questioned?" "yes, I've been doing some checking on and guess what I've come up with?" "I can't begin to imagine so enlighten me, will you?" "For starters, Claudia is very certain of Charles's involvement with another woman, but she doesn't know whom and I do!" Blake sat up in his chair starring into Bradford's eyes and asked, Brad do you know this for a fact?" "Yes Blake I do. I've observed them together and beside that, I've also learned through a couple of sources that she had been David Lansing's mistress for nearly two years. Her name is Regina Casper and she's employed in the building directly across the street from the firm, which incidentally, is very convenient for Charles. When Claudia was unable to reach him at the firm, he was having dinner with Regina Casper at the Hilton hotel in Universal City." As he was slowly sitting back in his chair Blake said, "so, she's the rationale for the bad blood that, existed between them and also Claudia's sudden marriage to Charles. I've always felt David was up to something and it wasn't Claudia's welfare that he was concerned about either." "Brad, I agree with you, it's time for Claudia to know what's in the letter. I'll telephone her to come to the office at her earliest convenience." I have no appointment s this afternoon so, I'm going to ask her to come in around one-thirty. Will you be free by that time, I'd very much appreciate it if you can?" Giving him a steady gaze he said, "you can count on it Blake." "Splendid, I'll have Jenny telephone her residence now." As Bradford and Blake were talking a much frantic Charles had recently discovered that is wallet was missing and telephoned Regina who suggested he check back at the hotel. Thinking he might have over looked it some place in the office, he searched again but it was no where to be found. Uncertain of where it might have been he went back to the hotel and spoke with the manager who assured him that no one reported having found *it, but he would make an inquiry among his staff. Leaving the hotel disappointed even more so he telephoned Regina to rendezvous with him giving her a certain location. "What if my wallet has fallen into the wrong hands, he asked himself?"*

Blake was sitting behind his desk and is thoughts were of Claudia and David's letter Thinking perhaps, it was for the best if Claudia is informed of the letter before confronting Charles. Bradford had telephoned him earlier stating e was enroute to his office and now he was awaiting Claudia's arrival. At precisely one-thirty p.m. Jenny announced "Mr. Colwell sir, Mrs. Carrington has arrived." "Thank you Jenny, please escort her in and when Mr. Maxwell arrives, just ask him to come on in." "Yes sir." He walked around the desk and met Claudia and Jenny as they were entering the door. Taking Claudia by the arm he said, "thank you Jenny." "You're welcome sir while gently closing the door behind her. He led Claudia to one of the chairs that were directly in front of his desk then walked round it and seated himself. Gazing deeply into her eyes Blake asked, "How are you my dear?" She looked away for an instant and back at him saying, Blake, I've given it a lot of thought and I'm seriously considering divorcing Charles, there should never been a marriage to begin with." He stared long and hard, at her before saying, "you sound quite certain of this Claudia." "I am, and my only regret in the matter is that, it has taken so long for me to come to this point. " She just completed her sentence when they saw Bradford entering through the door. With a broad smile on his face he said, "good afternoon you two, taking long strides towards the chair beside Claudia. "with a surprised look on her face, she smiled gave him a smack on the cheek and said, "good afternoon to you Brad, I wasn't aware that you were going to be here as well." Looking first at Blake then back at her he smiled and asked, is that going to be a problem Claudia?" "I don't believe it is especially since I'm in the company of my two favorite men she said smiling." That statement brought a hearty laugh from the both of them. Then Blake said Claudia, " I asked you to come into the office because Brad and I have concurred that there is some very important information that you have. As a matter-of-fact, but I was blinded by selfishness into thinking I was protecting you, and lost my true perspective regarding the matter, and I do apologize for it. Gazing hard at him then at Brad she asked Blake, "just what are you trying to tell me?" "Claudia to begin with when I was going through David's files I came upon a letter addressed to me and marked 'personal and confidential'. I was surprised and wondered just what it contained, when I opened it and began to read I was both shocked and angry. In David's own word's he stated there was a conspiracy between he and Charles. Your marriage to Charles had been orchestrated by him Claudia. " She sat directly up in the chair and wide-eyed exclaimed what?" "Blake stared directly into her eyes and said yes my dear, it appears that David made Charles a generous offer if he married you, with certain stipulations naturally, and he accepted." Blake observed her eyes as they began to swell with tears and she slowly eased herself back into the chair. His heart was aching at the expression he saw appearing upon her young face. Bradford could do nothing but hold her hand and the thoughts that were radiating in his mind could not placed into appropriate language. Finally, she looked at Blake and asked, "Blake did my mother, have any knowledge of this?" He gazed directly not her eyes and said, "No Claudia. And neither did I." "Exactly what were the stipulations, in the agreement she asked him?" "He said, according to the letter the terms set forth were, contingent upon two things, you and your mother was never to learn of the agreement and Charles was to severe all ties in his present relationship prior to the wedding date that was to be scheduled. It appears that David didn't trust him anyway because after the agreement was signed and with Charles's knowledge, he set up a contingency plan. He stopped there gave Claudia a concerned look and asked my dear, are you certain of wanting to hear the rest of this letter?" She took a deep breadth exhaled and stared at Bradford for an instant then at Blake and responded, "yes Blake and this time, please don't try to shield me from this horrible mess." He began, well three months later, somehow David learned that Charles hadn't resolved the Relationship and had deliberately reneged on the agreement so, David gave him his first and final warning. There's no statement confirming this, but I believe that was David's rationale for terminating Charles's authority to act in the capacity as representative for the firm. Then realizing the extent of Charles's deception, he immediately began to put his contingency plan into effect and that's when he came to me infuriated, at that point I didn't question him, but did the paperwork as he requested. I often wondered afterwards just what all of that was about since I had no background knowledge of what had actually transpired between the two of them. However, what I believe to have been the final conflict between them resulted in David's recission of the agreement in its entirety. Now it has become clear why Charles was trying so desperately to get his hands on David's files., he knew what they contained, but what he'd planned to do with them, I have no concept. " Claudia looked away for a brief period then said Blake, Brad this seems like a horrible nightmare that's difficult to awake from. Why would the man considered to have been my father do such a despicable and unforgiving thing and just what was his rationale for it, she asked Blake?" Blake gazed at Brad who nodded his head in recognition that he understood. Bradford repositioned his chair to face Claudia more directly and gazing directly into her eyes said Claudia, "I realize all of this has come as a shock to you, but Blake and I have already discussed the fact that you should have all of the information. Since Our last meeting I did some investigation on my own and this is what I learned. It appears that your marriage to Charles was orchestrated by Lansing as one of opportunity for the both of them. " "Claudia stared at him wide-eyed and asked, what do you mean Brad?" Claudia, Lansing and Carrington were involved with the same woman in fact, I was told that she'd been Lansing's mistress for over two years and was having an affair with dear Charles at the same time. Apparently Lansing devised a scheme to get Charles out of the picture by making him an offer he knew couldn't be refused and therefore, he'd have her all to himself. But all of it backfired on the both of them as you can well see. She was the rationale for the bad blood that had existed between the two of them and Charles is still involved with her. Apparently your suspicions of him were correct. When you were trying to reach him and intercepted the telephone call from the hotel which incidentally was the Hilton, they were there having dinner and I've seen them together on two separate occasions. I'm truly sorry for all of this Claudia." She stared hard at him and then Blake and said, please don't be Brad because my plans have been to get a divorce from Charles since the Business scandal now, I have all of the ammunition that I need to get him out of my life forever. Now I truly understand why he tried to ruin the firm, I imagine he considered that to have been retribution for what happened between them. Well that's too bad, because I'm going to see to it that he gets all that he deserves. She stared at the both of them for an instant and said, "I don't know who the woman is and frankly, I don't care, but what I can't possibly comprehend is what woman that has any common decency would chose to behave in such a manner as this?" Blake gazed hard at her and said," Claudia my dear I can't give you an answer to that question." She then turned to Blake and said, " I would appreciate your assistance in getting everything I'll need for the divorce and in the meanwhile, its time to settle things with Charles. Her voice had a firm and determined tone in it. Blake stared at Bradford then focused his attention on her and in a tone of voice that was unlike his said, "Claudia please be careful when you confront Charles he is quit unpredictable and there's no way in estimating what his reaction is going to be." Bradford said nothing, but observed the concern that was in his voice as well as the expression on his face. Then he turned, gazed into Claudia's eyes and said, "if Charles give you any problems Claudia, you know how to reach me." She stared at him smiled and said, "thanks Brad, but I believe he's going to be more surprised than anything else especially, when he realize the charade is over and he's no longer to be a part of my life. It appears that I'm the only one who didn't realize what was happening." The final analysis was it had been a marriage of opportunity for the both of them. David was exerting his influential power to get the results he desired by relying upon Charles's insatiable desire for wealth and power, but he didn't have the last say after all, because Regina Casper was still involved with Charles Carrington.

After Claudia's departure from Blake's office, Bradford thought now was the appropriate time to question Blake. He had become extremely precarious of Blake's motive regarding her especially, after what he'd observed minutes earlier while she was there. As he sat there silent for a few minutes and was about to speak, Blake gazed hard at him and said, "Brad we've known each other for many years and I know you, something's disturbing you." Bradford looked directly into his eyes and said," You're precisely correct Blake and I can read you like a book. So I'm going to get right to the point. From the beginning my instincts have been telling me you're concealing something. I haven't forced the issue because we were trying to resolve the situation with the firm and I knew you had other things on your mind. I've been observing you and as you've stated before, we know each better than most people." Blake looked at the man in front of him, his inner thought was, 'oh, oh, now I know something's up.' "Now level with me Blake, just what is it that you're concealing and how does Claudia fit into the picture?" At those questions Blake said nothing, but stared at Bradford in total awe because he was totally unprepared for those questions. He sat back in his chair and gave Bradford a hard, steady gaze and said, Knowing you as I do Brad for sometime now, I've had the feeling that you would eventually get around to asking me the questions that were on your mind. I'm grateful to finally be released from this haunting secret that I've had to carry for over twenty-nine years. You see, this is a part of my life that I never told anyone and I regret not having told you sooner and the only people who knew the truth were Claudette, David and I. Brad, Claudia is my biological daughter, not David Lansing." He stared hard at Blake and exclaimed what!? "Yes, she's my daughter and that is something that Charles definitely isn't aware of, or he would've used it against her, I'm certain of it. "Blake why didn't you tell me this from the beginning?" He looked directly into his eyes and said Brad, I've been asking myself that same question repeatedly and frankly, I didn't know how to tell you. All I can do now is ask your forgiveness for having kept this from you, of all people and can certainly understand why you're angry." He stared at him for a full minute then in a soft tone said, "Blake, I'm not angry with you perhaps just disappointed that's all." "And you have a right to be Brad. Claudette and I had a short lived, intimate love affair. David learned of it and Claudette's pregnancy, he told her that he would raise her as his own. When I learned of this I was infuriated with her, but she said it was for the best because there could be a scandal. So she, David and I made a mutual agreement that Claudia was never to know. I thought about it for awhile and felt perhaps; she might have been correct. I didn't tell her exactly why I agreed, but only did so to protect she and our daughter from a scandal for as long as I possibly could, I never wanted it to be this way, but she asked me to make her a solemn promise that I'd let thing's remain as they were and I reluctantly agreed to do so. I told her since she'd made that choice. I would always remain, near my daughter any way I possibly could. I didn't quite trust David to hold up his end of the bargain so instead of leaving the firm I told him that I would remain the firm's Attorney and of course, he didn't object. He continued his life-style as always, which was fine by me. Now I wonder if I really made the right decision in agreeing with Claudette?" "I don't know Blake as I see it, you did what you thought was best for Claudette and Claudia at the time." "Brad do you recall during our visit with Chatsworth at the hospital when he said I had held something over David's head?" "Yes Blake, I do recall the conversation because it appeared to have been as much of a shock to you as it was to me. " "Well, he was speaking of the signed agreement between David, Claudette and I. "Oh yes, it was stated in the agreement that, biological is my biological daughter, And he was reluctant to sign it in the beginning, but I told him if he didn't agree I would make it known anyway. In spite of the way he treated her, I felt he didn't want anyone to know and he knew I was quite serious about it. Brad, I honestly don't believe I could've done it, but he didn't know that, But what I had no knowledge of was the fact that he'd informed Chatsworth of it and that's what surprised me." "Blake something has just occurred to me, is it possible that Chatsworth terminated his partnership with the firm because of you and Claudia especially, since he's aware of the truth, and remember his statement when he said, that she's gone through enough?' "You know Brad, I never considered the prospect, but you just might be correct." " And recalling the conversation, just what brought on the threat you made to Lansing might I ask?" "Brad, when I learned about the impending marriage between Claudia and Charles, I felt something wasn't right about it so I went to David and questioned him. I also learned that Claudette had intervened on Claudia's behalf, but to no avail. He and I had some very heated words and at the time, he assured me that he had her best interest at heart and mind you, I had no knowledge of what had what had already transpired between he and Charles. I know Claudia was coerced into the marriage because Claudette told me she heard Claudia tell him, that she didn't care enough; about Charles to marry him. I suppose she just became tired of arguing with him. David Lansing could be very intimidating and cruel in the worst way as well as being manipulative." Bradford leaned back in his chair crossed his legs and said, "I've encountered some very wicked people in this business, but David Lansing is about the worst and perhaps, it's a good thing that I never had the chance to meet him." Blake gave a hearty laugh and said, Brad, "I believe you're correct about that." 'Then on a more serious note Bradford said, "Blake you know Claudia should know be told, she has a right to know the truth." "You're correct Brad, but perhaps it would be best to wait until the situation between she and Charles is resolved first, because he has no part in this." "I agree with you, it's going to be difficult enough for the both of you as it is without having him in the picture. " Blake looked away for a moment then said, "Brad you're absolutely correct, I should no longer withhold the truth from her. " Bradford gazed into his friend's eyes and beholding the great concern that, was quite obvious and in a mild tone he said, "Blake, you've carried this secret for many years now it's time, to spare your self; from the guilt trip and do what you believe to be the right thing. It's not going to be easy, but I believe you and Claudia will make it through this." "Thank you, my friend, for those encouraging words perhaps, that is precisely what I needed to hear, he said smiling."

After a casual drive along the ocean side Claudia finally arrived at her residence. She thought to herself, 'It's now time for me to bring this charade that exist between Charles and I to a halt.' As she began to enter through the front entranceway she observed him sitting in the large chair opposite the bay window. He stared at her as she was walking into the living room, but said nothing. Hanging her lightweight jacket on the coat tree and placing her purse on the end table, Claudia turned to face him and in a sullen tone said, "I'm glad you're here because you've saved me the time and effort in trying to locate you." He stared at her and said, "Yes, I've been here for awhile." "Well, I'm pleased to hear that and I hope you've enjoyed your stay because you won't be here for very much longer, she said in a determined tone." He gazed into her eyes and what he saw was anything but pleasant. Thinking to himself, 'I wonder what's gotten into her, I've never seen her this way before and the expression on her face appeared to have belonged to someone else.' "Claudia, just what did you mean by that statement?" She stared directly into his eyes and said, "I meant precisely what I said Charles. You see, I understand now, why you were so anxious to get your lousy hands on my father's files, but what you weren't aware of at the time of your plotting, they had already been removed to Blake's office and today, I learned what it was that you were so interested in finding. He gave her a blank stare and said, "I don't know what you mean." "you're a liar Charles. In going through the files Blake came upon a letter addressed to him from my father, explaining everything that had transpired between the two of you .' He looked at her in apparent astonishment because he said nothing but stared at her, it was as if he was dreaming. When she came through the door he had no concept that conversation was going to take place. She continued in a soft, but controlled voice. "I know about the conspiracy between the two of you, he made you a generous offer and you accepted it because of your insatiable desire for wealth and power. The marriage was orchestrated by him which was no more than a charade. Oh yes I know, my mother and I was ever to learn about your agreement and you were to resolve the relationship with the same woman that you're playing house with now, before the marriage was scheduled to have taken place. I don't know who she is and I definitely don't care to, but I do know this for certain, she's welcome to you. I didn't want to marry you anyway and Now I know why he was so adamant and persistent about it, even when my mother and I both disagreed with him. If he was alive today, I would never have forgiven him because it's as if I was auctioned off to the highest bidder you, having been the greatest opportunist. Of course, it was a marriage of opportunity for the both of you. Each of you had your own agenda. You, believing you could eat your cake and have it too and he was to get you out of the picture so he could have his mistress all to himself. Charles gazed hard into her eyes and in a high pitched tone said, "that's a lie Claudia." She stared at him and calmly asked, " which part of what I've said is a lie Charles?" He just stared at her in total disbelief. She continued yes that's right Charles, your playmate was my father's mistress for over two years, you stupid idiot, why do you think he offered you the deal? "Apparently he learned that you had no resolved the former relationship as you agreed to do and that's when he stripped you of your authority to act in the capacity of the firm's representative. We never knew why he'd taken that action until reading the letter. I'm guessing he discussed the matter with you. But you didn't do anything about it so he took final action by making a recission of the agreement in its entirety. This is why you started the subversion acts to ruin the firm, you considered that as retribution for what he'd done especially, after you couldn't coerce me into giving you the authority that you assumed you should have. Now Chatsworth will have nothing more to do with you either. As a matter-of-fact, he terminated his partnership in the firm as well. So you see, you now have nothing which is what you deserve." He stood on his feet and looking at her through demeaning eyes that made chills run down her spine he said, "you're nothing but a frigid little snip." And for the first time, she was actually seeing the ruthless side of him. But she wasn't about to retreat into some skittish little shell. I've already informed Blake that I'm divorcing you, now you can go live with your mistress." By that time, he was becoming belligerent and began to make threats against her saying he wasn't going any place, she abruptly stood on her feet as he reached for her with such intensity that he stumbled just as she moved away escaping his grasp. She sought protection from him by running into another room and securing the door behind her. In an assertive, he asked her, "where do you think you're going your dear father's not here to protect you now? " She didn't respond, but remained silent as he continued to bang on the door with his fists. After what appeared to have been hours, finally there was silence, but she still didn't open the door for fear of his being outside just waiting for her. He couldn't get in and she definitely wasn't going out, so she just laid down across the bed, because she knew he would eventually get tired of waiting and leave. She'd fallen asleep and was awakened by the bright sunlight glaring through the large window. Looking at her wristwatch it was eight-thirty a.m. She went to the window and peered down stairs, Charles's car was gone. Letting out a big sigh of relief she thought to herself' good. I'll call Blake's office to see if he's in.'

"Good morning, Attorney Blake Colwell's office." "Good morning, Jenny, this is Claudia Carrington. Is Attorney Colwell in his office by any chance?" "Why yes, he is Mrs. Carrington, I'll ring you through." "Thank you, Jenny." "you're welcome, Mrs. Carrington and he's on the line." "Good morning Claudia my, you're up rather

early". 'And good morning to you also, Blake. And yes, I realize it is early, but I had a rather disturbing night and thought I'd better call you as soon as possible." He thought for a moment, 'I wonder if this call's about Charles because she has stated that she was going to confront him.' "What's wrong Claudia, he asked her?" "Last evening , I confronted Charles with everything including telling him that I'm divorcing him, and Blake for the first time, I actually saw the ruthless side of him. He became belligerent and began making threats saying he isn't going anywhere." "Wait a minute Claudia, did he strike you in any way, as becoming violent?" Blake to be perfectly honest about it, I believe he's very capable of it, I saw an expression on his face that was cold and demeaning. He reached for me with such intensity that he stumbled, I was able to escape his grasp and ran into one of the rooms securing the door behind me. He banged on the door for what seemed to have been hours he finally stopped. I sat down on the bed and apparently feel asleep because I was awakened this morning by the bright sunlight glaring through the window. I didn't hear anything and when I went to look down stairs his car was gone, I don't know when he left, or where he went to. "Blake was silent for a brief period then said, "this is precisely what I was afraid of Claudia. We know he's very unpredictable and at this point since everything is out in the open, there's no way of knowing what he's going to do next. I'm going to call Brad and apprise him of the latest event, then place a call to the firm and have Charles come into the office. I believe it's time to apply some pressure here." "You just might be right Blake, but what if he isn't at the firm?" " then I'll just leave a message that it's imperative for him to contact me as soon as possible. In the meanwhile, I I suggest you take every precaution until this situation with him is finally settled." "All right and for now, I'm going to take a shower, get dressed and take care of a fer necessary things. I'll be speaking with you later and I'll have my cell phone on if it becomes necessary for you to contact me." "That's a good idea and be careful my dear." After the conversation with Claudia was completed, Blake sat quietly staring out of the office window. He had become deeply disturbed by what had happened and thinking to himself, 'he'd better not ever go as far as to lay a hand on her. I'd best telephone Brad and apprise him of the incident and the sooner the better, there's no telling what that arrogant ambitious young idiot might attempt to do next. "Hello Brad this is Blake, I know it's still quite early, but did I disturb you?" "No Blake you didn't, I've been up for quite sometime now, but your voice tells me something's wrong, what is it?" "Brad, will it inconvenience you to come here to the office as son as you can, Claudia called me a short while ago, and I do believe we're going to have a problem with Charles after all?" "Oh I see. There's no need for you to say anything more Blake I'll be there as soon as I can. In the meanwhile, I suggest that you try reaching him and have him come in to the office. I believe it's about time to have a serious talk with Charles, apparently he has some unresolved issues Blake."

When Bradford arrived at Blake's office he apprised him of the conversation he'd had with Claudia and told him that Charles was on his way there also. Bradford stared at him and in a soft mild tone said," I can hardly wait to see what he has to say Blake." About fifteen minutes after Bradford's arrival the secretary announced, Charles's arrival and Blake asked her to send him in. As he entered the door Blake called his secretary asking her to hold all his calls. Giving Bradford a disgruntled stare he asked Blake, "what is he doing here this time Blake?" Blake gazed hard at him and said, "have a seat Charles. Brad is here at my request furthermore, I don't have to justify my actions, but you have a

Lot of explaining to do. " "What do you mean by that Blake?" "You know precisely what I mean and I'm definitely not in the mod this morning foy coyness. Why did you threaten and try to intimidate Claudia last evening?" "Is that what she told you, he asked Blake?' "Never mind what she told me, what I'm interested in knowing is why?" He glared at Blake with hostility in his eyes and an arrogant tone said, "I've told Claudia before you're nothing but a meddlesome old man who's always interfering where you shouldn't." Blake

observed Bradford staring hard at Charles and thought to himself,
'Oh, oh I'd better say something and like yesterday.' "Blake said,
"hear me well Charles because I'll not repeat myself again. When it
comes to Claudia, that is my business whether you like it; or not and
I want you to understand this, what you and David Lansing did, was
the most despicable act I've ever known. When you teamed up with
Chatsworth to ruin the firm and was caught, you might have thought
you had problems then, but let me enlighten you , your problems are
just beginning. Claudia has knowledge of everything including your
extra martial affair with Regina Casper who by the way was David
Lansing's mistress for nearly two years. That, was his rationale
for wanting you out of the picture, so he'd be free to have her all
to himself, but ironically enough, it backfired on the both of you.
And you've been seen with her on two recent occasions." "That's a lie,
he yelled." Bradford stared at him and said," you're the one who is
lying Charles. I saw you with her twice, once at the restaurant and
again at the Hilton hotel in universal City, And you were with her
having dinner there, when Claudia intercepted a message that was
obviously, meant for you, confirming the reservation for two. Which
incidentally, was at the time, of your supposedly scheduled out-of-
town trip that, no one was aware of." "And what were you doing
checking up on me, he asked in an arrogant tone?" "No, I was tailing
you to find out just who was taking up so much of your time, when
you told Claudia that you were spending those ours at the firm."
"Blake said, Claudia has decided to divorce you and since she's the
sole owner of the firm you get nothing." Charles stared at him with
a defiant and obstinate expression and said," for your information
Blake, it's not going to be that easy for her to get rid of me because
there was a contract and I still have a fourth share in the firm." Blake
gave a hearty laugh and asked, "Is that what you believe Charles
because if it is, I'm afraid you're in for a very rude awakening?"
"What do you mean by that?" Blake was silent for a very brief period
the leaned back in his chair and staring hard at him said," One of the
essential elements of a contract is an agreement. And an agreement is

formed when an offer is made and accepted as was in your case. There are requirements to an offer, An offer expresses the willingness of the offer or to enter into a contractual agreement regarding a particular subject, the marriage. It was a promise which, is conditional upon an act. In your case, there were two acts. Claudia and her mother were never to learn of the agreement between the two of you and you were to severe your ties with the other woman namely, Regina Casper, a fore bearance that is given in exchange for its performance. As far the contractual intention the offeror which, was David must intend to create a legal obligation or must appear to intend to do so. And in this case David only led you to believe he'd carried it out. He didn't trust you so he formed a contingency plan by terminating the offer, once the offer terminated it cannot be revived. According to his letter you reneged on the agreement. His recission of the agreement was the termination of the partnership so was the one-fourth share in the firm's holding's. He'd already minimized your authority to act as representative for the firm and now, you're left with nothing. The recission of the agreement was David' final opportunity for self-satisfaction." He stared at Bradford then Blake and yelled," this was all his idea he came to me." Bradford gazed at him and said, "that might well be, but you were anxious to agree with him, he didn't force you into it, did he Charles?" He just stared at the both of them as if he was in complete shock. Blake looked at him and said, Charles as of now, I suggest you get your things and move some place else and I believe the sooner you do this the better." Bradford turned directly to face him and in a mild, but stern tone said, "Charles here's a peace of advice, if Blake has to call me that you've harmed Claudia in any way, you'll wish that you were some place out of the country and perhaps more difficult to reach." He looked at him and asked, Are you threatening me Maxwell?" "No, only fools make threats Charles, I only make a promise that I'm certain to keep." Blake stared at Bradford and knew he meant every word he'd spoken to him, and apparently Charles knew it as well and said nothing. Two weeks after leaving Blake's office Charles had moved out of the residence.

Claudia also filed for the divorce which, he tried talking her out of getting, but apparently she'd had enough and told him no, it was over and that was that! She informed Blake, that she would begin spending more time at the firm and decided she'd be taking fewer trips in the future, because she wanted to keep abreast; with what was going on in the business. He complemented her on her decision and said he believed, that she had made a very wise choice and she agreed.

Blake telephoned Bradford asking him if he could come to his office that afternoon? He replied yes and asked what would be a convenient time for him to come? Blake responded that around one p.m. Would be just fine because he had no further appointments scheduled for the afternoon. As he was sitting behind his desk, Blake's thoughts were of Claudia and her mother and the heated argument between he and David Lansing upon learning of Claudia's impending marriage to Charles. He recalled speaking to him regarding the marriage and wasn't convinced of his motives. Later, Claudette informed him that when she learned of David's plan she became irate over his actions and pleaded with him on Claudia's behalf, but with intimidating eyes the expression she was all too familiar with, he told her the matter was settled. She stated that she'd asked him point blank, what was he up to this time, and why he hadn't discussed it with she and Claudia, why not allow Claudia to choose for herself? But at the same time, while asking him those questions, she also remembered, how cruel he could be. Nevertheless, she was determined to stand her ground, later that day, she had a private discussion with Claudia. Then thinking,' I should never have allowed, David's threats to intimidate me. How can I possibly make Claudia understand that, it was because of my love, for her and her mother and I only wanted to protect them, that I didn't force the issue. Now I must face what I've always refused to accept and that is the grim reality of the possibility of losing her perhaps forever; the one most important thing that matters to me in life.'

Suddenly, there was a light tap on the door interrupting his thoughts and abruptly looking up he said, "come on in Jenny." She said, "Excuse the interruption Mr. Colwell, but Mr. Maxwell is here sir." "Oh yes, please send him in and thank you Jenny." "You're welcome sir, responding as she was leaving out the door." Bradford immediately came in and Blake walked around the desk and shook his hand saying, "I'm pleased that you could make it Brad." He gave a hearty laugh and asked, surely you had no doubt Blake?" Blake also laughed and replied, "not in this life time, have a seat Brad." "Have you heard from Claudia recently he asked Blake?" "He replied yes as a matter-of-fact Brad, I have. She informed me that Charles moved out of the residence two weeks after he was here and she's also filed for her divorce from him." Bradford gave him a smirk and said "Oh you don't say , well he received his just dessert I would say now Claudia can go on and enjoy the life that she so richly deserve Blake." "Amen to that, Brad. "By the way, she also decided that she's not going to be taking a lot of trips anymore, she plans to spend more time at the firm, her words were, 'so she could keep abreast of what's going on there.' "And I agreed that she had made the right decision." Bradford stared at him and said," Blake I believe she's going to be all right. After all. She is Blake Colwell's daughter while giving him a wide grin." "He laughed and said you're precisely right Brad and that's one of the reasons I asked you to come here. You see, I've been doing a great deal of thinking regarding our conversation and Claudia. You were correct in advising me to inform her of her true heritage and she does have the right to know the truth, all of it! I've come to realize that my greatest fear was in loosing her if she knew, but I'm afraid there no way of getting around that, my only hope is that she will find a way in which to forgive me for not having told her sooner." "Blake, I believe you're under estimating her. Yes, she's going to be angry, that's to be expected, and she's also going to be asking you, a number of questions because they will be important to her, but as I see it, all you have to do, is be honest with her. Give her your rationale, for having done what you thought was right at the time, and let her take it from there, he said." He gazed hard at him for a brief moment, then said, "Brad if only what you believe is correct, then I can deal with it." She's your daughter Blake, her mother is no longer here to give her an explanation, as to why the decision to keep her biological birth a secret, but you are here. And it's now up to you my friend, and the sooner, I believe the better. Enough time, has already passed for her not to have known the truth. You've always loved he and that will not change, but you will have to tell her that. I'm certain you realize as I do Blake, there are no short cuts to this." He stared ahead for a moment then said, "I believe the best place for me to do it is here in my office, I'll call and ask her if she's free this afternoon?" Bradford gave a hearty laugh and said, I think that's great Blake. It's a good start in the meanwhile, I'm going to run an errand and return to my office, you don't need me here when you and your daughter become acquainted with each other and one piece of advice, enjoy what you will have together life is short lived." Blake gazed hard at hi smiled and asked, "since when did you become a philosopher Bradford T. Maxwell?" "Oh you know me, I just call it as I see it, he said smiling." And that my friend ,is one of the many things I've always admired in you Brad, you've never pulled any punches." "Now there you go getting all mushy on me and that's my cue to get out of here. Let me know how things turn out with you two, will you?" " I certainly will and thank you again for being such a devoted friend." "No thanks are necessary, I'm just pleased to have been a part of it Blake," he responded as he was leaving." After Bradford's departure Blake leaned back in the chair and closed his eyes for a moment thinking of how he was going to break the news to Claudia. 'Oh well, here goes as he began to dial the firm's number'. "Hello Claudia this is Blake." "Blake what a pleasant surprise. I was thinking about you earlier and wondering what you were doing this afternoon?" "Oh really now! As a matter-of-fact, I'm calling to ask you the same thing because I have something very important to tell you?" She was silent for a moment then said, "I hope it's good news for a change, she spoke, smiling to herself." He smiled to himself and said, "I hope it is, my dear. Will it inconvenience you to come into my office this afternoon?" "No, not at all in fact, things are rather slow right now anyway. What will be a good time for me to come?" "I'm free for the rest of the afternoon, so how about two-thirty?" "That will be just fine with me, she replied." "Good. I'll be expecting you then, he responded with a large smile.

Claudia arrived at Blake's office at precisely two-thirty sharp and was met at the door by him. She didn't see Jenny behind her desk and asked Blake, "Where's Jenny today, I don't see her?" "Oh she asked to take the afternoon off for a scheduled appointment." She smiled and said, "oh, I suppose I've become spoiled by her presence whenever, I come into the office." He laughed and said, "I will certainly convey that sentiment to her." They walked into his private office and he led her to the chair opposite his desk then walked around it and seated himself. My dear, you're looking very beautiful today, as usual and you appear to be happy." She blushed and said, "I haven't felt this good in quite awhile. I can only contribute it to finally having Charles out of my life." "I take it then that he's no longer annoying you, he asked?" "Precisely, and I'm very grateful for the peace of mind that I now have." He took a long hard look at her smiled and said, "I'm very pleased to hear that Claudia. Now to get down to why I asked you to come here, it's past due time for you to know the truth, I've been carrying this guilt for past twenty-nine years and I'm growing weary of it." She stared at him for a moment and seeing the seriousness that suddenly appeared on his handsome face, she smiled and asked, "what is the guilt that you've apparently been burdened with for so long Blake? "As he began to speak, she observed a gleam in his eyes. "Claudia I was sworn to secrecy by your mother twenty-nine years ago, that I would not divulge this information and I reluctantly did so because it was against my better judgement. At the time, I was quite angry with her and didn't understand why she requested that of me until, I read her Journal and only then did I comprehend her motive and her actions. "She *gazed at him for a brief period of time and asked, does this have anything to do with Mother because for sometime, I've known that you were in love with her?" He gave her a rather startled look and asked her, "how on earth did you reach that realization Claudia?" "When she passed away I saw how deeply it affected you and it really confirmed my belief when you asked Brad if you could read her Journal." "You know my dear, you're very much like your mother, she was a very perceptive woman as well. And to answer your question yes, the secret has very much to do with your mother and you. You see Claudia, I'm your biological father, not David Lansing." He observed an expression of apparent shock and disbelief, that was slowly appearing on her face and he pleaded with her, to please hear him out. As she gazed directly into his eyes, hers began to swell with tears, but she managed to maintain her focus and asked, did he know?" He looked directly into her eyes and said, "Yes, he knew, you weren't his child." "What happened, when he found out?" "Nothing, your mother told him the truth and actually, there was nothing that he could say because at the time, I didn't know for certain that he was involved with another woman, but apparently Claudette did and she told him so. As a matter-of-fact, he was the one who suggested that you were to be reared as his child. Your mother assured me that it would be alright." I became angry with the both of them and stormed out of the door. A few hours later after I had cooled off, I telephoned Claudette that I was coming to the house because we had to talk further and she agreed. When I arrived there David was present also. She asked me if I'd given it some thought and I said yes. I made it perfectly clear to David that I would remain with the firm as the Attorney and I was always going to be a part of your life and he agreed. So the three of us agreed, but it was you mother the decision to keep your birth a secret because she didn't want you to grow up with a stigma. I agreed because I loved you and your mother and only wanted to protect you from a scandal. I wasn't concerned about David because he couldn't afford to have one either and I knew this. I do believe if things had worked out differently, she would have told you herself because you meant more to her than anything in the world. Our relationship wasn't anything to be ashamed of. David spent more time away from her than with her and after awhile she became lonely and I've loved her since we were in college. After the agreement between the three of us, she decided that we shouldn't be involved any longer, but had me promise that I'd always remain close to you." He looked away for a moment and said, Claudia I've been wrestling with this for many years and often wondered if I made the right decision by agreeing with your mother?" And then I began having a fear of loosing you forever, if you knew the truth about our relationship. I didn't want to tell you until our situation with Charles was resolved because it doesn't concern him what so ever! My dear I sincerely hope that some day you will find it in your heart to forgive both your mother and I." She didn't say anything, but rose from her chair and walked over to the window. It was apparent that after learning the truth and for the very first time in her life, Claudia began to realize the true significance of having been entangled, in a swelling web. As she stood there looking out the window, it was as if her life was becoming more complex with each passing day, and the reality of it all, was the simple fact, that she'd grown up, believing and accepting the things that were told to her. Now, she was feeling as if she'd been hidden the dark shadows of life, having grown up beneath the wings of a man who was characterized by those who really knew him, as being a vicious tyrant who resorted to what ever means necessary in order to achieve his desire. Blake said nothing, but focusing hie eyes directly on her, 'he wondered because of her silence, if he'd lost the one thing in life that mattered to him most and as he did so, his heart was aching?' After what seemed to have been hours .but only minutes, Claudia turned and walked slowly back to her chair and sat down. She gazed directly into Blake's eyes and softly asked, "Is there anything else that I should know about?" He leaned forward returning her gaze and in a concerned tone he smiled and said, "to answer your questions no my dear, and only Brad is aware of our relationship this is everything and the truth." Never altering her gaze on him she said, "you know, this is quite a bit to absorb. As I stood at the window my thought reverted to David Lansing and I recall as I became older, hearing remarks of his unsavory life-style and how could my mother tolerate being with him? I never said anything to her about it though. I had wanted to many times." She stared at him and asked, "were you aware that she enjoyed taking long walks?" Blake looked at her smiled and said, "yes Claudia I am. "She returned the smile and said, I believed they helped to relieve her loneliness because she was alone a great deal of the time. I believe I was around fifteen and one day as we were walking along the path I just happened to look at her and I could see the sadness in her face. And I happened to ask her what was wrong although, I already knew the answer because David had gone on another one of his supposedly business trips that were becoming more frequent? "She just looked at me smiled and said, "Darling, I am very pleased that you're here to share these walks with me. I don't know what made me say it, but I looked at her and said, mother I wish uncle Blake was my father. I recall she stopped in her tracks, gave me a strange smile and asked, Claudia why do you say that?' " I said because he's always here and we have so much fun together. She held my hand smiled and said, 'Blake is a wonderful man and I am certain he will always try to be near you'. "Now I'm beginning to understand the feelings I had about you when I was growing up. It was as if there was something special between you and I that was never present with David. I suppose a great deal of it was contributed to the fact that he never once gave me the affection that you did and I could never understand why. Oh, he would give an occasional kiss on the forehead, but that was just about it. You know Blake right now, I'm quite angry. We don't know what the future hold, but while the three of you were trying to keep my birthright a secret did it ever occur to any of you that I just might be interested in knowing the truth?" Blake gazed steadily at her and she could see the sadness that appeared upon his face and his eyes began to swell with tears. Ashe softly said, "Claudia you have no concept of how many times through the years that I desired to speak with you regarding the subject we're having today. But then I recalled the vow I'd made to your mother and I just didn't feel justified in betraying her. Yes, I've always felt that you had a right to know the truth and I conveyed this to your mother, but she was determined to let things remain as they were and of course I didn't question her rationale for it. I realize this undoubtedly the most difficult thing you've ever had to face. I came very near doing just that when I learned about the planned marriage. I went to David and we had some heated words regarding you because it was beyond comprehension why all of a sudden you were engaged to someone you hardly knew. And even then I felt there was something wrong, but he assured me that he only had your best at heart. Now we both know that was a lie." She stared at him for a minute and in a very soft tone asked, "does anyone else know about this?" He looked directly at her and said "yes, Brad knows and I believe Steven Chatsworth does also. As a matter-of-fact, Brad conveyed to me that he's been suspicious from the beginning." She smiled and asked, "just how did he arrive at that conclusion I wonder?" "Well, he reminded me of our conversation when we were discussing the case involving the scandal. He stated that there appeared to be something exceptional about the case and asked,' what was my stake in all of it?' Of course, I gave him the answer that we had reservations regarding Charles's loyalty that was all. He didn't buy it nor, did he force the issue. After the case and your situation with Charles had been resolved, he came to me and point blank said he knew I had been concealing something and wanted to know precisely what it was and how did you fit into the picture?"*

That's when I finally decided it was time to do the right thing. Your mother is no longer here but I am, and I believe she would agree with me." Out of curiosity she asked, "Why do you believe Chatsworth knows?" "Do you recall my informing you, that he'd terminated his partnership with the firm?" She looked at him and said, "Yes, I remember and wondered why the sudden change of heart?" "Well, he said something, that was quite surprising and strange at the time. Brad and I discussed it later. He stated that he was doing it because you had suffered enough for something that you had nothing to do with, and I could also destroy the papers that were in my files . Then he laughed and said 'oh yes, I know about the threat you were holding over David's head before Claudia's marriage to Charles, he told me all about it.' His vendetta was against David Lansing, for what he'd done. You see my dear, he was blinded by so much hatred that in his mind, the firm was representative of him." She stared at Blake in total bewilderment and asked, "just what was the threat he referred to?" He smiled and then with a serious expression on his face he stared and said," I informed him, that if I ever learned that he'd orchestrated your marriage in any way to Charles, I would openly acknowledge you, whether he and Claudette agreed with me or not." She gazed at him smiled and asked, "you would have done it?" He smiled and said "Yes Claudia, I would have, but what is still a puzzle to me is, what had your mother planned to do with the Journal and I do believe she wrote it to expose him to the world for what he did to your grandfather ?" She stared at him and said, "I can't begin to imagine when she'd planned to do it because no one ever knew she kept one, but we know the truth, don't we?" "Yes that's true perhaps now, she and your grandfather will rest in peace after all." She looked away for a few minutes then back at him and saw the deep sadness that had appeared upon his face. Her heart was aching at the sight of the man sitting behind the desk in front of her and thought to herself,' how could I not have loved this devoted and loving man who has always been in my life?' She leaned back in her chair and gazing directly into his eyes smiled and said "you know, I'm finding all of this to be quite a bit to absorb and it's going to take time for me to sort things out in my mind. I realize that under the circumstances you did what you thought was best at the time now there is only you and I. Regardless of how much regret there is in this, nothing is going to change what has happened. I've always loved you and that will never change, even now." Blake stared at her with tears in his eyes and said nothing, but listened as she spoke. She said, "I never realized until now, how complex my life could become and how difficult it had to have been for you all of those years as I was growing up, for the most part this is absolutely frustrating. I grew up under the wings of a selfish dictating tyrant whom I called father and now I've been informed that the man whom I always referred to as uncle is actually my father, the one I wished for at age fifteen how ironic, to say the least." Blake cleared his throat before speaking then said," my dearest Claudia, this is a lot on your plate to absorb and it's going to take you as well as myself some time. But as for myself, I've been relieved of something that had become a haunting nightmare. And I never meant to cause you any pain and in time, I hope you can find it in your heart to forgive me and accept me for who I am, I've always loved you even before you were born and nothing can ever change that." She said "up until today, I always took it for granted in knowing who I was, but now that's all changed because there's a new chapter in my life." Blake looked at her with great admiration and said darling, let your heart dictate to you. She stared hard at him laughed and said "My goodness, you haven't called me that since the day I graduated from college, you kissed me and expressed how proud you were." He looked at her smiled and said " I was and always will be, no matter what decisions you make because I'm certain they will be the right one's for you." Her eyes swelling with tears, she stood up walked around his desk and gave him a big kiss and hug and said, you sly old fox I love you and how can I not forgive you" He gave her a tight hug and said" and I love you, you mean more to me than anything in this world Claudia." She gazed at the wall-mounted clock and asked him "what do you say to our going out to dinner this evening?" He gave her a big smile and said" if you're gamed, so am I." She said "good then it's settled. I'm going back to the firm and check on a few things first. What time do you want to go?" He looked at her with glittering eyes and said, "when ever you're ready, just give me a call. In the meanwhile, I'm going to check tomorrow's schedule for appointments and see how early I'll need to be here then I'll close the office. Usually , Jenny arrives here before I do anyway." She walked around the desk picked up her purse smiled and said," I'll see you a bit later then." "yes you will, he said smiling and holding er hand as they walked through the door." As she gently closed the door behind her, Blake remembering her words when she 'stated a new chapter has begun in her life.' He thought 'Lord in spite of everything that has happened in our lives, am I going to be fortunate enough to enjoy my daughter the way I've desired for so many years? I can only hope so because she deserves to be happy, and we've missed out so much already. Now all can do is be patient and wait on time, because I will not pressure here in any way. The decision is entirely up to her, and whatever way she does decide I'll support her and honor it'.

Two days later, Claudia telephoned Bradford. "Hello Brad, this is Claudia, I'm only a short distance from your office and wonder if it will be an inconvenience for me to come there, say in about twenty minutes?" "And a pleasant hello, to you Claudia. No, it will not inconvenience me at all; I'll be expecting you." After replacing the receiver, Brad leaned back in his chair and with a deep smile thought, 'I'm quite anxious to learn , how she and Blake are coming along in their relationship? It's going to be difficult at the beginning, for the both of them, but I'm confident they'll survive the ordeal with love, forgiveness and patience.' While waiting for Claudia's arrival, he returned a few telephone calls that he'd postponed earlier. Suddenly, there was a soft tap on the door and he abruptly took long strides and opened it. With a wide smile and bow he asked, "does my fair lady wish to enter this humble domain?" Claudia laughed out loud and said, "Bradford T. Maxwell you're absolutely nuts, and gave him a big hug." He took her by the hand and ushered her to the chair opposite his desk. He asked, "would you care to join me with a cup of freshly brewed coffee madam?" She gazed at him, began laughing again and replied, "yes, I would thank you." He brought a serving tray sat it down on his desk and poured each of them a cup of coffee after which, he walked around the desk and seated himself. "Well I must say Claudia, you're looking very radiant today and happier than I've seen you in awhile." She gazed directly into his eyes and responded Brad, you can't begin to imagine just how pleased I am, to hear you say that. I had some business to take care of down town this afternoon and I thought perhaps if you weren't tied up, this would be a great opportunity for me to thank you." He stared at her through slightly slanted eyes and said, "Oh, to thank me, for what Claudia?" "For being an open-minded and unbiased friend for starters Brad. Blake and I spent an entire afternoon together after that, we went out to dinner and had a lovely evening. " Brad said nothing, but kept his focus on her and for the first time, he saw sparkles in her eyes as she spoke. "First of all before I get carried away with my enthusiasm, to answer your question for what? You inspired him not to fear in acknowledgment to me that he's my biological father and to explain the rationale for secrecy. When I first heard the truth, there was anger and disbelief, but after listening to him and seeing the regret, sadness and grief that came upon his face, the anger left me. I informed him that I've always known something, but I couldn't explain what it was. There was always a special bond between he and I that wasn't present with David Lansing. When I was fifteen David had gone on one of his supposedly out-of-town business trips. Mother and I were walking down the path and I recall telling her that, I wished uncle Blake were my father. She stopped in her tracks gave me a strange smile and asked, 'Claudia why do you say that?' I said because he's always here and we have so much fun together. She held my hand smiled and said, 'Blake is a wonderful man and I'm certain he'll always be near you.' Brad, as he was talking I began to understand all the feelings I was experiencing towards him while growing up. Oh David would give me a kiss on the forehead occasionally, but that was about it. I also asked him whose decision was it to keep my heritage a secret all those years? And he said, the three of them agreed that it was the best, but he only wanted to protect us from a scandal and did so reluctantly because mother had him promise. 'He said that someday, he hope I can find it in my heart to forgive him.' She looked away for an instant then gazed into Bradford's eyes and asked, "Brad, how can I not forgive a loving devoted man who has been with me all my life?" Bradford stared hard into her eyes and said, Claudia, that is something you'll have to decide, no one can do it for you. But in all fairness, I entreat you to embrace Blake's apology because as I see it, you both were victims of circumstance and that cannot be changed." She said "Brad, I've already lost one parent and I don't want to lose another one as well, it's just going to take me sometime to adjust to this new chapter in my life. Then as if to be recalling something significant she said" you know, growing up I believed most of the things told me, but the reality of it all is my life up to this [point, has been a lie. I still recall David's controlling behavior. He never once asked how I felt, or what I thought about anything. He just simply made all of the decisions for me. He was the same with my mother and he could be very demanding and persistent in getting what ever it was that, he wanted. I always assumed that she was content to let him take control her life that is, until I read her Journal then, I understand her purpose." Bradford began to observe a note of bitterness in her tone as she spoke of David Lansing, but did not interrupt her he thought it best to let her get it out of her system. She said, "you know the most ironic part about it is I never wanted to marry Charles anyway. He was much too arrogant and self-centered for my taste and I didn't love him. But that never mattered to David. Now I can understand why it wouldn't have. Mother was a stunning and endearing woman who seemingly remained loyal and the background. One day I was entering the study she was on the telephone with one of her friends and I over heard her say 'unfortunately, I've had first hand knowledge of what happened to those who openly opposed him in anyway. She never knew I heard, that part of the conversation and afterwards, I often wondered just what the conversation was about for her to have made that kind of statement. It's difficult for me to forget how he treated Chatsworth's sister and to learn that he'd orchestrated my marriage, that was the last straw. I didn't feel that my father could be that kind of man. Now, I'm pleased to know he's not, and I'm proud of the man who is *my father. I'm certainly not going to allow the bitterness of the past to interfere with our newly-found relationship, she said with a smile." Bradford stared into her eyes smiled and said" Claudia, I'm very pleased to hear you say that because I believe the love that Blake and you have for each other, will weather any storm that might come your way. At least now, you know who you are and some people, would envy the opportunity that the both of you have so; my suggestion is this, cherish every moment that you can spend together; and take nothing for granted, life is so short lived." She stared at him and with tears in her eyes she said, "Brad, I can truly say I understand the feeling's that my father has for you, because I've come to feel the same way and I'll always love you, for being the man that you are." He looked at her smiled and said, "that's the greatest compliment I've ever received, thank you Claudia." She said, "You're more than welcome, my handsome prince and I don't expect things to change overnight. The realization of it all is, I've inherited, 'a bitter legacy', but I'm going to work hard at doing whatever; it takes for us to really get to know each other better, in this new light of things." He laughed and said, "I have no reservations, regarding Blake's efforts. I can see him, bursting with pride as always whenever it came to you, and remember this, life offers no guarantee. Take it one day at a time and enjoy every moment of it!*

'Synopsis'

Claudia Carrington had lost both parents in a sudden tragic accident and inherited the family's wealth. Shortly after the deaths occurred, the name of the family's business was implicated in a large scandal and a private investigator was hired to search out the truth and bring a resolve. At the conclusion of the investigation, it was determined that the silent partner and her own husband had been directly responsible for creating the scandal. Unfortunately, that was only the beginning of what was yet to come.

Claudia's walls came tumbling down when it was revealed that she had been entangled; in a constant swelling web of deep family secrets, conspiracy, deceptions and betrayals. Claudia experienced shock, disbelief and anger having learned, the man whom she referred to as 'uncle', was in fact, her biological father. Her lasting reflection was-She had regrettably inherited 'a bitter legacy'.

'Biography'

As a favor to an old friend of many years, Bradford T. Maxwell, a no non-sense Private Investigator with a reputation for being resourceful, dangerous and lethal was asked to investigate a large Business Scandal. He was to search out the truth and bring a resolve. As the investigation progressed, Maxwell became precarious of the man's motive and his instincts led him to believe something was being withheld!

www.ingramcontent.com/pod-product-compliance
Lightning Source LLC
Chambersburg PA
CBHW022051020426
42335CB00012B/634